The Birth of American Tourism

D1474057

The BIRTH *of* AMERICAN TOURISM

◄§ ?◄

*New York, the Hudson Valley,
and American Culture,
1790–1830*

Richard H. Gassan

University of Massachusetts Press
AMHERST

LC 2008021777

ISBN 978-1-55849-665-1 (paper); 664-4 (library cloth)

Designed by Steve Dyer
Set in Galliard by dix!
Printed and bound by Sheridan Books, Inc.

Library of Congress Cataloging-in-Publication Data
Gassan, Richard H., 1958–
The birth of American tourism : New York, the Hudson Valley,
and American culture, 1790–1830 / Richard H. Gassan.
p.   cm.
Includes bibliographical references and index.
ISBN 978-1-55849-665-1 (pbk.: alk. paper) —
ISBN 978-1-55849-664-4 (library cloth : alk. paper)
1. Tourism—New York (State)—History—19th century.
2. Tourism—United States—History—19th century.   I. Title.
GI55.U6G37 2008
338.4'791747043—dc22   2008021777

British Library Cataloguing in Publication data are available.

To Lisa

The Brothers,
A Pastoral Poem

These Tourists, Heaven preserve us! needs must live
A profitable life: Some glance along,
Rapid and gay, as if the earth were air,
And they were butterflies to wheel about
Long as their summer lasted; some, as wise,
Upon the forehead of a jutting crag
Sit perch'd with book and pencil on their knee,
And look and scribble, scribble on and look,
Until a man might travel twelve stout miles,
Or reap an acre of his neighbour's corn.
But for *that* moping sort of Idleness,
Why can *he* tarry *yonder?* — In our Church yard . . .

WILLIAM WORDSWORTH, *Lyrical Ballads,*
2nd ed. (London, 1802)

Contents

Illustrations follow page 84.

Acknowledgments

I COULD NOT HAVE WRITTEN this book without the friendship, guidance, and assistance of a host of friends and colleagues. First, I am grateful to Stephen Nissenbaum, who helped me clarify my intentions early on. I am indebted to Gerald McFarland, whose sage advice, calm help, and warm encouragement were critical to the completion of this book, and I owe much as well to Dorothy McFarland, who offered insightful commentary. In addition, Margaret Hunt of Amherst College and Dona Brown of the University of Vermont provided important suggestions at early stages.

I could not have gotten to where I did without the love, encouragement, and assistance of my immediate family, Martha Oehler, Larry Gassan, and Ann Somerhousen; Lisa Welsh, who has been there far longer than both of us realized; and Tomi Anne Gibson, Sabine Dietrich, David Ornstil, Michelle Decker, Erik Gilg, Kris Woll, Tom Holmes, and Colleen MacCormick.

At the University of Massachusetts it was my pleasure to meet and work with Brian Bixby, Patrick Crim, Allison (Dunn) Delnore, Laura Donaldson, Christopher Franks, Harry Franqi-Rivera, Joseph Gabriel, Julie Gallagher, Tom Holme, Noel Hudson, Lincoln Lounsbury, John Lund, Tom Rushford, Julia Saari-Franks, Julia Sandy-Bailey, Christoph Strobel, Bethany (Zecher) Sutton, Jeff Vogel, and Peter Wong, who created an energizing and collegial environment. Aviva Ben-Ur, Bruce Laurie, Brian Ogilvie, Manisha Sinha, Ron Story, and Mary Wilson provided sustaining encouragement there.

A word of thanks is due the librarians and archivists I had the pleasure to work with, particularly John Hench, Caroline Sloat, and Vincent Golden at the American Antiquarian Society, a trove of critical materials where this project was first begun, and the staffs at the New-York Historical Society, the Southern Historical Collection, the Massachusetts Historical Society, Historic New England (formerly the Society for the Preservation of New England Antiquities), and the New York Public Library.

For their support in the now distant past, I want to thank Darcy Gingerich, Rosemary Finnearty, Larry King, Wenda Williamson, my many former fellow workers at Ohio University, including George Bain, and particularly those from the Ohio University Department of Geography, especially Hubertus (Hugh) Bloemer, Nancy Bain, and, of course, the great Hugh Wilhelm. Donald Jordan was a key inspiration in my decision to become a historian.

My thanks to Martin Johnson at Northern Illinois University Press, Jeff Hardwick at the Smithsonian Institution Press, Bob Lockhart at the University of Pennsylvania Press, and Robert Jones at Fordham University Press, all of whom in various ways spurred me to make this a better book. A special thanks goes to the staff at the University of Massachusetts Press, especially Clark Dougan. I am grateful as well to the anonymous readers of the Press.

Finally, I thank my colleagues in the Department of International Studies at the American University of Sharjah, United Arab Emirates, especially Nada Mourtada-Sabbah, former department chair, and my other friends there, including Isa Blumi, Jeremy Bendik-Keymer, Anatoly Kharkurian, Neema Nouri, and Pernille Arenfeldt; also Tom DeGeorges, Mark Fiocco, Steve Keck, and Meenaz Kassam—all of whom make it a very nice place to work.

The Birth of American Tourism

Introduction

❧ ❧

FRANCIS DALLAM TOOK only two weeks of vacation in the summer of 1827.

He could have taken much more: he was from an old-line Maryland family, with solid wealth; rents from land holdings in Maryland, Tennessee, and Kentucky; several slaves; and a position as the collector of taxes for the city of Baltimore.[1] Although he had a sizable family—he and his wife had six children—he took this journey without them, traveling with just one other male friend and, probably, a slave.[2]

This was not going to be a leisurely trip: he planned a tight schedule, never budgeting more than two days in any one place. But his time wasn't entirely taken up by traveling. His journey was sped along by a new transportation infrastructure, including stagecoach lines traversing improved roads and, most crucially, fast, reliable steamboats operating on regular schedules. These connected the major cities of the country with a whole new set of tourist destinations developed in the preceding two decades. Dallam's itinerary would touch on the most popular of them, all located in the Hudson River valley. These places had made themselves tourist-friendly by building some of the nation's largest hotels, offering entertainment brought in from major cities, and easing access to nearby natural attractions.

Dallam's vacation began on a Thursday. He left Baltimore by steamboat and by early evening had reached Philadelphia, where he spent Friday. Early on Saturday morning he took another steamboat to New York City, arriving in the early evening. After a Sunday in the city, he boarded a third steamboat early Monday morning for the journey up the Hudson River. After a stop halfway between New York and Albany at the Catskill Mountain House, where he spent a morning hiking and admiring the view, by Tuesday mid-afternoon he was on his way, once again aboard a steamboat heading north. After a night in Albany, he arrived on Wednesday afternoon at his northernmost destination, Saratoga Springs, six days after his departure.[3] After spending only slightly more than a day there, Dallam began making his way back south on Friday morning. After side trips to other Hudson Valley sights—the terminus of the Erie Canal, a stopover at a Shaker village—by early Tuesday he had reached New York, where his steamboat docked at its home berth at the foot of Courtland Street. It took him only another two days before he had safely returned home, where "thank God I found all my family and friends well and much pleased to see me."[4]

An enduring stereotype of antebellum travel holds that tourists of this era spent months or even years on long and leisurely journeys, most often in Europe. That Americans of the 1820s or 1830s could, and did, travel within the United States; that they would do so for leisurely purposes; that these trips would be of limited duration; that they would be undertaken not only by the idle rich—these are very new notions. Francis Dallam's short vacation was, in fact, far more typical than the travels of that tiny group of Americans of the antebellum era who were able to spend long summers at Newport or Saratoga Springs or the Virginia Springs. His journey, with its constant motion and limited duration, was an example of the new tourism of the 1820s: fast, short, efficient, and above all, remarkably modern.

Tourism arrived in America with surprising rapidity. At the end of the eighteenth century, even in 1810, it did not exist; by 1820 it was a flourishing industry. It emerged in the Hudson River valley north of New York City—because of a confluence of historical accidents, including the valley's proximity to the most rapidly growing financial and population center in the United States, its remarkable scenery, and its geographical position as a waterway that connected some of the country's most sought-after destinations.

The tourism that developed in the Hudson Valley marked a radical break with the past. Before this time, in both England and America, leisure travel had been an aristocratic luxury.[5] In the 1810s, though, people from outside the tiny sphere of American aristocrats began to travel for leisure, both up the Hudson and beyond, to Niagara, Canada, and elsewhere. At first just a trickle, by 1830 it had become a flood. The emergence of these travelers was increasingly noted in magazines and journals of the day, and their example became embedded in the minds of readers, many of whom could not yet afford tourism. The example of this small but highly visible and growing group of tourists became the dominant model.

The presence of tourism signified larger structural changes in American society. For example, tourism is almost pure consumption, a purchase of experiences that leaves little residue in the way of tangible products. In New England, in parts of Pennsylvania, and in some of the more conservative subcultures of the United States, there had been a tradition that discouraged consumption.[6] And yet, for various reasons, many of these regions embraced tourism.[7] Even among groups who had already been more inclined to consume, tourism was a spur to more conspicuous consumption. As tourism became ever more widespread into the 1820s and 1830s, its popularity marked the beginnings of a profound societal shift, as America firmly embarked on the road to a modern consumer society, a process that would not attain maturity until the 1890s.

The emergence of tourism happened at a decisive time in American society, when Americans were in the process of defining their national identity. Travel played a vital role in that process by heightening the value of American scenery and locations and by asserting an equality between America and Europe. The most visible and profound components of this shift were the nation's first major artistic and literary movements. America's first successful authors, such as Washington Irving and James Fenimore Cooper, wrote some of their most famous works specifically for the tourist market, a market composed of their best customers—the gentry. Other artists were also directly influenced by tourism. Seeking an audience, seeking patrons and customers, they created works that appealed to the gentry, the key tourist class. These painters would go on to found the country's first significant art movement, the Hudson River School. The works of these writers and artists further spread the idea of tourism and its leading American destinations.

This outpouring of American culture in the 1820s came at a pivotal time. In the 1810s, critics both at home and abroad saw American culture as merely a pallid imitation of that of the Old World, particularly England and France. In fact, Americans did take nearly all of their cultural cues from overseas, importing books, paintings, theater, and music. The few American artists and writers who could support themselves by their art usually attempted, somewhat unsuccessfully, to imitate what was already being produced in England and Europe. An American artist was not entirely schooled unless he had gone to Europe to study. Of course, some Americans objected to this situation, but very little was produced prior to the 1820s that could change this opinion much. Tourism, however, would help to change it. By celebrating American scenery and creating a market for American scenes, the new tourist-related culture signaled that a dramatic shift had begun.

The transmission of information about tourism closed the circle: by 1830, virtually all literate members of the upper classes—the gentry—knew what tourism was, where it happened, and how people should react to it.[8] The omnipresence of the Hudson River valley in that cultural material made it emblematic of all American tourism. This particular type of tourism had traits that were products both of their time and of the unique situation of the valley: pilgrimages to wild-seeming scenic spots that were, in fact, well tamed; a fast pace of travel for the time, where the illusion of leisure was balanced by the desire to move onward; the use by these tourists of very specific pieces of art and literature to interpret their surroundings; and the tourists' insistence on recreating an atmosphere at their lodgings that as closely as possible reproduced the comforts of home.

This idea of tourism was defined and dominated by northerners, especially New Yorkers, and it was successfully propagated throughout the nation in a wide variety of media.[9] This version of tourism became central in the American consciousness and would be the model for all American tourism in the nineteenth century.

What Is Tourism?

Although existing definitions of tourism are frustratingly weak, it is clear that tourism is a kind of travel that creates an illusion of novelty while remaining within a narrow range of comfortable, societally defined boundaries. If the tourist's travel experience ever lands significantly outside those boundaries, the journey begins to resemble adventuresome travel as it loses that crucial element of comfort. These boundaries are defined by three key components: a compelling destination with homelike accommodations, a comfortable travel infrastructure, and a cultural infrastructure that gives the tourist a model of thinking about what he or she is experiencing.

The most crucial element is a compelling destination. Why go there at all, unless there is some essential attraction? In the United States, the first true tourist attraction was Ballston Spa in Saratoga County, New York, founded as an elite retreat in the 1790s and by 1804 the site of the country's first major hotel outside a city. That hotel, the Sans Souci, and the others that were built near it—by the 1820s, the region had the largest non-urban concentration of hotels in the country—represented the creation of that essential part of the physical tourist infrastructure. Later, the focus shifted and became more diffuse: for most of the 1820s it was in upstate New York near the Hudson River, but by mid-decade the construction of the Erie Canal began to send many tourists westward, to Niagara Falls. It was at about that time that tourism to other places began, for example to the White Mountains of New England. Keenly aware of what had worked or failed in the Hudson region, these upstarts strove to replicate that original success. In many cases, the most successful of these sites drew tourists away from the older ones, and as the first wave left, a new wave of less wealthy, less elite tourists would move in. This early pattern of tourism would repeat itself in the decades to come, as tourist areas were created, became popular, and then fell into a relative decline. They would be forced continually to reinvent themselves—or face irrevocable decline. This pattern would emerge as early as the 1830s at places like Saratoga Springs, where new methods of drawing tourists—horse racing, for example, or casinos—would have to be found.

The second element of tourism is the physical transportation infrastructure. Getting to the place is crucial, and the faster the better. The quality of transportation has to be acceptable to the tourist: Too dangerous, and families will not come. Too slow, and all but the most determined or leisurely are excluded. Too expensive, and only the very wealthiest can afford it. In fact, speed can be seen as a measure of expense; even the most affluent Americans could rarely afford to abandon their affairs for months at a time. For the Hudson River of the 1810s and 1820s, the factor of speed would be satisfied by the steamboat, which connected to coaches and regular stages for the non-river portions of the journey. Only a few years later, by the early 1830s, one of the country's earliest railroads would be built to cover precisely that stage, as a link was completed between Saratoga and the Hudson River. That new era of railroad travel, not discussed here, would be the next stage in the evolution of tourism.

The third element is perhaps the most elusive: a cultural infrastructure. When tourists arrive somewhere, there has to be a story. Why are they there? Sheer physical beauty can carry a fair amount, but some element of romance must make the place sparkle. The cultural infrastructure of Hudson Valley tourism began with the writings of Washington Irving and James K. Paulding, continued with those of James Fenimore Cooper, and was manifest in the art of Thomas Cole and others. Together, these men helped create an image, an ideal, that the tourist could use to redefine what he or she saw while traveling. A vibrant cultural infrastructure can smooth over the unfortunate realities a traveler encounters; it can add a romantic patina to places that could be, under other circumstances, rather ordinary.

In this book I explore how these three elements came together in one place and one time, the Hudson Valley between 1817 and 1820. In setting such an early date, I am pushing back the first emergence of American tourism decades earlier than has generally been thought. Although the kind of tourism described here is not the mass tourism of later eras, it was in fact the model for everything that followed.[10]

As they make their way through this book, readers may ask themselves where the other attractions of the antebellum era fit into this story. Where is, say, the South? or New England?

Before the Civil War, the South did have a small infrastructure for a few visitors. But these destinations were limited mainly to the mountain springs in the Appalachians between what is now Virginia and West Virginia, certain upland retreats in South Carolina, mountain springs in Arkansas, and the like, and were restricted to aristocrats (the tiny number of extraordinarily wealthy slave owners, essentially) until after the Civil War. Even though they did undergo some growth in the late 1830s, southern resorts of this era were always on a much smaller scale than those of the North. They were carefully organized to separate exclusive from common spaces and were much more difficult to reach than northern resorts.[11]

One other important difference between the two regions in the experience with tourism lies in how it was publicized: the southern leisure travel experience was never as widely written about as that in the North. Partly, this stemmed from the print culture of the era, heavily concentrated around the cities of the Northeast, which featured writers who tended to treat the South as a distant province. Most significantly, however, northern tourism overwhelmed southern tourism in terms of sheer numbers: the northern travel experience was much more accessible, cost less, and could be done at greater speed, all of which drew increasing numbers of the upper middle class into leisure travel. Southern resorts never catered to these classes in the years before the Civil War, whether because they refrained from improving accessibility (by investing in transportation infrastructure, for instance) or because they never offered lower-cost options. While travel in the South was noted in magazines and journals, it never reached anything like the frequency or visibility of northern travel.

And what of New England? This book describes the tourist infrastructure created before 1830, and although the first New England tourist sites were created in the 1820s, the scale and scope of those sites would be only a fraction of those in the Hudson River valley, and would not begin to approach their importance until the 1830s and 1840s.[12] Further, the creation of tourist areas in New England was a direct outgrowth of what had happened in the Hudson Valley: the development of rural New England came only after the Hudson Valley had gotten Americans used not only to viewing their own country as inherently scenic and attractive (at least potentially) but also to the very idea of tourism.

Why Tourism?

The story of American tourism is one of America itself. In a society that is intimately shaped by the forces that took shape in the nineteenth century, it is valid to ask, "How did we get here?" In and of itself, tourism is (and should be) a small part of a greater picture, but it is an early warning of changing times. Although nothing that happened in the antebellum era approaches anything like the consumerism of later eras, there was a definite shift in how Americans sought out goods and experiences, and that shift happened in the period covered in this book.

Another central characteristic of tourism is that it appeals to people with some disposable income. The formation of a middle class—described elsewhere—began in this era.[13] Tourism points to the first stirrings of a middle class. Certainly, the tourists of this era would, in later times, appear to be fairly well off, but they are definitely not from an independently wealthy group. Their concerns—speed, cost, moral reform—would begin to shape the tourism they participated in. Eventually, tourism itself would change to meet their needs—but that transformation would take decades to be completed.

In this epochal era, the appearance of tourism was a symptom, a sign, and a driving force. In this book I will explore some of the many aspects of this phenomenon, in a world that is simultaneously very familiar and very foreign.

❧ 1 ❧

Laying the Foundation

ONE DAY IN 1792, Nicholas Low, one of America's richest men, began an unusual project. He ordered that a substantial inn be built, complemented by a bathhouse, on one of his poorer and more remote properties, a tract of sandy, forested land in upstate New York. What made this even more unusual was that the inn was to be located near another inn, one that had itself just been improved at considerable expense.[1]

The bathhouse is one way to understand what was happening there. Low's inn and its rival (later to be called the Aldridge House) were located at Ballston, a small cluster of cabins about thirty miles north of Albany, a full day's ride. The little village, named after Eliphalet Ball, its first pastor, had been founded in 1770 at a cluster of mineral springs believed to have medicinal properties. A few miles from the village lay another set of springs known to the Mohawks, the villagers' predecessors, as Saraghoga ("the place of swift water"). The villagers called those other springs "Saratoga," and to connoisseurs of such things, the water there was considered superior. It was the water that put Ballston on the map.[2]

Even before the Revolutionary War, enthusiasts had known of this extraordinary collection of springs for some time. During the war, the area gained wider renown when battles around nearby Bemis Heights became collectively known as the Battle of Saratoga. In the years that followed, seekers of mineral water formed a small but steady trickle of visitors to Ballston. Enough of these strangers had come by the late 1780s that one settler, Benajah Douglas, began to call his cabin an inn, and in 1787 he and

9

his neighbors built a slightly better inn along with a hovel they deemed a tavern.[3] Elkanah Watson, another wealthy local landowner, stayed at the shabby little place in 1790 on the way to inspect his upstate holdings. To get to the famous waters of the spring, he later wrote, he had to step through a "quagmire."[4] When Timothy Dwight, president of Yale College and a noted theologian, came to Ballston in 1792, he found just "a miserable cottage or two" surrounded by "an absolute forest, spreading every way to a great distance."[5]

Intrepid travelers came despite this desolation, and their steady patronage meant that by 1792 Benajah Douglas was able to expand once again with the intention of making a truly remarkable hotel. Rising up out of the quagmire, it would stand in stark contrast to its humble neighbors, as if one of the large, fashionable homes found on the streets of Philadelphia or Boston had been transplanted wholesale into the wilderness. When it was completed, the first feature visitors encountered was a long, broad porch (called the "piazza") that extended across the front of the house. Rising above that was a plain but elegant Georgian facade. Just inside the centrally placed front door rose a set of stairs that led to four bedrooms, while to the left and right two sizable public rooms extended, rooms that in a private home would have been formal parlors. The architecture spoke to one intended market: families to be sure, but more specifically, genteel women. Up to that point, as it would remain for some time to come, the springs was a male-dominated space mainly because of the dismal accommodations. Douglas knew that if a wider population were to come, they would expect a place that could be inhabited by members of the genteel classes. Although his ambitions were high, it would be another decade or so before that group began to come in any numbers. But this building was a crucial beginning.[6]

It is ironic that Douglas's inn (later called the Aldridge House after the proprietor in residence) was built without the involvement of Nicholas Low. After all, Low owned nearly all of the area surrounding the springs, having inherited a huge swath of land in Saratoga County from his father. But never slow to see an opportunity, he quickly grasped what the Aldridge House meant and leaped to take advantage of it. First, he ordered a survey of his tract, and the surveyors sketched out a plan for a much larger village at Ballston. They laid out streets and defined numbered lots that would become available for sale or lease. To complement or counter the Aldridge House, he built his own guest house, complete with a detached bathhouse.[7]

Low was taking a significant step: he was going to create, in the deep woods of upstate New York, the first American spa culture. Modeled on European examples, it would be populated by his family, friends, and acquaintances. Through his influence in New York society, he would make it popular. In the process, he would make a healthy profit.

When Dr. Benjamin Waterhouse, a prominent physician (the first to inoculate against smallpox in the United States) visited Ballston in 1795, he was favorably impressed. He found "a pretty large house for entertainment, with neat bathing-houses, and shower-baths for the convenience of invalids," surrounded by a forest of "lofty pines, which are overtopped by others," that "cover and ornament the hills." The springs were located "in the bottom of a valley, or excavation, forming a kind of bason [*sic*], of about 50 acres in extent." In all, he was optimistic: "The valley of Ballstown [*sic*] and its environs may be made an enchanting spot, equal, nay superior in some respects to any of the watering places in Europe." But between the lines, it was clear that beyond the springs themselves and the mineral water, there was very little to draw a visitor. A few amenities, he suggested, could make the place a little less shabby. One of the springs, for example, could "be converted by the hand of taste into an ornamental fountain," while "a little higher up orchestras for musick may be erected, and even houses for entertainment built."[8]

Clearly, Ballston lacked even the most rudimentary elements of a fashionable destination. Despite these shortcomings, however, it drew increasing numbers of well-to-do visitors. For example, in August 1797, James Read, a merchant from Delaware, found that his fifteen fellow lodgers were "in general . . . Genteel men." All were from New York City, except an unnamed gentleman from Trenton and a Virginia congressman, Richard Brent.[9] Over the several weeks of his stay, Read found that amid the "constant succession of comers & goers," he did not feel uncomfortable with a single visitor: "I have not discovered any thing uncommon in point of character amongst them."[10] One of the key factors, beyond the spa's curative powers, was the power of Nicholas Low's influence: his extensive business network, his chain of acquaintances and friends, and his personal stake in Ballston helped this rustic little spa become *somewhere*.

The steady patronage of wealthy people led to better facilities. Sometime between 1795 and 1800 a forty-foot-long wing was added to the house, making a dining room downstairs and more bedrooms upstairs. In 1800, the dining room was extended by about twenty feet, providing room for more bedrooms upstairs. The new rooms above the addition were basic, "proper for gentlemen only," in the words of a visitor, Abigail May, as they were furnished only with "a window, bed, table, and chair." Aldridge had declared to May that that when the extension was complete he could "entertain one hundred people," but she was skeptical.[11] One hundred visitors, she guessed, could be accommodated only if they were crammed, sardine-like, three to each small room. However many could truly be accommodated, by the standards of America in 1800 the inn was spacious and comfortable. And although it would not be as large as Aldridge's, Nicholas Low's inn, known as "McMaster's" after the two brothers who ran it, was also dramatically expanded in this period to meet the pressure of visitors.[12]

Ballston now had two inns that aspired to gentility. In 1800 it was given a grander name: Ballston Spa. But it remained a scruffy little place, described by Abigail May as "peculiarly wild and rude." The spring was surrounded by "half burnt trees and stumps, and decayd logs," and she suggested that "art might do a great deal here, without destroying its wildness." Any improvement would be a welcome way to take "advantage of the prospect," or view.[13] Another 1804 visitor from England described the area as "the very home of savages," where "nothing but tall forests of pine" stood. Low's inn was to his eyes a "miserable boarding house" where everyone "performed every necessary evolution in concert" and where the proprietors were "astonished at our asking for basins and towels in our rooms," suggesting instead that he condescend to "come down to the *Public Wash* with the other gentlemen in the morning."[14]

Better facilities would come soon. With the continued and eager patronage of crowds of New Yorkers, an increasing number of southerners, and even a smattering of foreigners, Ballston Spa's prosperity increased. Nicholas Low was now making regular visits to the village.[15] He decided to both enhance his investment and conclusively overshadow Aldridge's establishment. In early 1803 he instructed his agent at Ballston, George White, to build a large new hotel, to be called the Sans Souci.[16] By midsummer, the outlines of the project were visible, as noted by one visitor, the future author Washington Irving: "Mr Low is building a new house for the accommodation of Boarders[.] it will be very large & on the most commodious style."[17] It may have been the largest in America, as some published sources have claimed; in any case, it certainly was, as one historian notes, "the first large resort hotel in America," the first and largest outside of the nation's urban areas.[18]

The Sans Souci was about 160 feet wide with two wings, or pavilions, extending about the same distance back, and it had enough rooms to hold 150 or more guests.[19] It was an impressive building, painted white with verdigris shutters. Supporting it were a number of outbuildings, including a kitchen, icehouse, washhouse, bakehouse, stables and a coach house, and a laundry.[20]

Low's investment in the hotel was significant, and the existing receipts show that even furnishing the rooms to a minimum level—two or more chairs, a bed either three and a half feet (single) or five feet (double) wide, a table, and a side table—meant that by the time of its opening for the summer season of 1805, the hotel was equipped with 425 chairs and about 110 single and 32 double beds, costing $270 in all. The grounds around the hotel were landscaped with gravel walks and newly planted elms, shrubs, and lawns. Low had created a structure that aspired to the level of comfort available at the European spas. But he aimed for more, as his investments in landscaping demonstrate: he wanted to create a resort spa on the British model, one where an entire experience could be purchased, where members of the gentry from all over the country could come and sleep in style.[21]

Why Spas?

There were two main reasons that spas were seen as desirable destinations for travelers. The first stemmed from the long history of spas and mineral waters in Great Britain and Europe. Ancient beliefs ascribed healing powers to mineral waters, attracting large numbers of the sick to the spas that were erected wherever they were found. The very sick were joined by the not-so-sick and the "worried well," and by Roman times a spa culture had developed in Europe, creating places where the wealthiest and most privileged would come to heal and, not incidentally, to socialize. In Britain, spa culture had gone into a steep decline during the Middle Ages but was revived, with the help of royal and noble patronage, in the sixteenth and seventeenth centuries. By the mid-eighteenth century, spas were practically an industry. A large number of well-frequented, highly developed sites were available for the British gentry, including Bath (haunt of kings and queens), Tunbridge Wells, and, to a lesser extent, Harrogate and Bristol Hotwell.[22] The kind of medical problems mineral water was supposed to cure ranged from the remotely logical—kidney and liver ailments—to the outright impossible, including fractures and bleeding. Some practitioners did not see the need for specifically mineral water, arguing that mere application of cold water was enough to cure most ailments.[23]

Americans, too, believed in the curative powers of mineral water, and began frequenting springs as early as the 1660s. The numbers of people traveling long distances to these springs, located in Connecticut, Pennsylvania, and Virginia, would remain small for another century, given the difficulties of the journey and the nonexistent accommodation once there. A tiny social vogue for visiting springs began in the 1760s, particularly at the Virginia Springs and to a much lesser extent at Stafford Springs in Connecticut, but this was never widespread and was virtually obliterated during the long years of the American Revolution.[24] By the 1790s, though, when Nicholas Low was considering this investment in his distant holdings, the economic and social climate of the United States had begun to change. With the Revolution now long over and the first tiny glimmers of prosperity beginning to show in the country's urban areas, he could begin to capitalize on the longstanding desire to use these apparently special waters for curative purposes. In doing so, Low understood that a developed spa at Ballston not only would enhance the value of his otherwise poor and sandy land, but would also further cement his social status.

Although the social aspects of spa life were prominent, health drew, and would continue to draw, thousands to the springs. The tension between Low's two objectives were acutely observed by Abigail May over the summer of 1800. She wondered why "people should resort to a watering place for pleasure," to "dance and sing, while disease and death continually stare them in the face."[25] May herself was one of the sick, stricken with an unexplained affliction that had disfigured her hand. Outwardly she was quite healthy, save for the cloth wrapped around her hand. In private, she despaired at what had happened to her, and she nearly fainted in pain when her doctors manipulated the hand in an attempt at therapy.[26]

Using the best knowledge of the day, the doctors at the springs prescribed a standard treatment: she had to douse the hand in mineral water once a day. She was also ordered to drink several tumblers of mineral water. And she was to take daily shower baths in mineral water, making her entire body wet. Initially, these full-body showers had been quite a shock, but by the heat of August she had come to look forward to them. The shower was a primitive apparatus, basically consisting of a bucket that dumped water on the hapless invalid. Penciled graffiti covered the inside and outside walls of the old bathhouse, and May recorded some of the couplets describing the terrors of the shower:

> What freezing terrors chill the soul before you pull the wire
> As o'er your head the waters roll—you're ready to expire.

And

> Tis hard to think that it must come—
> Sooner the better for twill make you run
> I did not make a very long stay
> Before I pulled the wire, and ran away.[27]

The water was supposed to be cold for therapeutic purposes. The concepts of hydropathy, a form of medicine that would grow in popularity throughout the nineteenth century and has since almost entirely disappeared, were based on the effectiveness of either hot water (as held by the Romans, among others) or cold water (as at Saratoga). These therapies, it was argued, would cure most illnesses.[28]

Baths and bathhouses were radical departures for most Americans, who rarely washed more than their faces and hands, and then not more often than once a day; the concept of a daily bath or shower was almost unknown. Only the lure of a health benefit could induce most people to bathe much more than the customary amount. Full immersion baths, though, had already been in use at other American springs for more than fifty years, since immersion was considered another therapeutic use for mineral waters. But the social trend toward daily bathing, begun in the late eighteenth century among the wealthiest Americans, would take a century or more to become truly central to American life.[29]

It might seem strange to later generations that mere mineral water could have been seen as such a panacea as to draw sick people from hundreds of miles away for treatments that in hindsight seem almost laughably inadequate. The answer lay in the medical beliefs of the time. There has been quite a bit written about the respect held for mineral springs,[30] and the waters of Ballston Spa were reputed to be some of the best, "beneficial in an innumerable variety of maladies."[31] Abigail May found that her fellow sufferers "daily drink the waters" to cure "Salt Rheum, Schropila, Rheumatism, and various other disorders." And the treatment may have been effective: at least, May reported, her fellow sufferers seemed "to feel a reverential surety of relief."[32] The springs were so popular that a "catalogue of human infirmities" visited them, composed of the "nervous Rheumatic spasmatic crazatic stehatic hypatic goutatic somatic and all the atics."[33]

Every Sunday the out-of-town visitors were joined by great numbers of sick residents from local communities as far away as Albany who would bring their battered bodies to the spring to drink the water: "They flock'd in wagons[,] on horseback and on foot . . . the seats round the spring were instantly filld and resembled a booth upon the Common [on] Election day."[34] But it is not known how effective these treatments were. For those with chronic conditions, mineral waters could not have done much. The treatment the doctors at Ballston prescribed followed the most learned medical advice of the day. We now know that mineral water won't cure skin cancer, as Tobias Smollett suggested in 1752, but the topical use of acidic or astringent water probably was quite efficacious for some skin diseases.[35]

Verified stories of those cured by mineral water were almost certainly outweighed by the tales of people who tried the treatment without any visible effect. For example, Thomas Handasyd Perkins described one of his traveling companions, a Mrs. Magee, as laboring "under the effects of a stroke of Parylitic." Although they had come all the way from Boston to visit Ballston Spa and Saratoga Springs in the summer of 1800 with "hopes [that] the waters woul'd prove efficacious," all indications are that Mrs. Magee did not find the relief she had sought.[36] As for Abigail May, she arrived cautiously hopeful about the possible efficacy of the treatment, a hope that hid a deep undercurrent of despair.[37] By the time she arrived at the spa, she had been suffering from her affliction for about two years and had exhausted all other remedies. Sadly, the treatment would be useless. In late August of 1800, after three months without discernable improvement, she decided to return home to Boston. Passing through Albany on her way home, she decided to try one last regimen. There, a Dr. Stringer was using an exciting new discovery, "Oxygen Gas, or vital air." Aware that it was one of the "most approved method[s]," she hoped that she would be another of the "several extraordinary cures" attributed to it. But it was as ineffective as all the rest: she died in early September, just days after she had returned home.[38]

Water was also occasionally used to ameliorate another problem: alcoholism. Dr. Adam Alexander, a Scottish emigrant to Georgia, went to Ballston Spa in June 1801. Although he never says it outright, he seems to have gone to cure what might have been an unhealthy dependence on alcohol. On his arrival he drank the waters and "got immediately fonder of them, than of any Liquid I ever tasted." But he "contracted a violent cold" six days after his arrival, and "could use them no longer." After eleven days of this, he left for Schenectady. He reported that he had "tasted no kind of Spirits since my being at the Springs—One Glass of Wine & a Hopp & a few Glasses of Porter in the whole of the last six days, is all I have drank," assert that he has developed a "sudden distaste of Strong Drinks" that "has been attended with no inconvenience that I can perceive." There is no evidence of how conclusive this cure was, as his letters make no further mention of alcohol.[39]

After its completion in the spring of 1805, the Sans Souci stood alone, the nation's largest single hotel outside the major cities. But like many large projects, it was never really complete, and in the year following its official opening, Nicholas Low continued to make improvements. For example, the primitive bucket-over-the-wall arrangement Abby May experienced in the bathhouse was changed, and a number of bathing tubs were installed along with a "showering bath." The building itself was enlarged. Although the expansion was not completed in time for the first season, in the fall of 1805 a new gaming house was built. Equipped with a backgammon table and five new billiard tables hauled in from Albany, this facility would prove to be quite popular and lucrative: by 1812, it was turning over $170 in the season, which lasted less than three months, a significant sum for the time. Finally, in the west wing of the hotel a bar was built. Mineral bathing, gambling, and gaming created a complete experience for the hotel's visitors.[40]

The life of the spa had a very definite rhythm based on the calendar. Its high season, August, was dictated by the weather. By then Ballston would be comfortably and reliably warm, briefly shedding its tendency toward the cool and damp. Conditions elsewhere provided the push: August could be counted on to make New York, Philadelphia, Boston, and the other cities of the coast unbearably hot and humid. For many the heat was strongly associated with disease, as garbage heaps festered and water supplies were fouled. For those who could afford to leave, August was the month to flee northward.

We know a great deal about life in Ballston during the summer of 1800 through Abigail May's remarkably and meticulously detailed journal. She arrived at Ballston in late May of that year and left at the end of August, just before the "fashionable" season would end.[41] At first, May was one of only a handful of guests. The vast majority of these early-season visitors to Ballston had come for their health; some suffered from near-crippling illnesses. There were so few such visitors that May was able to describe many of them individually in her journal, neatly recording their names and where they came from. But that would change with the arrival of June. By then, she had given up trying to be encyclopedic, deciding that she would instead choose to name "only those for whom I feel invested."[42]

The early-season guests generally had come to treat their maladies with the mineral waters. They were not there to be amused; many truly were ill. But the others—the rare pleasure traveler, the chaperones, the family members of the sick—faced an enormous problem: entertainment. In the early summer they passed the time in conversation, along with a bit of singing. But as the days melded into late June and more pleasure travelers began to arrive, a critical mass was reached: the social season had begun, and more serious diversions would have to be concocted.

On June 24, 1800, the entertainment commenced. It was also the sign that "the season" had officially begun. That evening, Ballston held the first dance of the year. It was at Aldridge's, where Abigail May was staying. There had been talk of holding a dance before then, but the most crucial factor in deciding whether or not to dance was the number of women at the springs: until late June, the population had been overwhelmingly male. Although the female contingent that late June night was still only a "small set," in the words of Abigail May, it was sufficient. It included "all the young ladies from the other house [McMaster's] added to the such of us [here] who could dance." Each of these young women, some of whom perhaps would have been overlooked in the ballrooms of Manhattan or Boston, were danced to exhaustion by the large number of willing men.[43]

A number of factors help explain why there were so few women early on. Travel, for example, was much more challenging in the late spring, when the roads were likely to be quagmires. Also, women, particularly young women, almost never traveled alone, so they needed at least one chaperone or guardian, but optimally more than one. Most often, the traveling group in this era was composed of some portion of a family. Abigail May, for example, left home with her mother and a much younger brother. Hers was a special case, however; most often, the presence of a father or older male would have been deemed necessary. The masculine presence was perhaps the most important factor. Only a tiny number of male Americans could afford to leave their businesses or other interests in 1800: even among the nation's aristocrats, the maintenance of fortune took up a fair amount of time, and frivolous travel was rarely justified except for health reasons. August, then, would prove to be the month when everything could be combined: the steaming cities of the coast, those small but nagging health problems, the word of mouth about the fun to be had in Ballston, and the requirements of the family's health. Taking three or four weeks off, then, once every few years, became more plausible. But the number of people who could face the rigors of travel in this era was quite small, and the numbers at Ballston were consequently not very large by the standards of later generations. Still, by late June in 1800 there were enough visitors at Ballston to put on a dance, and dance they did.

The 1800 season progressed; June turned into July, and the frequency of the dances accelerated. At first, they were held only once a week. By mid-August, they were being held nearly daily, an increase that, fortunately, was accompanied by a significant increase in the population of danceable women (although they would remain in the minority). All of the dances were held in the largest room in Ballston, Aldridge's new long dining room. To make room for the dancers, the inn's large dining table had been pushed to one side, and the inn's adjoining parlor was used when the numbers overwhelmed the dining room.

The increasing frequency of dances demonstrated the change in the kind of visitors who had come to the village. The quiet group of late-May health-seekers had been transformed into a loud, lively, and fun-seeking group. It wasn't until early August that the shift from sanatorium to vacation resort would be complete: Abigail May described the diverse group around her as presenting "an epitome of mankind," with a social life so intense that Aldridge's had become "no home for invalids."[44]

Although May was a young woman, attractive enough to draw attention, she counted herself among the invalids. The sole reason she had come to the springs was to heal her hand, a condition that had blighted her life for nearly two years. She had abandoned romance, writing that her mind had "been tried and purg'd from all thoughts which might lead me to look on any man other than as my friend and my brother."[45]

But she could, at times, be drawn away from these somber resolutions. Her first distraction came just a day after she had written those words, when a "series of small quiet attentions" were given to her by a young Mr. French of New Haven, who probably was a student at Yale. It began when he favored her with a "delightful stroll." The next day, they took another walk together, and again the day following. After that, she confessed to her diary that she found him "one of the most pleasing interesting young men I ever met with." He would soon have to return home, to her sorrow, but there would be others. There was the handsome young doctor attending her, Dr. Anderson; later, she would be taken with a widower, Mr. Cain.[46] Abigail May had discovered one of the less hidden secrets of Ballston: although visitors repeatedly told themselves that they were there only to benefit from the healthful effects of its mineral waters, in fact—especially by midsummer—life at the spa was much more about being social than about being healthy.

Other major activities included rumor-mongering and gossip. All of this was typical of the instant-small-town atmosphere of this small society of some two hundred visitors, not counting servants and children.[47] Newcomers were met with intense curiosity and their behavior was closely followed. Every new arrival was quickly categorized. In this atmosphere, rumors could quickly grow and fester. May herself became subject to a rumor that left her fuming for days: she was reported to be the "intended" of a young man, Mr. Howard. The May family group had encountered him soon after they left home, and he had joined them as they journeyed to Ballston. He stayed only a week at Ballston before returning home alone. "I was quite shock'd when first told of it, and now find tis current all round—even in Troy," she wrote. "I hope in mercy Mr. H. will never hear of the report . . . it really (I am such a fool) makes me unhappy. I never would have consented to his coming if I had surmised it would lead to such reports."[48]

May was experiencing the extension of drawing room culture that characterized life at the springs. This was a culture shaped by the ever-changing cast of characters, the thrills of flirtation and the entertainment that the visitors created for themselves. There were risks to leisure, temptations that could lead visitors out of their normal circles.[49] For example, May always found it difficult to observe the Sabbath as she had done in Boston. She was not a very pious woman, but she liked a measure of decorum and found it vaguely unsettling that "there is nought here to remind one to keep holy the Sabbath day—no bells call to worship—piety here has no monitor, except those innumerable benefits which fill emotion and ought to awaken it." This telling phrase, "ought to awaken it," is demonstrated by her Sabbath behavior: the same paragraph, she explains that "3 Beaux kept with us thro' the day and we read eat [ate] drank talk'd walk'd. . . ."[50] And she was not alone; other visitors complained that people simply were not pious on Sundays at the Springs.[51]

The temptations of being away from more sobering models affected many visitors. May noted disapprovingly that "by all accounts" there was gambling at "the other house," meaning McMaster's, where it was "carried on with a high hand." Fortunately, her own house was more sedate: "tis that," she noted approvingly, "which makes the distinction between the houses very proper."[52] It was logical that Nicholas Low's house would allow for such activity, so common among the gentry in New York, since his inn was intended to be a social outlet for his set. As for drinking, many drank more than just water at these places, but often reassuring letters were sent home declaring that abstinence was the order of the day. For example, James Read wrote his wife that "scarce any thing is drank at either house besides the spring water" and that "we live very regular."[53] But in 1804

Low's business agent reminded him that his bar at McMaster's, also a billiard room, brought in "about $10 p Day in the season." Obviously, not everyone lived so "regular."[54]

But more dangerous vices loomed; threats to maidenly virtue abounded at the springs. Abigail May had found most of the young men too flirtatious and all too prone to posturing. Some were, in her words, "very wild," including the New York attorney general, a Mr. De Peyster, scion of a prominent and wealthy New York family.[55] Like vacationers everywhere, in any age, the spring's visitors were immersed in an atmosphere of freedom that seemed so far removed from their homes that they could do almost anything at all without consequences. For example, Abigail May tells of the (possible) fall of a young woman she called "Miss Kissam."[56] May described her as a vulnerable young woman staying alone at the spa, living at McMaster's without being "under the protection of any gentleman." She caused scandal early in her stay: she was seen consorting with "those high blades Bowers Baldwin &c." May suspiciously noted that although she dressed with "great taste" and moved "like a fairy," she displayed a "voluptuousness and *expression* in her every look" that was "not exactly characteristic of delicacy or even decency."[57] And, it turned out, her concerns were justified. Several weeks after Kissam's arrival, May described a "most improper situation" the young woman had fallen into.[58]

One of the men at the spa—"a man—a villain—by the name of Gilliam"—had been paying "very particular attention" to Miss Kissam and she had returned his interest: "she imprudently walk'd rode and conversed with him frequently."[59] But when he "offered himself to, and was rejected by her," he began spreading gossip about her. Gilliam "told the gentlemen round, scandalous—(I hope) falsehoods about her." May records that he claimed that "he could have her whenever he chose, for she loved him to distraction." A family friend of Kissam's, Randeleer Schuyler, a member of the prominent Schuyler family of Albany, heard these stories and warned her away from Gilliam. Schuyler told her that Gilliam was "a needy adventurer . . . induced by her little paternal fortune" to seek marriage and that he was a "gamester debaucher, and every thing that was bad." Societal restraints swung into action, and the situation was quickly remedied. May tells us that Schuyler "sent for an officer and put [Gilliam] under arrest for a £1,000 he owed him" and then sent for Kissam's mother. Without delay, the young lady was bundled southward and was returned to her mother's arms in New York City. May hoped that she had remained "an innocent artless girl, as I wish to think her, and believe she is." In her journal, she went on to chastise the girl's mother, questioning how she could "place a child (an only child) in such a situation."[60]

Society at Ballston was a direct extension of the small circle of acquaintance, rumor, and kinship of the upper classes of New York and Boston. It is possible that Miss Kissam was rescued just in time from the arms of an adventurer and so avoided a major scandal. She was protected at Ballston, just as if she had been in the drawing rooms of New York. The brief sense of freedom she experienced at Ballston Spa had been illusory; she found that the embrace of society was very close indeed.

The summer season of 1800 drew to a close: the guests left, May returned to Boston, and by early September the houses were again nearly deserted. The wealthy Boston merchant Thomas Handasyd Perkins found in September 1800 "but few people at Aldridges," with only twenty-four in residence. He disconsolately wrote that "it is but 3 weeks since they numbered upwards of an hundred & there were as many more at McMasters." The summer had gone, and the visitors with it. There would be other summers.[61]

In later years, Ballston continued to prosper, no doubt helped by word of mouth among Low's fashionable friends in New York. As early as 1802, it began to get wider exposure, publicity that touted its virtues beyond its remarkable mineral waters. For example, an article ran that year in the *Port Folio*, one of the nation's leading magazines, described the village as "an agreeable place of summer resort" where people were "determined to make each other happy," in which they "rarely miss their object." This happened, the article continued, despite its location, which "presents little to invite the curiosity" and was "totally destitute of natural advantages," set in a "dreary and marshy hollow, surrounded by high and barren hills." The article noted, probably hyperbolically, that the area was now drawing large numbers of beautiful and eligible young women to it, that "the eastern and the southern states vie with each other in transmitting their brightest beauties to enliven this barren valley."[62]

This points to one emerging aspect of the spa's role as social center: it was becoming a place where young people could find each other, or where they could be brought together. That is precisely what happened to

nineteen-year-old Eliza Southgate of Salem, Massachusetts, who visited
Ballston Spa in late August 1802 with her family friends Richard and
Martha Coffin Derby.[63] At first, she was put off by the atmosphere of will-
ful fun and leisure: she described it as "one continued scene of idleness and
dissipation" where "we do nothing that seems like improvement." But
rather than condemn it, she found it fascinating. "I think there is no place
one may study the different characters and dispositions to greater advantage," she wrote to her parents, noting that she had met "the most genteel
people from every part of the country." A kind of informality reigned,
where "ceremony is thrown off and you are acquainted very soon." In this
environment, where it could be safely assumed that all were of the same
class, the formal strictures of parlor life were loosened. From this group
she had no problem finding "some agreeable, amiable companions," a clear
indication that Ballston was beginning to fill one of its most crucial later
roles, as a kind of "marriage market" for antebellum America.[64]

Although there was a kind of informality, the people Eliza Southgate
met there were safe enough that she never felt threatened. The environment had been created to ensure that only the right people would appear there; others would be ostracized or shunned. But while staying at
Ballston, the young woman experienced a life-changing event. In a letter
to her mother, she said that at the springs she had "received more attentions [from men] than in my whole life before. . . . [And] among the many
gentlemen . . . was one I believe is serious."[65]

The group she was traveling with had initially run into a Walter Bowne
of New York City, who happened to have had the same accommodations
in Albany. Like them, he had planned to go onward to the springs, and by
happy coincidence they all left Albany together. While at the springs, they
were in close enough proximity for them to bump into each other; when
the party went on a jaunt to Lake George, he joined them. Eliza Southgate, in her letter explaining all this to her mother, was interestingly cir-
cumspect about what her chaperones, the Derbys, felt about this: "Mr. and
Mrs. Derby were all very much pleased with him, but conducted towards
me a peculiar delicacy, left me entirely to myself, as on a subject of so much
importance they scarcely dared give an opinion."[66] By this point, Bowne
had become a full-fledged member of their party, and on their departure
from Ballston he traveled southward with them. They spent a few days together at Lebanon Springs, near Albany. By the end of this period she had

spent every day for four weeks with him, and she "probably had a better opportunity of knowing him than if I had seen him as a common acquaintance in town for years." Because springs society was so much an extension of the world outside, she came to know people who knew him: "There are so many *New Yorkers* at the Springs who knew him perfectly that I easily learnt his character and reputation." He was, she wrote her mother, "a man of *business*, uniform in his conduct and *very much respected*." And she noted that despite her relative vulnerability so far from the parental embrace (a situation she described as "truly embarrassing"), his conduct had been impeccable. It was "such as I shall ever reflect on with the greatest pleasure,— open, candid, generous and delicate . . . he advised me like a friend and would not have suffered me to do anything improper." Eliza Southgate and Walter Bowne were married in late April of 1803, eight months after they had met.[67]

Their honeymoon tour took them to New York City, where they spent several weeks, and then to a spring at Bethlehem, Pennsylvania. They then came back to Ballston Spa, where they spent several weeks. On their return, she and her new husband settled in at his home in New York City. Eventually, Bowne would serve as mayor of the city for a term. Their marriage was the perfect product of the springs experience: two wealthy families were united in a way that probably would never have happened before the creation of Ballston.[68] This would happen repeatedly in the coming years. For example, Southgate would later tell her mother in an 1805 letter how John R. Murray, the eldest son of the wealthy New York businessman John Murray was "at last" in love (he had turned 30, and Eliza Bowne had worried that he would never marry) with a "Miss Rogers from Baltimore, whom he met at the Springs"—a woman he would marry the next year.[69] Just as with the British spas, Ballston Springs had become an ideal location for the young elites of America to shop for mates.

After the 1802 *Port Folio* piece, Ballston began appearing more frequently in the New York press. A pamphlet-length paean to Ballston was published in 1806, for example,[70] and a satirical essay about the town appeared in Washington Irving's *Salmagundi*, the most popular magazine of 1807. *Salmagundi* was gossipy and filled with inside jokes, some of which remain funny to this day. Each issue was enthusiastically received and discussed at the dining tables and salons of the city; it became the talk of the town.

Washington Irving coauthored the magazine with his brother William and with James Kirke Paulding, who would go on to have a rich career as a humorist and commentator.

"Style at Ballston" appeared in the October 15, 1807, issue. To write it, Irving drew on an 1803 trip he had made to Ballston. Then an aspiring young lawyer-in-training, he had not been impressed: in an unpublished travel journal he wrote about his feelings of exclusion and distaste for a scene that would not accept him.[71] In his article, Irving took the resentments and slights he may have felt in that fashionable and connected crowd and slung them back in the form of satire. His theme the idea that the spa was a place that "originally meant nothing more than relief from pain and sickness." Over time, though, Ballston had gone through a metamorphosis. At first, the pleasure found there was like that of "a sober unceremonious country-dance." The village in this halcyon time had been "emancipated from the shackles of formality, ceremony and modern politeness," a "charming hum-drum careless place of resort." Everyone was "at his ease, and might follow unmolested the bent of his humour—provided his wife was not there."[72]

But this bucolic and simple place had undergone a baleful change: "Lo! All of a sudden *Style* made its baneful appearance," and pleasure that had "taken an entire new significance": now it meant "nothing but STYLE." This state of affairs had been created by "the worthy, fashionable, dashing, good-for-nothing people of every state" who flocked there "not to enjoy the pleasures of society, or benefit by the qualities of the waters, but to exhibit their equipages and wardrobes, and to excite the admiration . . . the *envy* of their fashionable competitors." This may have reflected Irving's own experiences at Ballston. Perhaps the young man had not been able to present a stylish wardrobe or the overly precious manners of the aristocracy. In "Style at Ballston," he channels his bile at a number of targets. For example, he writes acidly of wealthy southeners such as "the lady of a southern planter" who squanders "the whole annual produce of a rice plantation in silver and gold muslins" or the planter with "a thousand Negroes at home" whose conspicuous consumption includes arriving at the springs with "half a score of black-a-moors in gorgeous liveries." Irving contrasts these decadent southerners with a "northern merchant, who plods on in a carriage and pair" with "no claim whatever to *style*." But he imagines a comeuppance. The southern "tyro of fashion" driving the elegant coach quickly spends himself into bankruptcy and has to slip away in a common stagecoach.[73]

Irving is also cutting about the relatively desolate and scrappy location of the spa. For entertainment, "every one chooses his own amusement," whether it is taking "a ride into the pine woods [to] enjoy the varied and romantick scenery of burnt trees, post and rail fences . . . scrambl[ing] up the surrounding sand hills . . . [to] take a peep at other sand hills beyond them," or taking a "stroll along the borders of a little swampy brook . . . watching the little tadpoles, as they frolick right flippantly in the muddy stream." Some visitors "play at billiards, some play the fiddle, and some — play the fool—the latter being the most prevalent amusement at Ballston." In all, the place offers "a delicious life of alternate lassitude and fatigue, of laborious dissipation, and listless idleness." But he proposes improvements: all Ballston needs is "good air, good wine, good living, good beds, good company, and good humour." If it had them it could become "the most enchanting place in the world—excepting Botany-bay, Musquito Cove, Dismal Swamp, and the Black-hole at Calcutta."[74]

Irving's cynicism was a clear reaction to the popularity of Ballston among certain members of the New York elite, although it was also typical of all of *Salmagundi*, which was intended to strike a world-weary pose against the frenzy of the popular. The piece is an indication of the spa's reach during this crucial time. Indeed, in 1809 one wealthy southern visitor called it "the most fashionable place in America" for the three months of the summer.[75] This class of visitors ranged from the governor of the State of New York, the state's attorney general, and several generals (active and retired) to a scattering of prominent foreigners. As evidenced by Abigail May's description, a certain number of the respectable upper middle class like clergymen and academics also came for several days at a time. However, Ballston's relative distance still made it very remote for even those in the wealthiest classes, although it could now, by one estimate, hold something in excess of two hundred visitors at a time.[76]

And so, despite the prominence of its visitors and increasingly important role in New York society, the problem of getting to the spa would continue to limit the size of Ballston for another decade. Because getting to Ballston was so time-consuming, those who could visit were restricted to those who were willing to spend days or even weeks just to reach it, much less to spend any time there. But new technologies lay just within reach, and their impact would profoundly shape the future of the spa.

Travel

Until 1808, just getting to the springs could be an ordeal. While summertime travel from Albany to Saratoga or Ballston was predictable enough—the roads were rough and dusty but they were passable—travel up the Hudson River from New York to Albany could be quite a trial. For long stretches the river cut through rugged terrain, and until the 1840s a direct road would remain financially impracticable to build. Travelers were therefore reliant on water-borne travel. Isaac Weld, traveling from New York City in 1797, was lucky enough to reach Albany (about ninety river miles) in only two days with the wind and tides favoring him. Dr. Adam Alexander, traveling in 1801, was not so lucky. It took him a total of six days to make his way from Albany to New York: two days waiting for any wind whatsoever and another four days tacking against an unfavorable wind down the river. And John Pintard, a prominent New Yorker of the early nineteenth century, wrote of two brothers who sailed from New York, one for Albany and the other for England. Both arrived at their destination at the same time—twenty-four days later. Prior to 1807 there were no regularly scheduled sailings and no established shipping lines. A traveler had to hope that a vessel was available and heading to a reasonable destination.[77]

The chancellor of New York State, Robert Livingston, had experienced these delays and frustrations. Hs estate, Clermont, lay on the river, and he had regular business both in Albany and New York. Undoubtedly he had often experienced the vicissitudes of Hudson River travel. Livingston longed for something that would transport him upriver with certainty, a boat driven by something other than the wind. In short, Livingston yearned for a steamboat.

America had already seen such machine. For one summer, in 1790, John Fitch, a mercurial inventor, had built and operated a steamboat on the Delaware River between Philadelphia and Trenton. It was a technical success—it maintained a schedule and had relatively few repairs—but it was a commercial failure. The reasons for this were complex, but two factors predominated. One was that the boat was extremely primitive, consisting mainly of a steam boiler set amidships with the smoke-belching contraption churning only feet away from the passengers' heads. Fitch, interested only in technical perfection, even resisted putting an awning over them for protection from the summer sun. The other factor was Fitch himself: he was so abrasive that he alienated customers and financial backers alike.[78]

But Livingston had noted Fitch's efforts and closely followed the developments in steamboat technology. In 1798, with an eye to the future, he pushed a bill through the New York legislature that granted him exclusive rights to run a steamboat operation on the Hudson. Those rights had originally been awarded to Fitch, but the failure of the Philadelphia line in 1790 and his suicide in 1798 had cleared Livingston's way. Although the governor objected to the bill as an unwarranted monopoly grant to a serving politician, Livingston worked the legislature, got his monopoly, and then used his powers as chancellor to override the governor's veto.[79]

Several years later, in the first years of the new century, Livingston was in Paris as the U.S. minister plenipotentiary. There, he encountered a vigorous and inventive young man, Robert Fulton. Fulton was the kind of person who was always in the right place at the right time. An ambitious and multitalented artist, engineer, and visionary, he had bounced about Europe at the turn of the nineteenth century in occupations ranging from the pet portraitist of a British aristocrat to itinerant weapons designer to inventor. It was in this latter role, as he ran his first experiments in steam navigation on the Seine, that he came to Robert Livingston's attention. Livingston had already funded one failed attempt by Nicholas Roosevelt to build a working steamboat, and he was always on the lookout for any new efforts. When Livingston saw Fulton's new machine, based on a modified version of Robert Fitch's old design, he was impressed. And although this particular boat would prove a failure, Livingston was confident that with a bit more tinkering, Fulton would succeed. With that in mind, Livingston approached Fulton and proposed that they build a boat in New York. He sketched out a vision for a steamboat line on the Hudson. Fulton, eager for official backing and deep pockets, readily agreed. In 1806, when Livingston resumed the post of chancellor, they returned together to the United States. Fulton promptly began building his new boat.

Fulton's connection to Livingston meant that when the *North River Steamboat* began its maiden voyage on the morning of September 4, 1807, it would be loaded with the elite of New York City.[80] Fulton did not disappoint: his steamboat made the run quickly and without breaking down; naturally, its first destination was the chancellor's estate, Clermont. Because of the distinguished crowd and the well-publicized effort, he was crowned the inventor of steam navigation in the United States over the hapless Fitch. To complete his triumph, Fulton soon married Harriet, Livingston's niece.[81]

The company that was formed around this first steamboat—only much later renamed the *Clermont*—was the North River Steam Company. The technical near-perfection of Fulton's boat and the company's protected status as a monopoly meant that Livingston and Fulton would prosper mightily, and as long as it held the monopoly on Hudson River steam navigation, the company led a charmed life. And although the steamboat would need extensive reconstruction at the end of its first season's work (six weeks after its maiden voyage), by March of 1809, eighteen months later, the company had earned a massive profit of $16,000.[82]

With this stunning success, his connection to Livingston, and the twenty-eight thousand acres of fine upstate land that had come with Harriet Livingston's dowry, Fulton had immediately joined the gentry class. His high status and instant celebrity helped to make steamboats fashionable. Perhaps more important, he was also able to make them *look* fashionable: he operated them in a manner that appealed to the genteel. Where Fitch had been interested solely in the engineering problems of his design, Fulton worked to create a comfortable atmosphere for his passengers, who paid the staggering sum of seven dollars each way.[83] In addition to a cabin with bunks, he offered good meals and a well-stocked bar, all designed with special attention to the comfort of passengers. To maintain decorum, he issued a set of rules that demanded cleanliness and order, and the company charged violators fines. In all, he worked to make value for money. Perhaps most importantly, the boat was fast: its maiden run was thirty hours and fifteen minutes, and he kept it to a sound schedule that earned the company a reputation for reliability. Finally, the boat was safe: unlike other boats, it did not blow up.[84] Of course, there were complaints. For example, unpleasant plumes of smoke and soot from the wood-fired boilers occasionally swept across the deck. But this was easily overlooked;

after all, this was an era in which every inhabited site in the world was more or less overwhelmed with soot from cooking and heating fires. His efforts to maintain the patronage of the wealthiest classes through the enforcement of genteel norms combined with the critical route his boat served, one that linked the two centers of power in New York State, the political (Albany) and economic (New York City), meant that his revenues would remain healthy. By 1814, Fulton had seen remarkable success and had expanded his fleet by an additional four boats. (His luck would run out in February 1815, when he died of exposure while walking back from New Jersey on the ice of the Hudson River.)

The steamboat was also crucial to the expansion of Hudson Valley tourism, as virtually all tourists bound for Ballston or Saratoga from New York City traveled on it. The inauguration of steamboats on the Hudson ensured fast and comfortable travel; with that, one of the most important elements of a tourist experience was now in place.

Entertainment

The steamboats that linked Albany and, by extension, Ballston and Saratoga to the major travel hub of New York City brought more than just tourists. Only a year after the first full season of steamboat service up the Hudson, traveling commercial entertainment arrived for the first time at Ballston Spa. This was a significant sign of the spa's arrival as a destination of import. The traveling entertainers of this era did not bother changing their routes to accommodate destinations where they could not make money or that took too much time to reach. The historian Peter Benes has described the patterns of itinerant performers, noting that the vast majority of them "limited their tours to principal seaboard cities, secondary ports, and deepwater up-river ports." Ballston Spa had become as viable a venue as any of the more sophisticated cities.[85]

The sort of entertainment that came was typical of the day. For example, the first to come to Ballston in August 1810 was a traveling panorama.[86] These long paintings were transported in special cases and at their destination were unrolled and exhibited in a wooden, stage-like frame hidden by curtains. When paying customers came to view it, care was taken to conjure an aura around the viewing, to create an "experience." The Battle of Arcola, the advertisements promised, would be "brilliantly illuminated," probably by a guide using a hand lantern in a well-lit room. Admission was set at twenty-five cents, which, although not dear, was also not cheap. This was the kind of exhibition that would have been rare in a place as far afield as Ballston or even Albany, although panoramas had long appeared in New York.[87] Another entertainment typical of the time, a "cabinet of curiosities," which came several weeks later, was announced by handbills. This collection of oddities was highlighted by a huge wax model of the 700-plus-pound Englishman, Daniel Lambert.[88]

The next step was the arrival of professional entertainers. These productions had a higher overhead, so it took until the summer of 1811 for them to arrive. When they did, quite a few came at once, including the "Equestrian Feats" of "Mr. Stewart, who has just performed to the admiration of all present." The day before, a "Signor Victoriani, a native of Italy," had walked "about 100 feet on a rope fastened to the top of the chimneys of two of the principal buildings," forty feet above ground without a net. Both of these performers had probably appeared in New York City just weeks before.[89]

Finally, the first traveling theater troupe, the "Company of Comedians," came to town in early August. They performed plays typical of the New York stage, including "the laughable entertainment" of *The Lying Valet* and, the following week, *The Tragedy of George Barnwell, or The London Merchant*.[90]

Both plays were staples of the theater in the Early Republic, and both speak of some key aspects of the spa's visitors.[91] *Barnwell*, an old warhorse first produced in 1731, was a morality play that warned rising apprentices of the consequences of vice and lauded and ennobled the work of merchants. It had often been used to educate apprentices in some of the pitfalls of their new relative freedom; thus more than a few of the spa's visitors would have seen it in their youth. Fortunately there was just enough salaciousness in the mechanism of the fall of the eponymous apprentice Barnwell to entertain the prurient. For the more proper, it was a solid morality play. *The Lying Valet* would have appealed to those not of the merchant class. Although it, too, was of some vintage, being first produced in 1742, it was, unlike *Barnwell*, a rollicking farce featuring sharp-tongued servants with an essentially virtuous (if somewhat clueless) hero and, unlike *Barnwell*, it had a happy ending. This was precisely the sort of frivolity that a spa crowd bent on entertainment would have sought. Like everything else associated with the spa, these entertainments belied its reputation as a resort for the sick and instead pointed up the new purpose of its existence, which was to be a destination for entertainment and fashion. Furthermore, the appearance of professional entertainment clicked the final missing piece into the picture of Ballston Spa to make it at least comparable to the spa scene in Great Britain or the continent. It was the fulfillment of Nicholas Low's dream of a perfect gentry refuge.

✑ 2 ✑

Inventing the Resort

Saratoga Springs

W HILE BALLSTON SPA was being built, the nearby springs at Saratoga remained quite rustic, despite the higher regard in which connoisseurs held the waters.[1] The springs had first come to the attention of outsiders after a legendary 1771 visit by Sir William Johnson, when one of the springs, High Rock, supposedly cured him of the lingering consequences of an old war wound, a cure so efficacious that the previously crippled hero purportedly walked the fifteen miles back to Schenectady. His accommodations at the springs were a Mohawk hunting hut covered with hides. In 1773, there was a brief attempt at permanent settlement, but it was abandoned in the face of the oncoming Revolutionary War.[2]

More people learned about the springs during the American Revolution, and at the end of the war in 1783, with the end of organized Indian resistance in New York, white men came to settle permanently in Saratoga. During these years, some famous visitors on their way to Bemis Heights diverted to Saratoga. They included General Philip Schuyler, who spent a summer at the springs in a walled tent, and it was legend in Saratoga that George Washington himself had come. In 1787, Samuel Latham Mitchill, a famous chemist and author, visited the springs. His published analysis of the waters would become a standard work for boosters of the springs and was reprinted in a wide variety of later works. At the time of his visit, Saratoga still consisted of only a single log cabin, the first settler's home, built in 1773 and reoccupied ten years later. A 1789 visitor was told that "wild beasts were very numerous and bold in the surrounding forest," and she and her fellow travelers spent a worried night there, having been warned that the wolves and bears "sometimes, when hungry, approached the house."[3] But steady hunting thinned the wild animals, and in 1789, inspired by the small but steady stream of visitors, Alexander Bryan, the owner of the cabin, made a modest expansion to it. That year, two other settlers came. One was a Vermont transplant, Gideon Putnam, who moved from Middlebury to Rutland and then to a leased three-hundred-acre tract near the springs. He immediately began logging the tall old-growth pines and transported them to the Hudson to sell in New York City. Another New England family settled nearby. A visitor, almost certainly Timothy Dwight of Yale University, came in 1791 to find "but three habitations and those poor log-houses." Despite these wretched conditions, they were "almost full of strangers, among whom were several ladies and gentlemen from Albany." Although he "found it almost impossible to obtain accommodations," he was able to spend the night. The area remained a wilderness: "for many miles" the tall pines extended, nothing but "perfect forest." In time, more New Englanders came to settle.[4]

And so while Ballston Spa was the destination of a high-class clientele, Saratoga remained entirely a backwater. There were hints, though, that it might someday overtake Ballston among the many connoisseurs of mineral water. For example, Dr. Samuel Tenney's 1793 analysis of the Saratoga waters called them a valuable resource and wondered why "the . . . physician, the chemist and the philosopher" had ignored them. To date, he mused, they had only "attract[ed] the notice, and excite[d] the admiration of the illiterate . . . the poorer sort of people." There were two major problems, he felt. One was publicity—the springs needed "a suitable introduction to the world." There was also the question of the accommodations and other facilities. Visitors needed "some convenient houses for boarding and lodging patients."[5]

Saratoga also lacked, in effect, the social connections that had made Ballston so fashionable so quickly. Without that fashionable word of mouth, Saratoga would have been forever destined to be the poor man's Ballston. But Saratoga was quietly improving, even as its reputation grew. For example, in 1795 Mitchill wrote a treatise on Saratoga Springs that was broadly excerpted in one of the more popular American books of the late eighteenth century, Jedidiah Morse's *American Geography*. Over the next generation, other geographies and gazetteers reproduced items from

Morse's book, so Saratoga gained national renown as a center for healthful mineral water.[6] By 1797 a visitor named James Read found "five or six excellent houses" at the springs. But during his visit he saw "very few visitors." Part of the reason, he mused, was that the food was just as dismal as it had been during his 1791 visit.[7] More visitors did come, probably in part as a spillover from Ballston. In 1803, Saratoga finally got a genteel hotel when Gideon Putnam completed Union Hall, a substantial structure some three stories tall and twenty-four feet deep. Putnam also built the springs' first bathhouse.[8] But Saratoga in these early years took a very different role than Ballston: its more plebian nature had already been hinted at in Samuel Tenney's 1793 work, and an 1804 pamphlet expanded on that characterization. Timothy Howe's *History of the Medicinal Springs at Saratoga and Ballstown* attacked Saratoga as a place of "drunkenness and profanity . . . vice and vulgarity" where "decent and respectable" inhabitants were scarce. He claimed that the climate of Saratoga was tainted with "air . . . infected with . . . effluvia that rise from the neighboring mill ponds," air that makes "the inhabitants universally . . . pale and sickly," affecting their "moral faculty" and creating the "general indolence and intemperance which characterizes the place."[9] This attack is deeply strange—unless one considers the context of the market the spas sought. For the partisans of each spa, it must have seemed that there were only a finite number of possible visitors, meaning that large sums of money and future fortunes were at stake. In fact, Ballston had already been warned: as early as 1802, the *Port Folio* had noted that "there appears a prospect of [Saratoga's] rivaling" Ballston.[10]

Ballston Spa did have some reason for concern. Saratoga was visibly growing, taking on more of the appearance of a town. Putnam expanded his hotel in 1804 and a year later bought a tract of land that included most of the major springs in the area. In 1808 he laid out a village. Its grandest feature was a 140-foot-wide main street named Broadway, along with sites for a cemetery, a church, and a school. At the end of each of the village's main streets were the town's main springs.[11] All of the side streets were likewise very wide, nearly as wide as Broadway.[12]

In 1808 another hotel, the Columbian, was completed by Jotham Holmes, but it was smaller than the Sans Souci and the Union. And Benjamin Risley, one of the other original settlers in the area, expanded his small tavern into the "Yellow House," as it was so prosaically known.

Other private homes in the area began to add rooms for in-season clients. But in 1811 Putnam built a clear rival to the Sans Souci, Congress Hall, which was just as large as Ballston's hotel. He did not have long to live, however; in 1812, he died of a lung inflammation.[13]

Even though Saratoga was rising rapidly, Ballston Spa was preeminent and would remain so for several more years. The differences were not limited to reputation: Ballston Spa was still significantly larger than Saratoga. One visitor claimed that Ballston could house nearly a thousand guests, and while that estimate seems high, the town probably could have accommodated around five hundred, about twice Saratoga's capacity.[14] There were also significant cultural differences. For example, as we have seen, Ballston, rather than Saratoga, was the destination of the itinerant entertainers. By 1809 there were at least two newspapers operating at Ballston, while Saratoga struggled to support one.[15] And in 1808 Ballston gained a lending library open to both residents and visitors; Saratoga would not get one until 1817.[16]

Given the speed of Saratoga's growth, the rivalry between the two spas would probably have been settled in only a year or two, but the summer of 1811 was the last flush of prosperity that either spa would see for some time. In June 1812 the United States declared war on Great Britain. The nation's feeble armies were mobilized for an invasion of British Canada; war would now rage across New York State for several years to come. This proved to be disastrous for leisure travel, as blockades and economic disruption cut deeply into the revenue of both rich and poor. Especially hard hit were the wealthy of New England, but traders and businessmen from New York also suffered. Both Ballston Spa and Saratoga Springs were badly hurt, as all forms of leisure travel effectively came to a end in New York State for the duration of the war. Throughout 1812 and 1813, battles were fought across the Canada–United States border, disrupting the peacetime lines of travel and closing the Niagara Falls area to leisure travelers. By 1814, the British were making raids down Lake Champlain.

Some histories of Saratoga claim that its decline during these years was due to the "restraining influence" of a temperance group that was founded there, perhaps as early as 1808, and that grew in influence in subsequent years. Its dreary restraints, they claim, drove away fashionable and fun-loving visitors to nearby Ballston Spa, which had no such agitators.[17] But the evidence is clear that both villages suffered equally during this period. One indication is the disappearance of all forms of paid entertainment from the villages. A "Panorama of Rome" was exhibited in the summer of 1812, the only entertainment offered that summer.[18] There were no other advertisements that indicated tourist traffic. In prior years, boarding houses had run advertisements in July and August; there were none in any of the local newspapers from 1812 through 1815. One intrepid soul, a Mrs. John Heard, who made the journey in 1815, during the first summer after the war, found "about fifty" visitors at Saratoga in July, a much reduced number from the seasonal height of years past.[19]

During this period the villages attempted to diversify their economic bases: the nearby town of Milton opened a factory; a shoe factory was opened in Ballston Spa, joining a very successful cotton mill there owned by Nicholas Low; and wool carding operations opened in both Milton and Ballston.[20] In 1816, the printer of the *Independent American* noted that "because times are peculiarly hard," all accounts had to be settled, and that although this announcement had run for a month, "few, very few have complied with its easy requirement." He finished with a warning: "Mark it—this is the last."[21]

Through the years of economic suffering, the spas remained in a state of suspended animation. Would their customers return? The stage had been set: a modern and efficient transportation infrastructure had been erected to bring tourists north from New York City, and not just one but two re-sorts had been built with hundreds of waiting beds. The moneyed gentry of New York City and elsewhere were primed for leisure travel. It would take only the return of peace and the slow arrival of prosperity to begin the first American tourist age.

Saratoga Springs

"The facility and economy of traveling, produced by the introduction of steam-boats into our waters," read the *New York Herald* in July 1816, "is a matter of surprise and felicity." A traveler, the article went on to report, could now journey from Philadelphia all the way north to Quebec City in as little as five and a half days, for only fifty dollars. Of course, such an ex-pense put this kind of travel beyond all but the wealthiest: fifty dollars could support a working family for months. But for the tourists of the time, it meant that there was now the possibility of spending just a week or two traveling to and from some romantic place rather than being absent from normal life for the entire summer.[22]

By 1816, there were the first signs of an economic revival at Ballston Spa. For the first time in years, a circulating library was advertised. In July it expanded to include a "Library and Reading Room" specifically directed to the "gentlemen and Ladies, Visitants at Ballston Spa."[23] But 1816 turned out to be a particularly unfortunate year for tourists and travelers, becoming known as the "year without a summer." It began mildly enough, with a warmish winter and less-than-average snowfall, but this drought lessened the forage for cattle. A warm, wet May ended with frosts on May 30 extending as far south as New Haven, Connecticut. Then the weather became as savagely unsummerlike as possible: snowstorms and more frosts arrived early June, and in mid-June the Catskill Mountains were still covered with snow. The weather there, the *New York Herald* reported, was succinctly described as "very cold, winds high, and frost severe." Deep frosts reoccurred in early July and again in mid-August, late August, and early September. All of this combined to make a dreadful growing season, as with each successive frost farmers lost all hope for any kind of crop. The cause of the unusual weather pattern was a titanic explosion of Mt. Tambora, a volcano in the Indonesian archipelago, in April 1815.[24]

The immediate impact was to suppress any desire to travel to the springs, although some travelers did come during the rare weeks of warmer weather. William Appleton, for example, arrived at Ballston Spa from Boston in mid-July after two leisurely weeks of travel. He stayed at Ballston for almost a month and made a number of trips to Saratoga, recording only that it was "very rainy" on August 4 and that August 14 was "rather warm."[25] Nonetheless, the number of tourists visiting the spas remained low, as is evidenced by the complete lack of entertainment advertisements for that year. Southern spas did prosper, though, as tourists from that region stayed closer to home. Beyond the weather, the nation's economy was still hard hit by the effects of the war, and the number of available prosperous travelers was much reduced from prewar levels.[26]

It would take another year before the tourists began to return in any numbers. The economy had improved just enough to allow the wealthy some leisure travel, although for others the economic impact of the war

would continue for several more years, and the financial panic of 1819 did
not help matters. The first glimmer that things might be turning for the
better came one day in August 1817, when professional entertainers reap-
peared for the first time since 1811. This traveling show, "just arrived from
Philadelphia," was, in the words of a large illustrated advertisement, the
"most Grand, Rich and Rare Collection of *Living Animals*," including a
"real Red African Lion" and an "almost full grown . . . Royal Tiger," all
housed in "strong iron cages." "Good Music on King David's Cymbals
and other instruments" was also offered.[27] The arrival of entertainers was
built on one key fact: the tourists were back. By the end of the season, the
newspaper reported that "near 1600" guests had visited "the four principal boarding houses, from the 18th of July, to the 10th of September."
That number included some of the most renowned personages of the
entire United States: General Winfield Scott, a hero of the recent war;
another American general, Henry Dearborn; and the Russian minister,
Mr. Daschkoff, "together with a considerable number of people from various parts of Europe." Ballston and Saratoga, the paper asserted, were "no
doubt the most celebrated Watering places in America." In fact, it claimed
(although with a bit of hesitancy) that "perhaps Europe cannot boast
greater."[28]

But although Ballston did not realize it, it was about to be eclipsed by
nearby Saratoga Springs, which was significantly better positioned for the
dramatic changes in the character and volume of tourism that were coming. A remarkable group of people were now setting Saratoga's agenda,
and their tireless efforts to promote and build the town would, by the early
1820s, make it the nation's preeminent "place of fashionable refuge," as one
local newspaper had it.[29] Although Ballston Spa would always have its
champions, its unchanging nature meant that it would steadily slip behind
Saratoga.[30]

Of this group of leading Saratogans, one man in particular would be
instrumental in securing the resort's prominence, lifting its name to a
national audience. Gideon Minor Davison had originally come from Vermont, a state hit particularly hard by the "year without a summer." Agricultural losses pushed thousands of Vermonters into upstate New York
and beyond. In 1817, probably as a part of that great outward migration,
Davison, then twenty-six, left Rutland, Vermont, for Saratoga Springs. He

was beginning a great adventure: for the first time in his life, he would be his own boss and would own and run his own newspaper.

Davidson had been born in 1791 in Middleton, Vermont, and at the age of twelve had been apprenticed to William Fay, the printer and publisher of the *Herald* over in Rutland. At the end of his apprenticeship, Davison went to New York City for several years, working with printers including the new printing partnership of James and John Harper (the famed Harper Brothers). He then returned to Rutland and went into partnership with Fay, co-publishing the *Herald* and printing popular books, pamphlets, and broadsides.[31]

There is some uncertainty about what drew Davison to Saratoga Springs. It is possible that he knew, or knew of, Gideon Putnam, the builder and proprietor of Saratoga's Union Hall, who had grown up in Rutland. Or perhaps he was solicited by the leading men of the village to start a newspaper. However it happened, by the time he arrived in town he was already well connected. On his first visit he met with the leading citizens, including the owners of the main hotels, the town's most prominent lawyer, and a medical doctor, John Steel, a widely quoted resident expert on the spa's water.[32] These entrepreneurs probably funded Davison in his new venture, since in a remarkably short time he had not only an entirely new set of type but also his own printing press—considerable investments of capital. On the May 26, 1819, the first issue of the *Saratoga Sentinel* appeared.[33]

The front page of that first issue proudly announced that the eight-page weekly paper would be printed "on a handsome sheet of large royal paper," and one can imagine the satisfaction Davison felt as he typeset those grand words. But he was not just going to produce a newspaper, he was also going to create a "a competent *Circulating Library*, composed of valuable, various, and well selected books [and a] spacious *Reading Room* [stocked with] the important . . . newspapers of our country."[34] Through his reading room and library, Davison planned to bring the world to Saratoga.

But he would also use his newspaper to bring Saratoga to the world. He lived in a remarkable time in American history—one author has called it "America's first information revolution."[35] By 1820, literacy had become widespread enough that most households had at least one person capable of reading a newspaper, particularly in New England and the Middle

States. Advances in printing, paper manufacture, and distribution made newspapers cheaper and easier to produce. By 1820, it was the rare town that did not have a newspaper.[36] The production of these papers often relied on a very small team, sometimes just one or two people, and they were often desperate for material. Consequently, most newspaper text consisted of material derived entirely or in part from journals, books, or other newspapers. In effect, the country was a kind of echo chamber for anyone who could put original material into print, as stories bounced from paper to paper. (One important factor was that the U.S. Postal Service, by law, carried newspapers for exchange with other papers for free.)[37] By creating a new, local voice, Davison could ensure that the news from Saratoga—his news, and the news his backers wanted to see—would reach the world. More important, his connections in New York meant that his paper would be distributed there. As a result, the *Saratoga Sentinel* was much more widely quoted than the small papers that had been produced in Ballston Spa and Saratoga. (Davison's newspaper wasn't Saratoga's first—there were at least six predecessors—but it was the most successful, with the longest period of publication to date and the most consistent tone and contents.)[38]

Davison was representative of the cohort leading Saratoga. Most were self-made men or from families of the lower gentry. Few of them were directly linked to the kind of New York elite represented by Nicholas Low. But because of the superiority of Saratoga's facilities and more effective publicity about the resort, that elite would be drawn away from Ballston with a speed that surprised many.[39]

Saratoga's rapid change was signaled by the opening in 1819 of the Pavilion, the town's first hotel larger than Ballston's Sans Souci. It would join Saratoga's two existing large hotels, Congress Hall and the Union Hall, along with the much smaller Columbian Hotel. The Pavilion had been planned as early as 1815 by Henry Walton, owner of much of the town of Saratoga Springs. It had been delayed several years until the business climate improved.[40] He ordered a Federal-style structure extending down the edge of an escarpment, two and a half stories high in the front and three in the rear. Like Aldridge's house in Ballston but on a much grander scale, it had a long porch or piazza along its front.

The hotel was completed in 1818 and took in its first guests in the early summer of 1819. The spas had seen large hotels before, but what made the Pavilion special was its setting. Walton, who had been educated in England during the Revolution, brought with him much of the British and Continental spa sensibility, reflected in his careful consideration of the grounds surrounding the new structure. An extensive garden, about a hundred thousand square feet in extent, was planned; one historian has called it the first park in the United States.[41]

More important, the Pavilion was heavily advertised in New York. Among the large display ads was one placed front page center in the *New-York Evening Post*, the city's leading newspaper. It touted the "extensive improvements," the "ample stock of choice WINES, and a variety of LIQUORS," and the beds, which were "large, and of the best quality." More significantly, it specifically addressed women, who were "assured that constant care" would be taken that the hotel would be "distinguished for [its] neatness." For members of the reading public, a "fashionable CIRCULATING LIBRARY and READING ROOM" had been placed "contiguous to the establishment."[42] This advertisement, which ran for weeks, highlights several crucial aspects of the new tourist culture. It was not particularly interested in health—the emphasis was on the resort's alcoholic beverages, not its mineral waters. It promoted comfort over privation for medicinal purposes. It recognized that travelers were readers, and reading would be a crucial part of the spread of the tourist idea. And it appealed to women, who tended to travel in larger groups than men, and never alone.

Until the United States Hotel was built in 1824, the Pavilion was the leading hotel in the area, attracting large numbers of visitors, many of them from the South.[43] But it was not just this one hotel that created Saratoga's reputation: the synergy between three high-class hotels pushed it to greater growth, as each competed to create the most stylish atmosphere, the most opulent furnishings, and the most glittering balls and entertainments. The hotels' need for more customers meant that they had to advertise as widely as possible, particularly in the newspapers of New York City.

The name of Saratoga was being marketed in other ways as well. Congress Spring water had been bottled as early as 1810, and in every piece of advertising related to that product, a strong effort was made to distinguish it from all others, a very early example of product branding. This creation of a brand was another key element in Saratoga's rise over Ballston Spa. By the end of the 1810s, the effort had paid off. Saratoga water was regularly being exported far beyond the springs, even to customers beyond the United States; in 1817, one traveler wrote that "they put it up not only for many of our southern cities, but even for the W.I. [West Indian] Islands." Two years later Congress Spring water was one of the main products at the country's first soda fountain in New York City. It was ubiquitous, becoming synonymous with healthful water. Even other spas sold Congress water; those who resisted soon had to give in to customer demand. For example, in 1820, Schooley's Mountain in Pennsylvania argued in advertisements that its waters would help those who had tried Ballston or Saratoga water "to no purpose." But by 1822 its advertisements were now promoting that the resort was offering "the Saratoga Congress Waters, fresh from the Springs . . . in bottles." Another spa with local popularity, New Lebanon Springs, declared in an 1823 advertisement that the "SARATOGA WATERS will be kept constantly for the use of the boarders."[44]

How Many Tourists?

For the period up to 1818, it is difficult for a historian to quantify how many tourists were visiting the spas. Certainly there was significant traffic of visitors: three major hotels at Saratoga Springs and one at Ballston Spa were being kept afloat by a traffic that lasted, at best, for twelve weeks of the year. Hundreds of hotel beds had been made and were being filled, and travelers' accounts regularly spoke of being turned away at the height of the season.

For the 1818 season we have the best existing estimate of the numbers of tourists visiting the spas, made by Gideon Minor Davison, the newspaper publisher. In June 1819 he presented a compilation of the number of the previous season's visitors, as taken from the registers of Saratoga's hotels, boarding houses, and inns. Davison realized that his system had shortcomings, noting that "a great number of itinerant visitors" stayed at lodgings all around the town outside of the large hotels. And the names of one-night visitors were never entered into the registers. But in his role as booster, he could then reasonably claim that his figures were conservative, that the spa in fact had many more visitors than his list would indicate.

Congress Hall	1476
Union Hall	823
Columbian Hotel	496
Dr. Porter's	295
Mrs. Sackrider's	113
Mr. How's	189
Mr. Sadler's	216
At sundry places at High Rock	259
At sundry other places	346
Total	4213

Of course, this seasonal total represents only the visitors coming to Saratoga Springs. It is a significant number, even if Davison had exaggerated by, say, 10 or even 30 percent. Ever the booster, Davison concluded the accounting with a ringing endorsement: "I cannot resist the idea that this [place] must become one of the first watering places in the universe."[45] Given what we know about Ballston's accommodations, perhaps another third had visited there in 1818. In all, then, perhaps some five thousand people had come to the springs that season, and that is an impressive number; to put it into perspective, consider that by 1820 the population of Albany County was around 36,000, that of New York City about 123,000.[46] Later in the summer of 1819, Davison claimed that the streets of Saratoga were filled with "a greater throng of visitants" than had been seen "since the settlement of the country," including a large number of "distinguished citizens" from not only "our own country . . . [but] numbers from Europe." Saratoga, he argued, had become the country's "favoured spot," one that attracted "not merely . . . invalids." It had become "the splendid abode of gay and fashionable life."[47]

Saratoga was becoming a real small town. For example, it was promoted in the eyes of the U.S. Postal Service from a hamlet to a village when the mail delivery was increased from three to five times a week, every day but Friday and Saturday.[48] That, too, would help out-of-town visitors to stay longer, since a remarkable number of them relied on the mails for comfort and even money, as their surviving letters show.

Davison began a campaign of steady promotion, most notably in a series of reports he began in 1819 that described what was happening in the town. These reports were almost always titled "The Springs." Issued several times a season, they were first published in Davison's *Saratoga Sentinel* but would be picked up by newspapers across the East Coast. Through this means, Saratoga, rather than Ballston, would become the name people associated with Hudson Valley tourism.[49] The campaign to carry Saratoga's name was remarkably successful. Its print presence combined with the spring's mineral water exports meant that by the beginning of the 1820s, most literate Americans knew at least a little something about Saratoga. The first years of the 1820s would carry that campaign home, as Saratoga's conquest of Ballston in the minds of fashionable travelers would be made complete.

A New World: Courtship and Tourism

Saratoga's rise was predicated on a number of factors, but one of the most important was the presence of large numbers of women. In particular, that presence created a new set of social opportunities. For many young people of the 1820s, the lure of this new world was irresistible. For the first time in their lives, they could meet people outside the usual circles of home and family. The tourist sites became an exciting venue for courtship and flirtation, of meeting and evaluation, a "marriage market." The hothouse atmosphere compressed time and accelerated the courtship process far faster than would ever have permitted under normal circumstances.[50]

Sarah (Sally) Ogden was a perfect example. A member of the American aristocracy, she traveled to Saratoga Springs in the summer of 1820. At twenty, Sally was one of the most eligible young women in New York City. She was described as charming, was considered good-looking, and was quite wealthy: her father, Judge David Bayard Ogden, was a prominent merchant and one of the state's largest landowners. Among other holdings, he owned tens of thousands of acres of land in upstate New York along the St. Lawrence River around the present-day town of Ogdensburg. Near there, on Ogden's Island (originally Isle au Rapide du Plat), he built a second home, a mansion where he lived with his wife, Rebecca Cornell Edwards, and their eleven children. Sally was their eldest daughter. She and her siblings went to school in New York City, where the family kept a stylish townhouse. After her time in school, Sally split her time between the upstate home and New York City, keeping in the thick of New York society. An active correspondent, she was kept abreast of events while out of town through regular letters from her cousin, Catharine Bayard, also from one of the city's most prominent families; it is through these letters that we know a great deal about the events of Sally's 1820 visit to Saratoga.[51]

She and her cousin had originally hoped to spend the summer of 1820 together at Saratoga, but Catharine Bayard went to Europe instead. Consequently, Sally went to the springs with other friends of the family, the LeRoys; they stayed at the Saratoga's premier hotel, the Pavilion. Although she had been pursued by scores of suitors, she was famously choosy about her potential mate, a quality that provoked gentle teasing from her cousin. Still, young men persisted, and during her time at Saratoga in late July and early August of 1820, it is clear that at least two poetic and sensitive young men had made an impression on her. One wrote her a longish unsigned poetical work, light in tone, entitled "Cupid's Visit to Saratoga in August 1820," which placed Sally as just one amidst a glittering group of immortals at the Pavilion Hotel. Although nothing came of this, Ogden preserved it in her papers for decades. She also kept another anonymous poem in a different hand, "The Stricken Deer," which likened the author to a wounded deer told by a "maid of matchless charms" that she "cannot love thee stricken deer."[52]

Perhaps one of these two suitors was the subject of a letter marked "Private" sent to her father by his brother, Charles L. Ogden, in late August 1820. In it, Charles reported that "my dear Niece, your Daughter Sally has made a serious impression on one of my Southern Friends Mr. James Potter of Charleston, So. Carolina." Ogden described the young man as having an "amicable disposition and correct habits," who was "less addicted to fashionable dissipation than most." He had just returned from a Grand Tour of Europe, where he had "ample time & resources to make his tour as advantageous as possible," having acquired "a better knowledge of the world, and a more refined taste in the arts and sciences." Having gotten that out of the way, he went on to note that this young man was quite wealthy indeed: his father owned a rice plantation near Savannah for which he "paid in cash between 2 & 300000 Dollars," and he had deeded half of it to his son. That half would be his once he came of age, so that "he is therefore quite independent already without looking forward to the

Death of his Father."[53] Although it is possible that Sally could have met the young Mr. Potter in the social circles of New York City, it is much more likely that the unique set of circumstances surrounding Saratoga Springs set the New Yorker and the Carolinian on the same course.

When Catharine Bayard wrote Sally Ogden in late August, she reported that New York society was buzzing about the events of the summer. She wrote that she was "frequently asked" about Sally, and she demanded of her friend and cousin, "Are you or are you not to be Mrs. James Potter?" By October, the answer was becoming clearer. Bayard wrote that the courtships around Sally "at present form one of the most fashionable topics of the day—causes of all sorts are attributed as reasons for Mr. P's unsuccessful negotiation." Potter was out, but Bayard reported that gossip in New York was suggesting another suitor, a "Mr. Betts," as the new, "preeminent" candidate. But there was at least one other suitor that summer. A poem, attributed to "ES" and titled, "To Miss S.O. on Returning to Her the *Ballston Poetry*," survives in the archives. This copy shows evidence of long and frequent examination, since the paper is folded and unusually worn even though it is still in good condition. It portrays Sally as living "in solitude . . . as frank, as free from earthly care, / As deaf to flattering fame." And it imagined her suitors being successful only

> When they had dared a nobler strain
> Beyond the *flights of fashion*
> And learn'd at last, to *feel* not *feign*
> Love's deep *domestic* passion.[54]

But Sally would ultimately reject all of them. We will never know why; perhaps her family disapproved of the one she really loved. One letter to her from her mother in 1822 seems to hint at this explanation: "I would prefer seeing you married, to man of Talents and respectability, with a mere competency to support you, than to a person possessing the former, without the latter—Where both are united, so much the better. . . . I would however recommend to be slow in deciding, & to reflect well—For it is better for you to remain under the Protection of your parents, single, & without the superfluous things of an expensive City, than to marry a man, whom you do not respect & love."[55] The message here is mixed—on the one hand, seeming to support her free choice; on the other, warning her that her choice had to be perfect. Apparently she did not return to Saratoga, or at least there are no existing letters that mention another vacation like the one in the summer of 1820.[56]

Sally Ogden was precisely of the class that had long visited the springs and other tourist sites. But the new tourist infrastructure began to give people who did not come from the elite social classes an opportunity to mingle alongside the elites without an introduction: tourist sites tended to allow nearly anyone with the money unfettered access. Although these outsiders were not necessarily welcome once they were through the doors, neither were they automatically rejected. In the past they would have been nearly entirely shut out of fashionable circles.

In the summer of 1817, Solomon Mordecai, twenty-five years old, was looking for a wife. An Ashkenazi Jew, he was the son of Jacob Mordecai, a German immigrant who had settled in Philadelphia in 1760. In the 1790s Jacob moved his family to North Carolina, where he ran a store. In 1808, after some business reverses and a short stint teaching at a local boarding school for boys, Jacob was approached to set up similar school for girls. His creation, Mordecai's Female Academy in Warrenton, North Carolina, quickly became successful. The family's Jewish heritage was associated in the minds of parents with academic rigor, and the family was only too happy to use this as a major selling point for their school. It drew students from across the South, the vast majority from Christian households, and prospered despite the economic disruptions of the era: in several years it had nearly doubled in size. Its success made the Mordecai family relatively, if precariously, well-to-do.[57]

Solomon Mordecai became a teacher at the family's school, along with his brothers and sisters. But in a community far separate from the small Jewish population of the Early Republic, Solomon had few, if any, opportunities to meet eligible young women. He therefore decided on a journey northward to look over possible mates. It would not have been proper simply to state his intention outright, however, so in letters written after he had set off, he explained to his older sister that he had been suffering from a number of stomach or digestive ailments and argued that he might, perhaps, choose to go to Saratoga Springs to repair his fragile health.[58]

Solomon's route northward allowed for some crucial side trips, stops at the homes of relatives and friends of the family—essentially, the bulk of the Jewish community in the United States—in Richmond, Baltimore,

Washington, and New York. He made a careful survey of the available young women at each site: since he wanted to marry within his faith, his choices in the small Jewish-American community were limited. For example, at Richmond, Solomon wrote that "Miss H. looks thin, and in appearance is much improved, she is serious & looks interesting as in my ken she never before did." This is not exactly a ringing endorsement and nothing ever came of it. After not finding anyone in Philadelphia he decided that after New York City he would go to Ballston—"either that or Saratoga—or both."[59]

At first Solomon intended to spend at most several days, perhaps a week, at Ballston Spa. But once there, he was very soon persuaded in "a conversation with some gentlemen who had been in the habit of visiting these springs" that going to Saratoga, whose waters "are a more powerful mineral," would be best. He did so, and although he found on his arrival that "the houses are all so full already (for it is deemed early in the season)," he was nonetheless able to obtain "a quiet room in a house not connected with the main building" at Union Hall.[60]

Solomon eventually spent several weeks at Saratoga, and he made a careful inventory of the women he saw. From the accounts in his letters, by this point he now appeared to be open to any potential mate, not just a fellow Jew.[61] For example, when he described a large group of two families, the "Coles and Skipworth" he pointed out a young lady, a "fair one" named Susie, "a fine girl & improves so much upon acquaintance." He would have accompanied them to New York were it not for her mother's "indisposition," although he was "by promise bound to meet Miss S. in Norfolk." But once again nothing came of it, despite his wistful hopes that "perhaps some fairer fair one may dispose of her heart to me *à bon marché*."[62]

Perhaps there were limits to the marriage market. Solomon is never explicit on the question of anti-Semitism, but it may have been a larger factor than he would admit in his letters. There may be a coded reference to it in his description of one encounter: "[I have been] introduced to but one young Lady, and her I have seen since only *en passant* and at Meal times— this is not my fault for I have no other opportunity of being in their company; and then soft looks is not the order of the day—Of her name and of the polite manner I received my introduction and that too from her father, I will let you know after the first frost of October."[63] Could this reference to the "first frost" be a coded reference to a cold shoulder from the girl's parents? If Solomon encountered anti-Semitism on his journey, he never wrote about it: either it was so common as to be expected and thus was not considered remarkable enough to mention, or perhaps he knew that it would be upsetting for his extended family group and spoke of it only in private conversation. It is also possible, although highly unlikely, that he truly never did encounter it. In any case, his ability to meet and mix with people outside his religion and class would become a hallmark of the American tourist experience. This cross-socialization would prove to be a source of some tension in the decades to come.[64]

Solomon Mordecai's travels represent a new turn in the tourist experience. His journey through the sites of what would very soon be dubbed the "Fashionable Tour" demonstrates that the dream and promise of travel had become available to classes outside the traditional elites. That process of transmittal would accelerate in the 1820s, as literature, art, and drama would all display tourist motifs. But for the members of the upper middle class, exposure to these motifs presented a dilemma. In order for the tourist dream to be acceptable to them, it needed to change from its earlier incarnation as an aristocratic leisure activity to one that had some greater purpose. And as travel became ever more accessible for more mainstream, middle-class Americans, the ideas and goals of travel would change even further. From that dilemma emerged the idea of travel as an instrument of self-improvemment. First, however, we can take a step back from that brink and instead examine how these ideas were transmitted.

3

The Revolution of Seeing

Tourism and the Founding of the Hudson River School

A TRIP UP THE Hudson River to Albany reveals a series of spectacular sights. Once clear of the New York City metropolitan area, the river cuts between steep mountains and sharply cut valleys. At times it opens into large bays, at others the cliffs close in tight to the water. Parts of the journey, even today, closely resemble what a traveler of 1820 might have seen, particularly at the river's wildest parts. To our modern eyes, this seeming wilderness is spectacular and exciting; we revel in its ruggedness. For most people in the United States of 1820, however, that wildness would have been at best worrisome, at worst absolutely terrifying. It was not something to be sought out, and only when it was tamed—the trees felled and the forest turned to pastureland, roads, bridges, and towns—could it become a pretty scene.

Before large numbers of Americans could be convinced to travel, several conditions would have to be met. One of the most crucial of these was a change in the appreciation of nature. If tourist travel was to be successful, it would need destinations that were pleasing to the eye. The evolution of the notion that raw nature was pleasant had already begun in England and Europe. In the United States, though, it was going to take a good while before it became widespread.

When Americans gazed on American scenery, they saw something that was visually far inferior to the Old World, where the weight and gloss of history provided those special elements that made for a truly scenic landscape. America, it was argued, was too young, too rude, too wild. The lack of ruins, the wildness of its nature—even in areas, like the Hudson Valley, where the major predators had by the 1810s been almost entirely driven away—all of this meant that it lacked scenic impact. This was an old set of attitudes. But in the first decades of the 1800s, new, radical ideas filtering in from Europe would profoundly change the way many Americans perceived their own scenery, redefining what a visitor saw when gazing at mountains or wild lands.

Beginning in the mid-1700s, European thinkers began to change their view of wild terrain. Nature, these writers argued, was the source of all that was truly authentic; in wildness was a source of inspiration and strength. This way of thinking had become widespread among intellectuals in France, England, and Germany by the late 1700s, but it would not be accepted in American society for some time. Radical in the 1810s, it began gaining a wider currency by the mid-1820s. This happened, in part, through the impact of tourism.

As Americans began to change how they thought about their country's nature, its depiction in American art likewise began to change. These new depictions in turn accelerated the shift in perception, shaping the way a broader audience of Americans thought about their country's nature. In the end, it would create significant cultural movements, ranging from a whole new school of American literature to the first truly American art, the work of the Hudson River School.

In the United States, these ideas came mainly through its former colonial owner, Great Britain. There, the change had begun with the writings of a group of theorists in the seventeenth and eighteenth centuries who postulated three basic modes of perceiving nature: as beautiful, as sublime, or as picturesque. Each view of nature invoked a particular set of ideals and notions, which in turn influenced the creation of a particular kind of art.[1]

Art created under the notion of the beautiful depicted a world that was ordered, perfect, and pastoral. This was an expression of a kind of utopian longing for an ordered landscape, a striving for perfection, something that was, of course, impossible through human agency. Its landscapes presented idyllic scenes that were peopled with idealized humans, beyond imperfection. The nature that was thus represented was of the "lion lying down with the lamb" variety, a world where God's hand had removed all evil. More often than not, the painter placed some evidence of human presence—a hut, a temple, a road—into his composition. Depictions of pure nature were avoided. The vast majority of American landscape art before 1825 was created under this idea.

The sublime was best defined by Edmund Burke in his 1757 treatise, *A Philosophical Enquiry into the Origin of Our Ideas of the Sublime and Beautiful*. In its earliest form, the sublime suggested a way of looking at nature that began with fear but then shifted into overwhelming feelings of awe and perhaps even despair at the power of God as expressed through his works in nature. Burke reasoned that a viewer could reach an ecstatic state while witnessing the raw power of nature through a combination of imagination, artistic taste, and judgment. This sublime state would overwhelm the viewer and create within him a fundamental and intense sense of the awe-inspiring power of God. In this state, his faith was made deeper and more profound. The thrill of fear involved in this sublime state would remind him inevitably of the apocalypse and final judgment, but it would also remind him of eventual eternal bliss. Burke felt that the sublime could be attained only while witnessing the raw power of nature in its most threatening but magnificent form: in the midst of a thunderstorm in the high mountains, for example.[2] He based much of his thinking on a body of travel writing that had begun to be prevalent in Britain beginning in the early eighteenth century, particularly from writers who had ventured into the Alps. Others in Europe, such as Jean-Jacques Rousseau, had contributed to a significant body of work idealizing nature, which, as Rousseau wrote in 1754, "never lies" and which calms and even civilizes; the wilder the place, the better.[3]

There was little or no acceptance in the United States of the sublime before 1800, and acceptance of it would come only slowly thereafter. Among the most educated elite, those most closely in touch with British and European trends, it was a familiar concept; however, they were in the minority.[4] In American painting and graphic arts, too, there were virtually no depictions of the sublime.

Part of the reason was technical. It was relatively easy to render the beautiful on canvas; when the artist was successful, the images were attractive and pleasant. Depicting the sublime was elusive since the artist had to convey not only the majesty and greatness of nature but also its terror. When the artist succeeded, the resulting images tended to be dark and difficult. Perhaps most crucially for patron-poor American artists, sublime images were difficult to sell. The market, controlled and defined by the wealthy patrons who commissioned and purchased paintings, tended to favor images that were much less fraught.

A middle ground was necessary: the picturesque, which sought a mid-point between sublime and beautiful in order to create images that invoked the sublime while still maintaining the forms that made the image acceptable to the viewers of the time. Its first and probably greatest proponent was another Briton, William Gilpin. From the 1760s until his death in the early 1790s, Gilpin produced a steady supply of books that not only defined the concept of the picturesque but also described places that exemplified that ideal.[5]

Gilpin's theories produced a generation of artists fascinated with nature and prepared to look at it with a new eye. Picturesque ideals, taught to the gentry and aristocratic youth, became mainstream in Great Britain by the turn of the nineteenth century and slowly made their way into the American gentry. Gilpin's influence was so pervasive that his work became the subject of a highly successful satirical parody, William Combe's *Dr. Syntax in Search of the Picturesque*, which was published in England in 1810 and in Philadelphia in 1812 and remained in print for some time in both countries. The popularity of *Dr. Syntax* is an indication that some Americans, at least, had been exposed to Gilpin's ideas, since the satire would not have had much impact without them.[6]

But Gilpin did more than just define aesthetic rules. He also defined a new type of travel, one that produced a new traveler: the "picturesque tourist." Imitating what Gilpin did in his books, travelers began journeying to picturesque sites and, once there, would "take a picture" or draw a sketch. Widespread in England among the upper classes by the 1780s, this trend was also slow to come to America. American cultural parochialism was one factor, but in truth, most Americans and most Europeans simply did not see America as having truly picturesque scenery.[7]

Influenced by several major trends, this attitude began to change; by the early 1820s, many critics had begun to call for America to impose some degree of cultural separation with its former colonial master. They detested that Britain still produced so much of what elite Americans read, saw performed in their theaters, listened to in their concert halls, and saw in their paintings. There was a rising chorus of complaints that called for the creation of uniquely American art, literature, and drama, a movement pushing for a redefinition of American culture.[8] One aspect of this cultural independence movement was an effort to celebrate American landscape and scenery, as exemplified by the rise of travel books about America. Another was the native romantic movement whose best known specimen was William Cullen Bryant's widely reprinted poem, "Thanatopsis" (1819), which combined a romantic morbidity with a fascination with nature. Still another major influence was the work of Sir Walter Scott and his series of wildly popular romantic novels about Scotland.[9]

The influence of Scott on Americans' perceptions of their own natural environment cannot be underestimated. He began writing novels in 1813 after an acclaimed career as a poet; in a short time he had produced a number of highly successful works. *Waverly*, the novel that would give its name to an entire series of books, was first published in England in 1814 and in the United States in 1815. It and its successors were bestsellers in both countries, particularly in America, where the lack of copyright protection by British authors meant that a number of publishers printed editions.[10] Scott's influence in the United States was widespread. Washington Irving, for example, considered Scott a huge influence and was thrilled to meet him in England in August 1817, just before Irving wrote his first collection of essays and stories, *The Sketch Book of Geoffrey Crayon*.[11] His highly romanticized and compelling depictions of the Scottish Highlands as a wild and untamed land populated with remarkable and brave characters probably did more to spread picturesque and sublime ideas in America than any other single factor. His writing was often imagistic, linking characters to scenery. For example, the two romantic interests in *Waverley* are Rose, a young, beautiful, and gentle lowland Scots woman, dark-haired and steady, and Flora, a Highland clan leader's sister, blond, wild, and spirited. Other romantic if doomed Highland rebels are situated amid sublimely rugged terrain, while steadier lowland Scots inhabit pastoral lands reminiscent of "beautiful" paintings. Scott was a clever manipulator of the ideas of nature and art fashionable in his time, and he included artistic references that were readily identifiable to his readers. For example, at one point in *Waverley*, he invokes the name of one of the most popular picturesque painters in Europe, Salvator Rosa.[12]

Scott was also a writer whose fiction very often had a journey as a key element. His novels were tightly tied to place—here, Scotland—with highly specific descriptions of landscape and clear identification of sites. Perhaps most important, though, was the notion that the protagonists' exposure to these landscapes was in an of itself a factor in their personal development. Landscape, romance, personal change, and adventure all combined in Scott's novels to create an aura of excitement around travel. Combined with the highly visual nature of his writing, tourism and the picturesque and sublime were all tightly intertwined.[13]

The popularity of his novels allowed the ideas of the picturesque and sublime to reach an audience that had not yet been exposed to them. Their wide acceptance in the United States certainly helped lay the groundwork for the acceptance of the sublime in the minds of American readers; no doubt, more than one tourist made the connection between Scott's Scottish Highlands and the romantically scenic Hudson Highlands. His ideas, translated in American minds to American scenes, began to wean Americans away from the traditional notions of what landscape types were worthy of artistic depiction. In the 1820s a new generation of American artists would arise to meet the challenge.

American Artists Discover American Scenery: William Guy Wall

America was slow to change, however, and the American art world clung to traditional ideas long after they had largely been abandoned in Europe. It was not that formally trained American artists did not know of the sublime; they were quite aware of the key principles and could have chosen, had they wished, to depict sublime American scenery. What prevented them from doing so was their patrons' reluctance to purchase such paintings. Although some art historians have argued that this stemmed from patrons' ignorance of the sublime, there is strong and consistent evidence in the diaries of elite travelers from this period that many of them, perhaps most, knew what the sublime was and where they should feel it.[14] Unfortunately, sublime images of the American landscape were simply not in fashion. What made them fashionable was tourism: tourism would play a central role in creating America's first true native art movement, the Hudson River School.[15]

Culture can swing almost imperceptibly slowly before suddenly and dramatically shifting course, and the perception of American scenery fol-

lowed this pattern in the early 1820s. One by one, the minds of elite travelers were changed through exposure to the new ideas of tourism, as they
encountered the newly prevalent travel literature and heard the experiences
of their friends and neighbors. As their minds changed, they created their
own impressions as they traveled the Hudson River valley to Saratoga
or Ballston. Each new piece of validation of the greatness of American
scenery added to their appreciation of what they saw. The emphasis in the
new travel genre on the primal importance of Hudson River scenery created a sense among traveling Americans that the Hudson River valley was
the most scenic area in the United States; only distant Niagara on the other
side of the Canadian border ranked higher. The valley ranked so high for
several reasons, including its unparalleled scenery, its proximity to the
major cities of the east coast, and its new, fast transportation web.[16] The
valley had become a training ground for a new way of seeing American
scenery.

This process began to create a market for American scenery, and it was
only natural that American artists would look to the Hudson Valley. One
of the first to do so was William Guy Wall, who arrived in America from
Ireland in 1812 and made a modest reputation for himself in the New York
art world with his oil paintings and watercolors.[17] In 1820, he was commissioned to paint a series of watercolors of the Hudson Valley. After a summer trip up the Hudson, Wall returned that fall with around twenty
different views of sites on the river. By the summer of 1821 a prominent
New York engraver, John Hill, had begun translating the images, and in
the fall he printed the first aquatints of them.[18] He and his printer, Henry
Megarey, conceived of a folio of prints based on the watercolors, a high-
cost and high-priced package they called the *Hudson River Port Folio*. The
Port Folio was a collective effort, a collaboration among at least four
persons: Wall himself; John Hill, the engraver, who in some cases modified the foregrounds and river activity; Henry J. Megarey, the bookstore
owner and artistic entrepreneur who financed and sold the prints; and,
finally, John Agg, who wrote texts introducing and describing each plate.[19]
Taken as a whole, the *Port Folio* is the first attempt to present America
with an image of itself that moved away from the "beautiful" toward the
picturesque.

The *Port Folio*'s twenty engravings were issued in five separate "numbers" or sets. Each number was sold by subscription for sixteen dollars, a

substantial sum at the time. Although there are no sales figures for the folio, it is known that after initial runs of one hundred or two hundred prints (depending on the engraving), additional runs of between fifty and sixty prints were pulled. The first set was issued in January 1822, the fifth in mid-1825. A projected sixth set of prints was never issued. This was a risky and expensive endeavor, and by mid-issue some questions had arisen as to its success. Henry Megarey had initially issued the plates in partnership with two other printers, but as a June 1823 article in the *New-York Evening Post* noted, his partners had dropped away: "We are sorry to learn that so little public taste for the fine arts yet exists in the United States," the paper sighed, "that the enterprizing bookseller who has ventured to enter upon [this] expensive project . . . is, from present appearances, likely to be a very considerable loser by his liberality." It hoped "for the honor of our country" that Megarey would "in the end be amply remunerated." Despite these concerns, eventually there was enough demand that the entire *Port Folio* was reprinted in 1828. In sum, the work sold well and widely, and it was ultimately one of the most successful artistic ventures of its time. As such, it represents the "arrival" of American scenery among the art-buying gentry.[20]

The first of the *Port Folio*'s scenes was the northernmost, showing the falls near the village of Luzerne; the last depicted the city of New York from Governor's Island. Taken together, however, the choice of images produces some surprises. For example, fully half of the folio's images depicted sites located on a relatively short stretch of the upper Hudson from Luzerne to Fort Miller. This area was rarely, if ever, mentioned as being the ideal scenic area of the river in the literature of the time, and Wall's choice of it as his subject speaks more of convenience than a concerted effort to choose strategic sites for his talent.

The remainder of the *Port Folio* fits better into the conventional wisdom of the time about the Hudson's scenic sites. Still, there are curious omissions. For example, city of Troy merits a print, but Cohoes Falls, just north of the city and universally mentioned as a prominent scenic place, does not. Two prints depict the city of Hudson, but the famed escarpment above Catskill is shown far in the background in only one view. Four prints are clustered at or just north of West Point, but the Tappan Zee and the view down toward New York—the conventional view—are not included. The last two prints, though, are natural choices: one shows the Palisades, the other New York itself. Wall painted several other watercolors, pictures that were not printed in the *Port Folio*. But of these, even at popular sites such as Cohoes Falls, he chose to paint not the waterfall that emptied into the Hudson but rather the bridge.[21]

This scheme does not represent the received wisdom on the Hudson's most scenic sites: there must have been another agenda at work. The agenda that does fit is that of a tourist's journey up the Hudson. The last ten images, in reverse order, represent the most prominent sights seen on a steamboat journey north from Manhattan. The prints themselves suggest this: in three of the four prints depicting steamboats on the river, they are steaming northward, toward the remainder of the *Port Folio*, toward the promise of the countryside.[22] The major steamboat stops on a summer trip are depicted: West Point, Newburgh, Hudson, Troy. This framework could explain the curious omission of a direct rendering of the hills above Catskill, since the artist may have been most concerned with capturing the site of the landing rather than the view from it. The remainder of the *Port Folio*, then, imagines a leisurely journey north from Troy along the post road from Albany to Glens Falls. Once there, the viewer, perhaps as the artist himself did, would then make visual day trips up and down the river to some of the prominent sights in the area.

Looking at the prints in the *Port Folio* today, one sees images that are, in general, placid and essentially pastoral, well within the "beautiful" tradition. They have little of the sublimely tangled nature of the works of later Hudson River School painters like Thomas Cole, with their dramatic rocks, twisted trees, and exaggerated precipices. Wall's watercolors present a Hudson prettily decorated with homes, country roads winding near the water, and boats peacefully sailing or steaming. He peopled each print with busy figures engaged in fishing, traveling, or trade: colorful common folk working, presumably, for the gentry, from which Wall's patrons came. His skies were marked only with the occasional thundercloud of summer, and, aside from the images of waterfalls and rapids, his depiction of the river itself reveals a placid and benign body. A sense of order prevails; human intervention trumps nature.

But artistic fashion in New York in the early 1820s was subtly changing. American artists, many of them European or European-trained, had long been aware of Romanticism and the artistic picturesque, but there was no demand for such scenes. As the 1820s progressed, the art-buying public—

in other words, the *Port Folio*'s potential customers—began to show some interest in the Romantic picturesque. And we see evidence of this in the overall package that the *Port Folio* was sold in, which contained not just the etchings but also textual introductions explaining the prints. It is these introductions that reveal the effort to recast Wall's "beautiful" prints into a product that evoked the ideals of the picturesque and maybe even a bit of the sublime.

For example, "Little Falls at Luzerne" depicts the short waterfall at that village. On the left bank of the river lies a mill; in the foreground, a fisherman climbs down to the river, pole at the ready. And across the river, beyond a fringe of trees, is a series of smoothly rounded pasture slopes. Maybe, if we peer past that smooth patch to the smoothly forested hills at the rear, we can glimpse a bit of the picturesque there, in those distant, forested hills. At any rate, the text wants us to see it: "These marked and irregular summits," that is, the rounded, sugar-loaf-form hills, "create in their frequent intervals, a thousand romantic glens and ravines, surpassing each other in wildness, and giving to the *tout-ensemble* of the landscape, a character of darkness and dreariness, amidst which the most morbid imagination might roam and revel with unqualified delight."[23] In a subtle way, John Agg realized that he was distorting the message of the prints. As another of the texts explains, these introductions allowed the reader to "call up a thousand associations of ideas, which clothe the artist's skill in new charms . . . which no richness of colours, nor ingenuity of touch, could otherwise impart."[24]

Beyond its value as an expression of an emerging interest in the sublime and the associated increasing interest in nature for nature's sake, the *Port Folio* is, in the end, a product molded to meet the expectations and desires of the art-buying public. The world of the *Port Folio* is made for the traveling gentry. Its implied viewer is a member of an educated, urban class who has chosen to leave the city to find peace and to the contemplate the riches of America. He is doing this despite the ready availability of Europe as a destination. The texts assume a viewer who is a seasoned traveller, one "accustomed to dwell on the calm and cultivated beauty of a European landscape." But this traveler is weary of urban life, and these views remove those woes, as the "View near Jessup's Landing" promises. It is "well calculated to produce a powerful impression" on a traveler who is "forsaking crowded cities and 'the busy hum of men' to satisfy the cravings of a romantic fancy." This urban aesthete "attaches value to the landscape in the exact proportion of its lonely grandeur and chaotic sublimity." This pilgrim will find, another text assures us, "a number of romantic situations and interesting promenades," places that are "beautiful, and well calculated to attract visiters [*sic*], whether in pursuit of health or pleasure" that are off the beaten tourist track. Finally, though, the majority of these sites are not *too* picturesque or *too* sublime: they offer a "cheerful and striking contrast to the rude and solitary grandeur of the [Hudson] Highlands."[25]

Beyond these soothing messages of health and peace, the social subtext of the introductions worked to reassure the genteel traveler of his place in the world. At the "Meeting of the Hudson and Sacandaga," the distant scenery had "a wild, ferocious, and solitary sublimity" (symbolized by a distant thunderstorm buffeting the rounded hills), but in the foreground, overlooking the falls, sit "two houses": one "occupied by Judge Rockwell, near the bridge," the other "in the possession of a magistrate and lawyer." Together, they "assume a proud pre-eminence over the rest of the straggling hamlet," located just across the river. To the side of the estate near the falls, fields hold stacks of freshly cut hay, a perfect metaphor for gentry control over the scruffy common element. And in "Fort Edward," a Native woman is depicted in the foreground, carrying a bundle. She appears to be leaving this place, where "the houses are but few in number, but there is a neat church, which is well attended." Perhaps one reason for her departure is a nearby fort, once the site of "much brilliant service" but at which now "the dust of the merciless Indian and the ambitious European repose in awful amity together." This is a place that unequivocally belongs to the United States and has been cleansed of its native peoples.[26] The *Port Folio* was a calculated package that presented a complete tourist experience for armchair travelers, filled with images that neither challenged nor threatened their world view. It was a precursor to what would follow, a movement to create an appreciation of American scenery and culture. Soon that movement would truly take off, with the emergence of a a major talent.

Founding the Hudson River School

In the summer of 1824, a young artist in Philadelphia was struggling to make a career for himself. His early work had not met with much success, as it was hobbled by the artist's wobbly sense of perspective and his awkward way with the human form. This artist, Thomas Cole, was well aware of the shortcomings of his style, and he had spent much of the preceding year studying the principles of Gilpin and others to improve his technique. But he was still not selling his paintings, and in April 1825 he decided that he might have better luck if he moved to the country's largest city, New York.

Cole took a small garret above his father's house, which one biographer called a "poorly lit closet." There he painted five small, imaginary compositions, studies partially based on the examples he found in the painting manuals he was consulting. When they were done, he was able to persuade a neighbor, George Dixey, a carver and gilder, to hang them in his shop. One day, George Bruen, a merchant and appreciator of the arts, came by and saw them in Dixey's window. He purchased four of them, providing Cole with a windfall that must have seemed staggering.[27]

Bruen now began to play a key role in Cole's life and career. Not only had he just infused thirty-one dollars into Cole's pocket, but he suggested that the young man needed to paint real subjects. Cole had not traveled much outside of the city, and Bruen suggested that he get out of town, go see some real scenery. Bruen probably had specific places in mind—he was a member of the traveling class—and he may have suggested particular sites to the young man. The record is clear that Bruen funded Cole's trip to some extent. And we also know that at some time in the late summer of 1825, Cole boarded a steamboat chugging north up the Hudson.[28]

The route he followed is traceable through a sketchbook he kept on the journey. These twenty-two landscape sketches outline a path that had been so worn by tourists that by 1825 the country's three existing tourist guidebooks were primarily devoted to describing it. Called the "Fashionable Tour," it signified the cheapest and fastest route to the most accessible scenic sites in North America. Beginning in New York City, Cole went up the Hudson to a point just north of Albany, and there he turned southward. He stopped at the Catskill Mountain House—a new, large, widely publicized hotel just completed on a mountain high above the Hudson River—and took in the nearby falls, and then he returned to New York. He did not go to Saratoga: it was not very scenic, and he could not afford it. A lack of funds is also the probable explanation for why he did not visit Lake George, universally acclaimed as scenic. From the sketches he made, at

West Point and at Cold Spring just across the river, at Troy, at Cohoes Falls near Albany, and at Catskill, it is clear that he was conveyed by steamboat: he sketched places that were at the line's standard stops. For a budget traveler in 1825, just a year after the Supreme Court ruled against the North River Steam Company, ending their monopoly on Hudson River travel and subsequently causing ticket prices to collapse, steamboat was the cheapest and most efficient way to travel.[29]

Several of Cole's sketches were made on the boat as it chugged north through the Highlands, both in the morning and in the early evening. He probably got off at West Point to make several more sketches of the area and of the nearby ruins of Fort Putnam. He then probably took another boat up to Troy, possibly at night, as there are no sketches between Putnam and Troy. At Cohoes Falls, he made four more sketches. Cole almost certainly had been told to go to Cohoes Falls, located on the Mohawk River just before it empties into the Hudson, since they were touted as one of the most scenic falls of the tour and had been described numerous times in print, as in, for example, Gideon Davison's 1822 tourist guidebook.[30] After turning southward, Cole went directly to Catskill, where he made six sketches, capturing various sights in and around Pine Orchard—a new mountain house had recently been built there and had been heavily advertised in New York's newspapers.[31]

Cole was evidently quite taken with Kaaterskill Falls, which he studied at various angles, making four detailed sketches in all: two from below, one at a distance and another from closer; another from the top; and one from within the overhang of the upper falls. These are some of the earliest images we have of the falls, and they show a well-developed tourist location. To the left stands an observation platform built on iron poles above a large rock.[32] To the right of the falls, the sketch depicts the guide's hut, which was set somewhat back from the edge and was fronted by a short railed walkway extending to the precipice. Cole populated one of his larger sketches of the falls with several tourists lounging on the rocks at the bottom of the upper leap. Overall, Cole was awed with the site: on the obverse of one sketch, he wrote that the falls had a "sublime view."[33]

Cole returned to New York, and within a few weeks he had created five paintings. Soon they were hanging in the window of a bookstore and picture shop owned by William Coleman. Two were views of Cold Spring and were purchased by a Mr. A. Seaton.[34] Another was a view of Fort Putnam, near Cold Spring. The other two, both views near Catskill, are the ones that made his reputation: they are considered to be the foundations of the Hudson River School.

One day not long after Cole had begun displaying the paintings, Colonel John Trumbull walked by the shop. Trumbull, whose depictions of patriotic themes and portraits of Americans of wealth and power had made him one of America's few famous artists, spotted *Kaaterskill Upper Falls, Catskill Mountains* and immediately purchased it.[35] He showed the painting to two other prominent artists, William Dunlap and Asher Durand. All three returned to Coleman's shop and purchased the remaining two paintings, *Lake with Dead Trees* and *View of Fort Putnam*. A short time later, Dunlap's triumphant article about Cole and his works appeared in the *New-York Evening Post* bearing the title "Another American Genius."[36]

We know from his writings that Cole was a lover of nature, a man who valued the turn of light and the play of color. And it is obvious that he was an appreciator of the picturesque. But we also know from his surviving correspondence that he was highly attuned to the desires of his patrons: he was an ambitious man who wanted to produce salable images that were admired and purchased by men of influence.[37] The paintings he produced after his trip came from a mix of these motives. They mixed his artistic desires with what he perceived would be salable to his target audience, to patrons like Bruen, to the other members of the traveling class. In fact, it is probable (although not provable) that Bruen himself suggested the subjects that Cole eventually rendered: even later in his career when he was much better known, Cole allowed and expected his patrons to have this kind of control over the content of his paintings.[38] At any rate, the five images Cole made were of places that he knew would appeal to those classes. The appeal of the two views of Cold Spring was that they depicted an area that had fairly recently become the site of a number of estates of wealthy New Yorkers who aspired to the status of old moneyed families, Livingstons or Van Rensselaers. His *View of Fort Putnam*, set on the Hudson in the same general area, showed a site that was prominently featured in the guidebooks of the day as the closest thing the United States had to a "mouldering ruin" (in the words of an 1822 guidebook), even though it had been built only fifty years before, during the American Revolution.[39]

But the two Catskill scenes are out of place with the others—either they are offered purely as scenic wonders, which they certainly were, or perhaps there was something more. And why Kaaterskill Falls? He could have chosen Cohoes Falls: it certainly had gotten enough attention from his pencil, and the guidebooks rhapsodized over it constantly. Naturally, we cannot completely know the roots of his decision, but the impressive result is not in question: the two Catskill paintings sold. One, *Lake with Dead Trees*, was bought by William Dunlap, who almost immediately resold it to Philip Hone, one of the wealthiest New York merchants, for twice what he had paid. Cole had precisely targeted his audience.[40]

But still: why the Catskills? The composition of the paintings gives us important evidence. As his sketchbook attests, Cole had rendered the images from life. In his sketches and in these early paintings, he did not do a great deal of artistic modification, which would have been allowable under Gilpin's picturesque painting scheme. But although *Lake with Dead Trees* appears to have been a close record of what Cole saw there, the other painting from the Catskill tourist area, *Kaaterskill Upper Falls, Catskill Mountains*, contains several elements of fantasy, one of which has a particularly loaded message. Barely visible in the surviving copy, there lingers at the very edge of the second leap of the falls the figure of a Mohawk Indian. Like the Indians populating James Fenimore Cooper's works, this figure, far more than a mere decorative element in a picturesque composition, had powerful evocations for the viewers of the time: a distant past, mournfully portrayed in a half-remembered golden light. This is the high romanticism of Sir Walter Scott's Highlands.

But what is the Indian doing there? One reason, certainly, was to add authenticity to Cole's painting in the same way that Cooper inserted Native characters into his novels. An Indian at Kaaterskill evoked a pre-tourist Kaaterskill Falls, a more "authentic" time than the present. Cole probably was aware of the tremendous appeal of Indian images, like those that Cooper used, among the art-buying public. He was careful, for example, to depict the Indian in as authentic a representation of Mohawk dress as was known at the time. His audience would have been quite aware of them.

But why put the Indian at the *edge* of the falls?

Cole may have been influenced by some of the stories that were reproduced in the tourist guidebooks available the year he traveled. In Gideon Minor Davison's 1822 guidebook, *The Fashionable Tour*, a "legend" is told concerning Cohoes Falls, one of the sites of Cole's trip: "An old tradition states, that a chief of the Mohawks, attempting to cross in his canoe, embarked too near the current of the falls, to escape their descent. Fineing [*sic*] himself unable to resist the influence of the tide, which hurried him fast to the summit, with true Indian heroism, he turned his canoe into the stream, assumed his station at the helm, and with a paddle in one hand and his bottle in the other, was precipitated over the brink."[41] In 1825, Davison's story was taken up by another guidebook author, Henry Dilworth Gilpin, and given several enhancements:

> It is said, that when the country was inhabited by the Indians, they were in the habit of transporting the skins and articles of trade in their bark canoes down the Mohawk, and when they arrived at the falls, they carried their boats around by land. In speaking of this circumstance, old Vander Donck relates the following anecdote:—"It chanced that an Indian, with whom I myself was well acquainted, accompanied by his wife and child, with about sixty beaver skins, was descending the river in the spring, when the stream is most rapid, intending to trade with the Netherlanders. Not being careful to come to in time, not regarding the current enough, and relying too much upon his own powers, before he was aware, he was carried down by the stream, and notwithstanding he exerted himself to the utmost when it was too late, the rapids precipitated him, with his bark canoe, his wife and child, his beaver skins and other packages which he had with him, from the top to the bottom of the falls. His wife and child were killed, most of his goods lost, and his canoe dashed to pieces; but he saved his life, and I have frequently conversed with him since, and heard him relate the story."[42]

Gilpin added the elements of pathos that were surefire appeals to the sentiments of the time: now he is with his wife and child, and he survives to tell of their deaths.[43] Gilpin added these flourishes to help sell his guidebook; Cole was almost certainly motivated by a similar impulse. But there may have been something deeper at play: Cole might have been trying to make a greater statement. This is discernable if both of these Catskill paintings are seen together.

Lake with Dead Trees, the other Catskill painting, is incongruous when compared to its four sister images. For one thing, it was probably about as far from the "beautiful" as Cole got, as it depicts one of the two ponds that feed Kaaterskill Falls. It is a small, calm lake ringed with picturesquely gnarled trunks of trees dead perhaps a few years. Rising above it is the nearby peak of Round Top. The subtext of *Lake with Dead Trees* is only understandable within the context of the history of the immediate area of its subject. The lake, called Parmenter's Pond, had been expanded by a dam that had been placed just atop Kaaterskill Falls. This manmade obstruction had backed water up into the lower lake, killing the trees around it.[44] In fact, because of the dam, the falls themselves did not run in the summer unless visitors paid the mill owner to release the water.[45] Kenneth Myers speculates that Cole may have been criticizing the desolation that ensued from human intervention by offering these images as symbols of the great changes underway throughout the region. Taken together, *Lake with Dead Trees* and *Kaaterskill Upper Falls, Catskill Mountains* appear to have been deliberately created as a pair; Cole, who was always interested in the symmetry of pairs and would build his later career on series of paintings, may have seen the two paintings as part of a whole. Both depict elements of the natural landscape destroyed by the modern world: on the lake, the grand trees, perhaps the lake itself; at the waterfall, the noble savage, perhaps the last of his race.[46]

After his initial splash, Cole went back to work in the winter of 1825–26. George William Featherstonehaugh, a British-born gentleman farmer and merchant, invited him to work at a painting studio on his extensive estate at Duanesburg, New York, a short distance from Albany.[47] There, Cole painted for his supper, producing four views of Featherstonehaugh's estate and a couple of other minor paintings. He had also gotten a prized commission from William Gracie, another wealthy New York merchant, who wanted him to render another view of the Kaaterskill Falls; it is possible he dictated the subject and maybe even the composition. Cole then produced an uncontested masterpiece, *The Falls of Kaaterskill*. This large canvas (43 by 36 inches) depicted both of the leaps of the falls from the front. A significant number of elements were changed, omitted, or added. For example, the view depicts the falls as if seen some fifty feet in the air, looking dead on at the falls. The curve of the rock has been flattened out, particularly on the right, and there are several imagined "picturesque" rocks. Cole omitted the tourist platform, the guide's hut, and the protective railing, all awkward artifacts of the commercialization of the falls. And the lounging tourists who populated Cole's sketches of the falls had been replaced by the figure of an Indian, standing, as in *Kaaterskill Upper Falls, Catskill Mountains*, at the precipice—ready (perhaps) to fling himself to his death.

Cole presented an ideal tourist vision of the falls, one unencumbered by the very tourism that had drawn to attention of his patrons and had allowed Cole to stand before them. Cole's idealized visions publicized his patrons' good taste and fashion. These men of wealth had commissioned these images to increase their social standing yet further, not only as proof of their generous sponsorship of this artistic superstar but also because the paintings they commissioned him to create depicted an area that had suddenly become the most fashionable summer destination in North America. Soon, Cole's paintings would be the center of an artistic revival in New York City, through the Academy of Fine Arts, an institution that would overthrow the old tyranny of the beautiful in favor of a new generation of artists working toward the picturesque. Images from his paintings would soon be widely reproduced in prints and even printed on dinnerware.[48]

⊷ 4 ⊷

Travel Literature, the Fashionable Tour, and the Spread of Tourism

B Y THE 1820S, a huge change had begun among those who could afford to travel. In Great Britain, the idea of travel for leisure had been widespread among the prosperous classes for more than thirty years. For a number of reasons, however, it had been very slow to gain any ground among Americans of that class. There were a number of reasons for that. In the 1790s, few Americans could afford to conspicuously consume; among those who could, it was not at all fashionable to do so. By the early 1820s, the number of wealthier Americans had grown significantly. In 1790, getting to the country's few resorts could take days or weeks; even prosperous Americans had to maintain their businesses, and few could afford the time away. By 1820, that travel time had been cut significantly. But the last and perhaps most important factor still missing in 1820 was that very few Americans had been exposed to the idea of leisure travel, at least in an American context: very little had been written by Americans about travel within the United States. This would change rapidly, though, and that change would occur in just a few years, in the late 1810s and early 1820s. One of the keys to the creation of a tourist society would be the transmission of that idea in print.

Travel Literature and the Idea of Tourism

The first exposure many Americans had to the idea of travel for pleasure was travel literature, a genre that most significantly consisted of personal accounts of travel but also included gazetteers and geographies. In the mid-1820s, though, a new subgenre of travel literature would appear, one explicitly aimed at the leisure traveler: the tourist guidebook. These books would help define explicitly what tourism was, where in America it happened, and how to do it.

In the late eighteenth century, American travel literature had been only a tiny part of the book market. But the number of travel books about the United States grew rapidly in the first and second decades of the nineteenth century. By 1810 travel books had become steady, if not necessarily spectacular, sellers—"medium appeal" books.[1] Initially, very few of these books described destinations in the United States; most were about subjects deemed "worthy," such as Italy, Great Britain, and other European sites. But that would increase dramatically after the War of 1812, in part due to a growing nationalist sentiment, in part due to a curiosity about America in the British reading public. (The book trade of the era tended to downgrade American-written books in favor of those by British authors. Part of the reason was that American publishers did not have to pay British writers any royalties; there was also an inherent snobbishness among American readers that favored British authors.)

American audiences examined works by British and other foreign writers with a skeptical eye, often criticizing them for their inaccuracies and condescension. But nonetheless these books were steadily purchased and read.[2] They made the Hudson and all of the main routes of travel in upstate New York increasingly prominent in the minds of their readers, as writers depicted their beauties and described accommodations and travel conditions. Most of their readers were of the armchair variety, but a growing number began to use travel books as guides for their own travels. In the first decades of the nineteenth century, there was also an explosion of magazines and newspapers, many of which contributed to a broad body of secondary literature (criticism and reviews) about these travel books, exposing even more readers to them.[3] The increasing output of travelers' accounts helped the reading public to become acclimatized to the idea of tourism.

Featuring descriptions of the cultural and natural American landscape, travel literature bestowed on Americans a more self-referential gaze, a process that helped them define not only themselves but also what in America was scenic, inspiring, or worth visiting. Travel writers in these years usually tried to give a panoramic view of the country, but in addition to the major cities a remarkable number of them visited Saratoga or Ballston. Generally, they offered brief sketches of the spas, and usually the medicinal qualities and chemical composition of the springs themselves were detailed.[4]

This new body of widely available travel literature exposed Americans to new ideas about scenery, wilderness, and nature. The rising tide of travel books was a part of a search by Americans for national self-definition, as such books helped define for Americans the places that were uniquely theirs. The sum effect of the steady repetition and wide distribution of all of these travel accounts was to increase the acceptance of travel and tourism among the gentry. In the years after the War of 1812, these gentry travelers would come to flood the main routes of tourism, especially in upstate New York.

The Fashionable Tour

The increasing number of tourists in the postwar period began to create a demand for information about travel and tourism. Publishers were a little slow to react. At first, they marketed general travel literature at travelers. For example, in June 1820, at the beginning of the tarvel season, an advertisement titled "To Travellers," was run by the A. T. Goodrich Company, New York's leading printer and purveyor of travel-related books and maps; it touted a gazetteer, John Melish's *Traveller's Directory*, in three different formats, "half-bound," "bound in a pocket book," and "ditto with additional maps." The same advertisement had listings for John Steel's pamphlet on the chemical properties of Ballston and Saratoga's various mineral springs, a directory of New York City, and "Goodrich's Map of the Hudson River."[5]

Through the 1820 travel season, this series of advertisements retained the generic "To Travellers" headline. But for the 1821 season, their orientation changed to tourists heading for the Hudson Valley and beyond. When they first appeared, in May, they advertised to "Travellers to the Lakes." By June the advertisements were aimed at "Travellers to the Springs, Lakes and Falls." By late summer, that had been changed to "Travellers to the Springs, Niagara Falls, &c &c."[6]

But all of the products listed were, in effect, multi-use products. Maps could be used by travelers or, say, by landowners. Likewise with directories. For most of this period, there were no published products intended specifically for American tourists. That changed in 1822, when the first tourist products appeared. As a part of his campaign to bring Saratoga Springs to Americans, Gideon Minor Davison introduced the first tourist guidebook ever published in America, *The Fashionable Tour, or, a Trip to the Springs, Niagara, Quebeck, and Boston, in the Summer of 1821.*[7]

Davison was also the first to commit to print the concept of a "fashionable tour" in America. The idea was based on the British tradition of having young men, generally from the wealthier classes, travel along a standard route on the continent of Europe as a kind of finishing experience before returning to their homes and (it was expected) a productive life. The European Grand Tour, based on much earlier pilgrims' routes, reached maturity in the seventeenth century and flourished until the French Revolution. The generation of conflict that followed crushed continental tourism; when Davison was writing his book, tourism in Europe was only just beginning to return, and it would take another generation before it returned to its earlier heights.[8]

Although he was the first to write of it, Davison did not devise the "fashionable tour" out of nowhere. His book codified and modified a route that had become the accepted path among highly adventuresome travelers prior to the War of 1812. Perhaps the first solid evidence of this route (although it is entirely possible that there were earlier journeys) is found in a series of letters written by a South Carolinian named Isaac Ball. In long accounts mailed home the summer and fall of 1806, he described the adventure he and members of his family experienced that year. They had left from their estate in South Carolina in June and sailed to New York City. After a pleasant time there, they began to travel what would become the route of Davison's Fashionable Tour. Beginning in New York City, they sailed to Albany, and then took the Mohawk River westward. When the river turned north, they continued west across New York State, skimming just north of the Finger Lakes Region until at last they arrived at Niagara. After touring Niagara, they took a boat eastward across Lake Ontario to Kingston, in what was then Upper Canada. There, they purchased a "batteau" (a boat paddled by "6 Canadians who were to work their passage"), and they traveled down the St. Lawrence, at one point through rapids made "more terrible" by an impending thunderstorm. After that exhilarating trip, they arrived in Montreal, where they stayed a few days before sailing to Quebec City in a sloop. Several days later, they returned to Montreal and headed south, probably down Lake Champlain to the Hudson and Albany. At this point, they had completed what would be the main route of the Fashionable Tour. Ball's route after Albany, which took them across Massachusetts to Boston and then south to Newport, Rhode Island, before their return to New York City, would be followed by others.[9]

Of course, this epic journey was undertaken by one of the wealthiest families in South Carolina. Their huge slave force, extensive landholdings, and family network gave Isaac Ball and his cousins the immense affluence and ample leisure time needed for an entire summer of travel. Few northern people of wealth wanted to be gone from their homes for more than a few weeks: most were still merchants, especially those from New York City, who would have acutely felt a long absence from their business.[10]

Moreover, the Balls were unusually adventuresome: few tourists of his class would have risked the rapids of the St. Lawrence, for example. Only after the infrastructure of travel was improved would this route ever be more than sparsely traveled, although there were still a few intrepid northern travelers who followed parts of what would later become the Fashionable Tour. For example, Mary Murray, the daughter of John Murray, a wealthy New York merchant, traveled to Niagara in June and July of 1808. Her experiences were less adventuresome than those undertaken by the Balls, but she nonetheless made the trip there and back, despite difficult roads and several dramatic moments.[11]

Mary Murray and Isaac Ball traveled before the War of 1812. With the end of the war, hundreds and later thousands more would follow. By 1818, for example, one writer complained to her friend that summer in the city had become boring: too many of her peers had gone traveling, including her best friends, "the two J. Le Roys," who had "gone to the Springs [and] they intend proceeding to Niagara, Montreal & Quebec."[12]

Gideon Minor Davison's guidebook was unique in several respects.[13] Perhaps most important, he organized his entries geographically: they pulled the reader along a very specific route. This broke with the conventions of a type of book it otherwise closely resembled, the gazetteer, which was a geographical dictionary featuring short capsule descriptions of places arranged alphabetically. Nor was it like a geography, which comprehensively described a place or region. It was like standard travel literature in that it described a route, but it differed in the way it was written. It did not have an narrative voice; instead, it had an omniscient, even commanding, tone: go here, then see that. (Later guides would add, in effect, "then think this.") For example, at Lake George, just north of Saratoga Springs, Davison writes: "There are few places where a greater variety of inducements is presented to the stranger than at Lake George. Besides the interest which is excited from an association of many important historical events, this place is rendered attractive by an unrivalled prospect of the beautiful and romantick scenery presented by the lake and its environs." Of Albany, which from "the distance of half a mile gives . . . a very favourable appearance," he writes. "But the first impression is rather diminished than increased by a more intimate prospect. Most of the streets are narrow and irregular; and with all the elegance displayed in the construction of the buildings, the stranger is too often reminded of the original settlers, by the frequent occurrence of their antique edifices."[14]

These innovations meant that Davison had invented what was in effect a new form, a subgenre perhaps, of American travel literature: the tourist guidebook. Since this was a new kind of book, Davison wanted to stay on more familiar ground, so he explicitly linked his book to the existing conventions of travel literature by subtitling it *A trip . . . in the summer of 1821*. This implied that the book was a record of a particular trip at a particular time. Even a cursory reading of the text, though, shows it to be nothing of the sort; later editions dropped the subtitle. Davison's other contribution was that his book was specifically directed at leisure travelers—tourists—rather than, say, commercial travelers, and it was the first to do so. In describing the Hudson River, for example, he declares that "besides the novelty of a steam boat passage, the Hudson river presents to the tourist, a variety of natural scenery, which it will be difficult to find elsewhere in a journey of the same extent."[15]

Davison chose an unusual format for his new product. Physically, it was small, pocket-sized. It was printed and finished cheaply. Printed paper covers enclosed a weakly stitched set of pages with ragged-cut edges and a text lacking illustrations or even a map. All of this signaled that the book was going to be used once or twice in the field and then tossed aside. New editions, it implied, would soon arrive to update its information. It did not look like travel literature at all; in fact, what it most resembled was one of the era's omnipresent almanacs.[16]

The readers of this new kind of book were not the people who purchased typical travel narratives. Davison as much as admits to this in his introduction. The book, he wrote, was merely "a small pocket volume of references" that contained "facts . . . interesting to the tourist," a reader who "seldom commands leisure for a more detailed description."[17] But at which leisure travelers, specifically, was Davison's book directed? The title gives a hint. The book promises to direct a traveler along a "fashionable" route. But for a tour to be fashionable implies that there already exists a group of fashionable people following that same route. Those people presumably would already know where they had been, where they should stay, and what they should see, and they would, presumably, return on their own steam. So those people were not Davison's market. The form of the book itself provides another clue, since it lacks the kind of high-style enhancements that would appeal to a wealthy audience, such as trimmed page edges, gold-leaf edges, and maps, lithographs, or other illustrations.[18] Its cheap printing quality points to the likelihood that the audience to whom the book was directed was less the "fashionable" visitor to Saratoga Springs than to the striver, a newly well-to-do traveler unfamiliar with the "fashionable" routes and sites.

This might have been a reflection on Davison himself. He was, of course, just a job printer—not in and of itself a high-status position. Although he was also the editor of the local newspaper, that, too, was not a very significant position. But he had aspirations. The combined reading room and circulating library was a good place to start. There, he would inevitably come into contact with the fashionable crowd that was coming to the springs. And he was making efforts behind the scenes to raise his status, particularly through a series of canny real estate purchases that by the time of his death in 1866 had made him a very wealthy man indeed.

Gideon Minor Davison's little guide and its description of the Fashionable Tour was a sign that a significant shift in the nature of American tourism was coming. Davison and his book represented the rise and appearance of a category of people at the spas that the founders of these exclusive places had hoped, in some ways, to exclude: the market was beginning to intrude on what had been an exclusive refuge. Saratoga itself was an expression of this. It was not Ballston, which more closely resembled the more exclusive southern resorts; for one thing, the sheer size of its tourist facilities meant that it would be very difficult to exercise the kind of control that society at Ballston had. Saratoga represented a new world.

Literature, the Hudson Valley, and Tourism (1817–1822)

Davison's guide represented one element of an emerging cultural infrastructure of tourism. Other key items began to emerge in this period that would have a far wider reach, as they sought to decorate the visual delights of the Hudson River valley with stories and legends, to create idealized visions of its beauties.

The first writer to do this successfully was Washington Irving. By the late 1810s he was a widely traveled and experienced writer well known to the New York reading public. His first major publication was a solid success, the 1807–8 magazine *Salmagundi*, and when his full-length historical parody *Knickerbocker's History of New York* was published in 1812, it sold well, making him a minor celebrity. Irving became a one of a small group of New Yorker gentry who had taken their name, the Knickerbockers, from his famous 1812 book. They feared the changes coming over the nation as it moved, in the 1810s and 1820s, ever more decisively away from the old hierarchical structures inherited from Britain and refined in America toward those allowing for far more social mobility. It is no accident that they were based in New York City, which was experiencing explosive growth during this period. Irving expressed this conservative Knickerbocker attitude in his writing. For example, the "Style at Ballston" segment from *Salmagundi* (discussed in chapter 1) was a recognition that tourism was a symptom of the beginning of the breakdown of the old order, as it allowed social mixing in a setting where the carefully structured protocols of city society were not easily maintained.[19]

Irving had grown up in comfortable surroundings and had never been forced to work for a living, but in 1818 he faced an unprecedented crisis: his family's business, the source of his income, went bankrupt. His career as a dilettante was cut short, and for the first time in his life he had to support himself. So he decided to become a professional writer—a radical step, as no other American had ever been able to earn enough solely from the pen to survive. But he pushed forward, and through the summer and fall of 1818 he wrote a series of stories that were collectively published as *The Sketch Book of Geoffrey Crayon, Gent.*[20]

The *Sketch Book*, with its colorful characters and stories of New York life, was an immediate success, bringing Irving far greater fame and fortune than he had yet experienced. Two stories that were particularly popular when it was published, "Rip Van Winkle" and "The Legend of Sleepy Hollow," have since become classics. Although nearly every story in the collection had a strong New York flavor, these two in particular relied on their Hudson Valley setting, a location particularly relevant for the traveling audience. In the years to come, travelers passing through on their way north from New York City through the Hudson Valley would come to associate the places they passed with Irving's stories: they added a romantic gloss to these places and locations.

Although it is impossible to prove that Irving deliberately chose his settings as a lure to draw readers, it is clear that Irving knew of the attraction that tourism had for the members of his social class. And the members of his social class, in a time when books were still relatively expensive, were the book-buying public of New York City. He knew that they would find these locations evocative and as much as says so in the opening paragraphs of "Rip Van Winkle": "Whoever has made a voyage up the Hudson must remember the Kaatskill mountains. They are . . . seen away to the west of the river swelling up to noble height and lording it over the surrounding country." A significant number of travelers who had "made a voyage up the Hudson" by 1818 were the tourists heading to the springs. Others had traveled to the statehouse in Albany for governmental or business reasons.

Once Irving set this scene, a scene that would be familiar to his readers, he began his tale: "At the foot of these fairy mountains the voyager may have descried the light smoke curling up from a village, whose shingle roofs gleam among the trees. . . . It is a little village of great antiquity, having been founded by some of the Dutch colonists in the early times of the province."[21] This is the village of Catskill, which lies just across the river from the town of Hudson, a main passenger stop on the steamboat line. Travelers along the river would have seen the "magical hues and shapes" of Irving's mountains. Especially prominent was the grand escarpment that rises above Catskill, a geographical feature often noted in travelers' diaries. Further, in this passage Irving added a layer of mystique by describing the village as being of "great antiquity." This description would have been laughable to Old World visitors, but for Americans it bestowed an authority and authenticity many found missing in their relatively new country.[22]

Irving set "The Legend of Sleepy Hollow" at a precise location in the Hudson Valley some miles south of Catskill, "in the bosom of one of those spacious covers which indent the eastern shore of the Hudson," on the shores of "the Tappan Zee . . . at Tarry Town." Irving used geographical identifiers based on river landmarks because he had come to know the Hudson well during the many hours he had spent chugging slowly up and down it. And he knew that his audience would know them, too, for precisely the same reason. His stories instantly made these sections of the Hudson River famous, and tourists traveling upriver now began to anticipate moment when Rip's home, the Kaaterskill Clove (derived from the Dutch word for "valley"), came into view.[23]

The scenic cachet of the Hudson River was a common theme in the New York State travel books of the day. But as we have seen, travel books prior to the 1820s tended to be written by foreigners, particularly Englishmen. The time was ripe for a high-profile travel book by an American, and when the first volume of Timothy Dwight's *Travels in New England and New York* was published in 1821, it was embraced, because here was a true American voice. Dwight, a grandson of the famed revivalist and evangelist Jonathan Edwards, was president of Yale College from the 1790s until his death in 1817. There, he reigned as one of America's cultural arbiters, producing sermons, inspirational works, and various other commentaries; his was one of the most respected voices in America.[24]

After his death, his nephew, Theodore Dwight, gathered the many accounts his uncle had written during his travels, which spanned more than twenty years, from the 1790s to the 1810s, and edited them for publication.[25] The resulting collection was published in four volumes. The language was casual, as if Dwight were writing letters home to a friend, a common device in the travel literature of the day. The book contained a vast amount of statistical and geographical information, but it also had lengthy discourses about the character and look of his various hosts' homes, the nature of the towns he visited, and the relative beauty of a number of prominent sights.

Dwight was a master traveler: he had made many journeys across New England and New York State, and his notes were voluminously detailed. Of the many places he described, though, he was particularly admiring of the Catskill Mountains, which he mentioned more than a dozen times across three of the four volumes. Dwight's book became a standard reference for the region and remained in print for many years, not only because of its thoroughness about New England and New York locations but also because of the weighty reputation of its author. As already intimated, it was also celebrated because it was a travel narrative published by an American, which was relatively rare at the time.[26]

Dwight, the burgeoning tourist culture, and the success of Washington Irving's tourist-influenced stories, in turn, influenced other writers. One of them would become the most successful writer of his day: James Fenimore Cooper. Cooper had been raised in wealth and privilege, but his family's fortunes began to collapse soon after the death of his father, William Cooper, in 1809. This was followed soon after by the premature deaths of a number of siblings. Probably the only factor that kept him from sliding into complete poverty was that he had married into the politically connected and tremendously wealthy De Lancey family.[27] But he had been as proudly reluctant to ask them for money as his father-in-law proved to be in providing it.[28]

After a tepid introduction to the writing world, he achieved amazing success with his second novel, *The Spy*, in 1821. Wanting to strike again while the iron was hot, he began *The Pioneers* while he was living in Scarsdale, New York. Despite his earnings from *The Spy*, he was still perilously close to financial failure, and he needed another bestseller. Most of all, he was worried that his good fortune would not last, since everything in his recent personal history had led him to believe that fame and wealth were fleeting.[29]

Cooper wanted more than money from *The Pioneers*. As much as he needed the novel to be a financial success, he also wanted it to serve as a vindication for his late father. The book was a thinly fictionalized version of his father's own story, indeed a rewriting of the history. In particular, Cooper felt that his father had been wronged in the courts and by the family's creditors, that his fortune and lands had been stolen by outsiders and opportunistic men. But Cooper's desire for success was just as powerful: he wanted to regain the gentry lifestyle he had enjoyed before the collapse of his family's fortunes. There are clues that to enhance its marketability he deliberately worked in references intended to appeal to the segment of society that dictated what was fashionable—in other words, the tourist class.[30]

A clear example is an episode he inserted into the story, one that is not, strictly speaking, necessary for the plot. In the scene, which comes about halfway through the book, Natty Bumppo, the old frontiersman also known as Leather-stocking, is sitting with the old Indian, Mohegan, who has long since been displaced from his former hunting grounds. Joining them is a tourist-surrogate, Edwards, a young, educated, and possibly noble guest in the village. Leatherstocking is remembering one particularly striking place. He tells Edwards that this place was "up on the Cattskills. You know the Cattskills, lad, for you must have seen them on your left, as you followed the river up from York. . . . Well, there's the High-peak and the Round-top, which lay back, like a father and mother among their children. . . . But the place I mean is next to the river, where one of the ridges juts out a little from the rest, and where the rocks fall for the best part of a thousand feet."[31] Natty is describing a high escarpment that rises above the village of Catskill, on the western bank of the river just across from the town of Hudson. On that escarpment, which Cooper made famous, a prominent hotel, Pine Orchard, would soon be constructed (see chapter 5). Natty expects Edwards, as Cooper expected his readers, to remember this dramatic site from their voyages north. Cooper also knew that this escarpment was familiar to his audience not only because of their travels but also through their (and his) reading of Dwight and Irving. At the time of its publication, Cooper wrote a friend that he hoped the book would make "American scenes interesting to an American reader"; to do that, he pandered to the traveling/reading class, a class already exposed to and therefore more susceptible to those scenes.[32]

Cooper then had Leatherstocking describe Kaaterskall Falls near the escarpment, another place that figured prominently in Dwight's work.[33] By 1821, the falls had recently become much more accessible to travelers, through a road that had been cut up the nearby valley:

> "But there's a place, a short two miles back of that very hill, that in late times I relished better than the mountains; for it was kivered with the trees, and nateral."
>
> "And where was that?" inquired Edwards, whose curiosity was strongly excited by the simple description of the hunter.
>
> "Why, there's a fall in the hills, where the water of two little ponds that live near each other breaks out of their bounds, and runs over the rocks into the valley. The stream is, maybe, such a one as would

turn a mill, if so useless a thing was wanted in the wilderness. But the hand that made that 'Leap' never made a mill! There the water comes crooking and winding among the rocks, first so slow that a trout could swim in it, and then starting and running like a creater that wanted to make a far spring, till it gets to where the mountain divides. . . . The first pitch is right two hundred feet, and the water looks like flakes of driven snow, afore it touches the bottom; and there the stream gathers together again for a new start, and maybe flutters over fifty feet of flat-rock, before it falls for another hundred."

"I have never heard of this spot before: it is not mentioned in the books." [says Edward.][34]

There are a number of ironies in this passage. Natty describes the area as "kivered [covered] in trees, and nateral," and that would have been the case in the time the book is set, 1793. But for Cooper and his audience, the immediate area around the valley was the site of a thriving tanning industry established in the late 1810s and early 1820s. Tanning required a large amount of wood bark, particularly the kind found on the tannin-rich hemlocks that stood thick in the Clove. The process also used great quantities of water to soak the skins. Skins were soaked a year or more, a stage that threw off hundreds of gallons of foul water. This industrial operation had transformed the Clove by denuding large swaths of it and by fouling the watershed.[35]

Natty also notes that "the stream is, maybe, such a one as would turn a mill, if so useless a thing was wanted in the wilderness." Dwight described the stream feeding the falls as a "millstream" with "a magnificent current." But as we know, the stream had been dammed to drive a mill since around 1819.[36]

Finally, when Edwards comments at the end of this excerpt that he had "never heard of this spot before: it is not mentioned in the books," he is referring, of course, to the very travel books that Cooper used to flesh out his descriptions. Natty's reply to him is even more telling: "I never read a book in my life . . . and how should a man who has lived in towns and schools know any thing about the wonder of the woods!" Cooper wanted to create an air of authenticity around his account, to clothe his descriptions in a way that hid what may have been his true sources. He wanted his readers to think of *him* as authentic, in contrast to the increasing numbers of tourists flooding the Hudson for whom nature was mere decoration, one more destination to visit and leave again. These mere tourists were, unlike him, reliant on the medium of print to find the sublimely beautiful sites that the natives of the area—including, by implication, Cooper—knew almost instinctively. This is one of the first appearances in America of themes that have become commonplace among travel writing: that tourists are merely sensation seekers who would not and could not possibly appreciate what they were seeing. Later in the 1820s, other authors would make these themes the basis for their books.[37]

But this was about more than just tourism. Like Irving, Cooper was a member of a class that feared and resented the disorder of the young republic. Through the 1820s and 1830s his books reflected his increasing distaste for a new trend in American politics, one that celebrated a new kind of political leader: the self-made man, the "man of the people." This trend represented a huge shift from post-Revolutionary generation of leaders and was driven by a national movement to grant universal white male suffrage. (Previously, voting rolls had been almost exclusively drawn from upper classes of society, generally limited to those who held a certain amount of property.) Cooper found this new class of politicians to be essentially base and craven as well as potentially corrupt. His fears stemmed in large part from what he had witnessed with his father, who he felt had been wronged and dispossessed by such men, and he would sound this theme several times in *The Pioneers*.[38] It was also a prominent motif in his next book, *The Last of the Mohicans*, published in 1826. In this novel, set during the French and Indian War, Cooper celebrated the sense of honor he perceived to be inherent in the old order, often casting his heroes as British officers or as members of certain Native nations. By creating a dichotomy among the Indian characters—bad and brutal versus good and honorable—he was reflecting the typical prejudices of the era about the still-existing Indians. In this scheme, the good and honorable Indians had departed, or soon would depart, while the debased, bad, and brutal ones remained. These prejudices were reflected in the scores of tourist accounts of visits to the Oneida reservation in upstate New York, where tourists described their displeasure at seeing Indians still living within the borders of the United States and moaned about the fallen state of the Indians of their time. But at the same time, Cooper also reflected the era's romanticization of the Indian, a trend that ignored the pesky persistence of living

Indians in favor of an idealized noble breed, now sadly departed.[39] Cooper and other writers and artists used these images of Indians as allegories for the Euro-American past, one that reflected a nostalgia about the pre-Revolutionary social and political order and that encoded a wish to a return to a time when the world seemed secure, settled, and orderly.[40]

Ultimately, though, the enormous popularity of Cooper's writings brought about the very change he wished to avoid in the very places that he had hoped would remain unchanged. Indeed, on the same mountaintop from which the fictional Leatherstocking had peered a large hotel would soon rise, and tourists were not coming to see the famous escarpment of Leatherstocking only. Tourism was spreading beyond the springs.

Ballston before 1800; watercolor by Sir William Strickland.
(New-York Historical Society)

An image of Ballston Spa from 1794 shows how remote the village was. Within a decade a hotel would rise there, and by the War of 1812 it would become the the single most important travel destination in the country.

THE
PAVILION,

Saratoga Springs.

---❋---

M.RS LEWIS,

Widow of the Late M.r Nathan Lewis

Respectfully announces to her Friends and the Public that
she continues the above Elegant establishment, which, in regard
to situation cleanliness and comfort cannot be surpassed.
Many improvements have been ma.. , the Beds are Large &
of the first Quality, the rooms are airy & Kept in the Neatest maner.

An abundance of the best Wines and Liquors shall be kept
constantly on hand, and every rarity the Country affords shall
always be procured for the Table.

An extensive Circulating Library and fashionable
Reading Room are contiguous to the Pavilio .

M.rs Lewis.

hopes by the many inducements offered to share a portion of
the Public Patronage and a continuance of that preference
with which she has hitherto been favoured.

N.B. the Post-Office is Immediately opposite.

Engraved by   R.Tiller J.r Phil.t

Pavilion Hotel flier. (New-York Historical Society)

*Advertisements for Saratoga's first tourist hotel, The Pavilion, were distributed
widely throughout the nation's cities when it was completed in 1819.*

Saratoga Springs. (New-York Historical Society)

A print of Saratoga Springs from 1817 shows the Congress Spring (foreground) with the Congress Hotel behind. It was the first year Saratoga overtook Ballston as the country's premier tourist destination.

Piazza of Congress Hall, Saratoga Springs. (New-York Historical Society)

The piazza, depicted in this 1830 print, was a standard feature of hotels of the era, used by tourists for displays of conspicuous consumption.

ABOVE: "The Falls of Cattskill, New York." (New-York Historical Society)

An 1831 print of Cole's Kaaterskill Upper Falls *demonstrates the broad secondary market for his romantic image of a tourist destination long since transformed into a commercial site.*

OPPOSITE, TOP: *Hudson River Port Folio,* Plate 1 ("Little Falls at Luzerne"). (New-York Historical Society)

Prints of William Guy Wall's paintings were sold as the Hudson River Port Folio *(1822–1825). Wall painted in the picturesque style, but by the time these engravings were made, tastes had changed, and introductory title plates attempted to push the gentle images into the realm of the "sublime."*

OPPOSITE, BOTTOM: *Hudson River Port Folio,* Plate 3 ("View Near Jessups Landing"). (New-York Historical Society)

America's first expensive art portfolio, the Hudson River Port Folio *was a failure; but in three years, particularly through Thomas Cole's work, the artistic climate had changed, and an 1828 reissue sold well.*

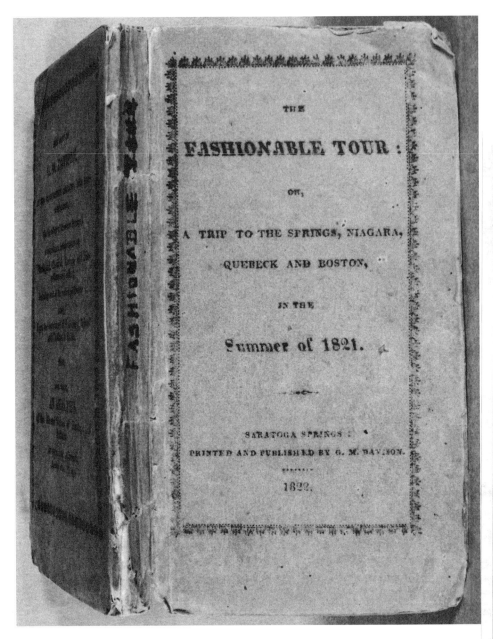

The Fashionable Tour by Gideon Minor Davison. (American Antiquarian Society)
The cover of the first American tourist guidebook, published at Saratoga Springs in 1822.

Washington Irving, from a drawing by Vanderlyn (1805).
(New-York Historical Society)

The young author from about the time his satire "Fashion at Ballston" was published in the first issue of Salmagundi.

"ALBANY."

Steamboat *Albany*. (Personal collection)

The Albany *was built and furnished at great expense to compete for tourists on the Hudson River. Deliberately expensive to ride, the steamboat and its partner ship, the* Philadelphia, *proved a failure over time, as tourists consistently chose economy over luxury.*

"View of the Catskill Mountain House, N.Y." (American Antiquarian Society)

Although only five years old when Cole made this engraving of it in 1828, the Catskill was already famous. Widely advertised, it became the model for thousands of mountain houses in the decades to come.

Niagara Falls by Minott. (New-York Historical Society)

Because of the difficulties involved in getting there, only limited numbers of tourists visited the spectacular site in 1818, when this image was painted. The completion of the Erie Canal just seven years later opened the way.

The Last of the Mohicans, Cora Kneeling at the Feet of Tamenund by Thomas Cole. (Wadsworth Athenaeum)

> *Cole's 1827 painting of a scene from Cooper's* Last of the Mohicans *first hung in the gallery of the elegant and expensive Hudson River steamboat* Albany.

5

Expanding Tourism
beyond the Springs
The Catskills and Niagara

A S OTHER WRITERS noticed the Catskill references in Irving and Dwight and Cooper, they, too, began incorporating references to the area in their works. For example, James G. Percival, a minor poet, issued his second book of poetry, *Clio* (volume 1), in 1822, and in it was "A Picture, Catskill Valley," which in turgid lines described a storm-tossed night as witnessed by an overheated, sensitive youth.[1] This level of literary attention—Percival's superheated Romanticism, Irving's whimsical tales, Cooper's dashing stories, and Dwight's stern but appraising eye—created a sudden opportunity for tourist development in the Kaaterskill Valley and up on Pine Orchard. So it is not surprising that a group of local entrepreneurs seized this moment to create a genteel tourist site there.

The official announcement came in early July 1823, when the *New-York Evening Post* published, over two days, a long letter signed "A Lover of Nature." It described in guidebook-level detail the charms of the Catskill mountains, including information about their geology and the views available from the top of the escarpment. But, most important, it noted that a "a company of gentlemen, at Catskill" had just completed a lodging place for travelers atop the "South Eminence." Previous visitors had had to make do, camping on rough pine boards at a refreshment stand that had been operating at the summit since about 1819.[2] The lodging place mentioned in the article was not much more than a large shack constructed from locally sawn hemlock boards and divided into men's and women's dormitories, a kitchen,

85

a large room rather grandly called the "ballroom," and a parlor. The bedding was loose straw for men, ticks (straw-filled mattresses) for women. Despite this roughness, it was an immediate hit. But, more important, a more permanent structure—a genteel accommodation—was also being built. When finished, the Catskill Mountain House would be an imposing building visible for miles up and down the Hudson Valley: three stories tall, sixty feet long, and twenty-four feet wide, its white-painted length facing outward like an advertisement from atop the escarpment, its front door leading out to a dramatic ledge jutting out over the steep cliff.[3] To support this, a stage line was set up to ferry visitors "immediately after the arrival of the steamboat" from Catskill to "the Mountain," an advertisement in New York newspapers announced several weeks after the opening.[4]

The "group of gentlemen" who created this tourist site knew their market. The temporary shack had its grand opening on July 4, the unofficial start of the tourist season, and they inserted the first article in the New York papers at the precise point in the travel season when southern tourists were heading north and when New Yorkers were pondering their summer journeys. But more than just a hotel was envisioned: the area would become something of a theme park, and the article glowingly described the immediate environs, including two small lakes stocked with fish just behind the nascent Mountain House. And, of course, Kaaterskill Falls awaited.

The publicity campaign was a major success, as is evidenced by the response the new tourist site received. Visitors in that first summer came from the first rank of New York society, including the governor, DeWitt Clinton, and, perhaps, Aaron Burr.[5] And it was not just New Yorkers who were drawn to the mountaintop. One visitor from the southern states was Elias Ball, another member of that fabulously wealthy South Carolina plantation family mentioned in chapter 4. He had arrived in New York City in early July as a tourist. Not knowing anyone in the city, soon after his landing he went "in quest of some acquaintances" but "could find none." The city nearly overwhelmed him. He wrote his uncle, who had already been to the city, that "you can readily imagine how a stranger must feel in so great a commercial town. " He found himself swamped by the sound, and he found the traffic intolerable. A traveler "can't hear himself speak, for the rattling of carriages over the stones is so great." Overall, he wrote, "there appears to be nothing but bustle and confusion during the hours of business."[6]

But the Mountain House was being advertised precisely to travelers like Ball, and just days later he was mounting the overlook above the Hudson. Ball's experience speaks volumes about how effectively advertised it was. He stayed at the Mountain House for several days, "much pleased with the very extensive view," and then "came immediately to the Springs," where he "passed a gay week." Later, he traveled northward to Canada and then south to Boston. He returned to New York by the end of August.[7]

The Mountain House's wealthy visitors opened a lucrative new market for entrepreneurs at Catskill as early as that first season. For example, as Ball made his way on the road up to the house, he encountered what was advertised as "the cave where Rip Van Winkle . . . had his long and comfortable nap of twenty years," "if ever such a person existed," Ball added, charmingly uncertain about the fictional status of Irving's character.[8] Another traveler, somewhat more certain about that, "could not help thinking of our friend and precursor Rip Van Wynkle" as he climbed the hill. He imagined that he might "expect to see the antiquated figure of the drowsy German Royalist starting up from his long slumber to wonder at the mountain rivulet that rolled by him, and the poor modern creatures that asked the aid of horses to drag them heavily up these dreary passes."[9] Rip Van Winkle became (and remains to this day) a minor industry in and around Catskill. By 1825 there was a "small cottage," staffed, one traveler reported, "by a Person called Rip Van Winkle," who, he wrote, "from W. Irvings discription [*sic*] of that oddity you would suppose he bore a striking resemblance." But his verdict for this non-event was crushing: he found it "tedious."[10] Other tourist experiences were offered on that same road, such as a caged bear advertised with an "attractive inscription, accompanying an admirable likeness, hung out on the exterior of his dwelling place—'3 cents for a sight at the Bear.'"[11] The finished Mountain House was inaugurated in 1824.[12]

The phenomenon of mountaintop structures was not limited to the Hudson River valley. In Massachusetts, on a June day in in 1821, a group of local villagers voted to build a mountaintop platform to serve refreshments to hikers atop Mt. Holyoke, above Hadley, Massachusetts. This mountain is part of a dramatic range whose summits command atmospheric views of the Connecticut River Valley; the southward view would be immortalized a decade later by Thomas Cole. This structure would never become as large as the Catskill Mountain House, and it would not be until the early 1850s that a truly genteel structure would rise there. Nonetheless, it was a sign of the spread of tourism beyond its hearth at the springs, since the majority of its patrons came from tourists journeying across Massachusetts to and from Saratoga.[13]

The Catskill Mountain House would lead to a craze for mountaintop lookouts, hotels, and other structures that would spread far beyond the Hudson Valley, eventually reaching into New Hampshire, Vermont, and upstate New York. The spread of these houses was itself a symptom of a far greater trend, as tourism itself spread. But even as it spread beyond the Hudson River valley, it was also expanding within the valley itself: Saratoga Springs was about to become the premier tourist spot in the country.

In the years just after the War of 1812, Saratoga and Ballston had entered a period of profound change that would transform the two villages. In the space of just a decade, from 1810 to 1820, Ballston Spa fell into a steep decline, from being the height of American tourism to looking fusty and old-fashioned. Not a great deal had changed; Ballston merely suffered in comparison to the stunning rise of its nearby rival, Saratoga Springs.

With surprising speed Saratoga had built itself into a thoroughly developed tourist destination. Saratoga's expansion from one hotel in 1812 to four in 1822 made it the single largest grouping of hotels in America outside the cities of New York and Boston, capable of boarding more than five hundred guests at a time just in the three largest establishments.[14] The largest, Congress Hall, could sleep at least two hundred, and the second-largest, the Pavilion, was able to put up at least 110. More significantly, the price of accommodations at the various hotels allowed for a relatively wide range of guests, and thus many more tourists were able to stay at Saratoga. Even those who were not of that early elite class of travelers could now partake of what had recently been a quite exclusive experience.

The most fashionable and expensive hotel rooms were at Congress Hall, where rooms could be had at ten dollars a week. The cheapest accommodations in Saratoga (outside private homes) were at Sadler's boarding house, which charged $2.62½ a week. In contrast, no new hotels had been built at Ballston Spa in this period. There, the prices of rooms remained as expensive as they had been in 1811, when rooms cost between four to eight dollars per week.[15] What is even more striking is that this growth happened in a period of deep economic disturbance. The Panic of 1819 was one of several banking crises that shook antebellum America. Businesses up and down the coast and far into the interior were forced into bankruptcy, and scores of banks failed. Despite that, investors continued to fund the building of hotels in Saratoga, and the spa grew steadily.[16]

The other indicators of Saratoga's growing importance were slower to manifest, but in time they came, too. In entertainment, for example, there was a slower growth than in the expansion of rooms. In 1817, entertainers still made Ballston their main destination, and from 1819 through 1820 Saratoga was visited only rarely by traveling entertainers, if evidence from the local newspaper is any indication (perhaps a side effect of the Panic). But by 1821, entertainers were bypassing Ballston in favor of Saratoga.

The growth of entertainment was perceptible. For example, on July 4, 1821, a Mr. Cristiani, who had been advertised in New York as a "professor of music" and composer to "all the Theatres of the Court of Spain," performed a number of unspecified "Italian" or "French" songs; perhaps the highlight of the evening was the singing of "Yankee Doodle . . . with variations."[17] His was the only advertised entertainment for that season. The big show for 1822 was a "Grand Caravan of Living Animals" that stayed for a week. It charged an admission price of 25 cents, with a discount for children. Both were traveling versions of shows that had played in minor New York theaters.

But the 1823 season began with displays that were more upscale; for example, paintings by John Dunlap and John Sully, two of the country's most prominent artists. More extravagant exhibits came as well, exhibits that required more space and infrastructure. For example, a panorama of the city of Boston was shown, along with views of ten named cities and "40 other Cities and Views, too tedious to mention, which are very interesting." Capping the season was "Mr. Frederick Brown, of the New-York, Boston and Charleston Theaters," who, in a one-man show, did his celebrated "Mail Coach Adventures," a description of the experiences of travelers, interspersed with comic songs, such as "Mail Coach" and "An English Song Sung by a French Gentleman." Brown's appearance in Saratoga is a sign of how much the village had grown in importance, at least in the eyes of entertainers. Unlike all of the earlier entertainers, Brown was a "name," a popular New York actor and mainstay of the theater who had appeared in plays throughout the 1820s in roles ranging from Macbeth to impersonations of other actors.[18]

The venues for these shows and exhibits also showed a dramatic change. Prior to 1824, all of these entertainments had taken place in various rooms at the major hotels (with the exception of the circus, which did its show in its own tent). But in 1824, Saratoga got what Ballston never had: a permanent theater and exhibition hall, the Grand Picturesque Theater, which was praised by the local newspaper praised for having "a pleasant, tasty appearance."[19] The theater was a part of a comprehensive entertainment package, as detailed in an anonymous letter (signed "W.") to the local newspaper from the summer of 1824: "We [now] have . . . healing fountains for the sick, rich viands for the epicure, choice wines for the *bon vivante*, the merry dance for the young and nimble, the circus for equestrians, theatricals for the Corinthians, rope dancing for the boys, servants and fiddlers, melody for those who have music in their souls, and, though last, not least, the great Mr. Goodacre is giving his celebrated Astronomical Lectures for the benefit of those, who, wearied with the dull cares of earth, would now like to wander among the stars."[20] The town was growing into a complete resort.

These vast improvements in entertainment and accommodations were matched by a highly improved transportation network. By 1824, it had become much easier to get to the springs. Travelers could now rapidly (at least by the standards of the time) come to Saratoga on the most modern transportation system available in the United States. "A person," one newspaper article claimed, could "leave Philadelphia at 6 o'clock in the morning, and arrive at the Springs the next day, at 4 P.M."[21] Part of the efficiency of this network came from a vigorous competition on the land elements of it. A number of firms had sprung up to carry passengers, and their competition led to innovations both useful and merely decorative. For example, the ride from Albany to Saratoga could now be made on coaches of "beauty and strength" that had been newly equipped with a remarkable advance: "elastic or spring cushions."[22] One passenger described her coach as being "lined on the inside with read [*sic*] Morocco and cushions of the same with spring seats, the out side [*sic*] was painted red with a deep border of green, yellow and a great deal of gilt." Clearly, this was more than just functionality at work, and she knew it: "This was merely done to induce Passengers to go in this line instead of the other."[23]

But innovation on one part of the transportation network had essentially stalled. The Fulton Company (now the North River Steam Navigation Company) had kept its monopoly on travel from New York City, and it had continued to keep fares high while avoiding expensive technological advances. Their enviable position collapsed suddenly in March 1824, however, when the Supreme Court, in a historic decision, ruled in *Gibbons v. Ogden* that the monopoly was unfair. The effect was explosive, as all riverboat traffic in and out of New York City was now open for competition. On the Hudson River runs, a rival line almost immediately began operating, radically undercutting the North River line's scandalously high fare of seven dollars each way. The impact was seen immediately: by May 1824, the North River line was forced to cut its New York to Albany fare from seven to five dollars. By June both lines had dropped weekend fares to two dollars, weekly rates to five dollars. By late July all fares were two dollars.[24] By 1830 fifty-cent fares would be common on all of the five lines running from New York to Albany.[25]

One traveler who noticed the effect of all this was a young Philadelphia poet, Charles West Thompson, who was traveling in the summer of 1824. He arrived in New York in late July, and after spending several days there with his five traveling companions, he continued north alone, spending the night on the water on a new steamboat, the *Chancellor Kent*. The impact of the new prices was apparent to him: "The unparalleled cheapness of travelling this season (being but 2 Dollars to Albany) has occasioned to be rather uncomfortably crowded, especially with regard to sleeping accommodations, although they are very large and well provided."[26] Although Thompson went on to find Saratoga Springs crowded, he was mistaken in attributing the throngs there to a three-dollar drop in steamboat fares. Most of what he experienced was the effect of the resort's increasing visibility and popularity.

Thompson stayed at Saratoga only three nights, like most of his fellow visitors. On his way back to New York, he stopped at the village of Catskill, where he took a carriage to "the pretty white edifice," the Catskill Mountain House, which he found "over crowded." The next morning, after an early rise, he and a friend hiked several miles and gazed, stunned and amazed, at the spectacle of Kaaterskill Falls, which they contemplated from "a platform erected on one of its overhanging precipices."[27]

To Niagara

The Niagara region also saw a huge change in the mid-1820s. Its development as a tourist destination was closely linked to that of the Hudson Valley. As travel and facilities in the valley improved, access to destinations beyond the valley became easier as well. When the Erie Canal was begun in 1817, the long haul across New York State to Niagara steadily improved, and as the number of tourists coming north from New York City increased, steadily increasing numbers took the time to go to the continent's premier natural landmark.

The distant dream of Niagara had long beckoned travelers. The very first accounts were relayed back to Europe in 1604 by Samuel de Champlain, who passed on secondhand stories but never saw the falls himself. The first witnessed record of them by a European, René Brehan de Galinée, stressed both their immensity and grandeur. Galinée called it "one of the finest cataracts or waterfalls in the world," and subsequent visitors such as Galinée's contemporary Louis Hennepin noted that although they were "the most Beautiful" falls in the world, they also were "at the same time most Frightful." This theme of fear commingled with beauty would become a mainstay of descriptions of Niagara for centuries to come.[28]

Travel to Niagara from places outside Canada had been difficult through most of the eighteenth century, as it involved crossing the territory of the Iroquois (Haudensaunee) Six Nations Confederacy, which maintained a close guard on their lands. Despite that, intrepid artists and travelers made their way there, and their paintings and illustrations of the falls were widely duplicated. Paintings such as those by Thomas Davies (1766) and Richard Wilson (1774) became symbolic of the grandeur and possibility of the American wilderness. Niagara shimmered in the distance, a place where the impossible had become manifest. On the other hand, the falls had become so regular a stop for any travel writer describing North America that by the 1770s some were refusing to describe the falls in their books, claiming that such passages had already become a cliché.[29]

After the Iroquois were defeated in the Revolutionary War, their lands in upstate New York were steadily constricted, and the area was opened to Euro-American settlement. Even for the hardy traveler, getting to the falls was a long and uncomfortable process; nonetheless, travelers did make the effort. Improvements made on the first leg of the trip, the journey from New York to Albany, made the trip a bit easier. Along the route from Albany to Niagara, too, the situation slowly began to improve as, in the first decade of the nineteenth century, settlers slowly began to fill the region, offering an increasing number of way stations, some improvement in the quality of roads, and other assistance such as the possibility of changing one's horse.

Once a traveler arrived at Niagara, the British Canadian side, which had been settled for a much longer time, offered far more in the way of accommodations and villages. This variety, though, did not necessarily represent any variation in quality: most of the inns were primitive. On the American side, there was only a small village, Lewiston, along with a scattering of tiny settlements associated with the chain of small American forts that lined the frontier. In 1805 the State of New York designated lots for sale in the formerly closed one-mile-wide margin of land it owned adjacent to the cataract. They were bought up by entrepreneurs intending to harness the water power from the furiously flowing Niagara River. These industrial goals meant that the property adjacent to the falls, where the water flowed fastest, garnered premium prices. But despite this great potential, development was slow to come because the main market for America goods lay far to the south, something that the Erie Canal was intended to remedy. Although the region looked poised for further growth, the disruption caused by the War of 1812 also slowed progress.

By 1808, when Mary Murray traveled from New York to Niagara, she found that there had been improvements for travelers. While the changes were primitive compared to those already happening along the Hudson, the area was nonetheless considerably improved. For example, there were "excellent" stretches of road near Utica, but when her party settled down for the night at a "Coffee House" there, she wrote that she could not "say much, particularly as it respects sleeping. We found Bugs plenty, and were oblig'd to put our beds upon the floor." Soon after Utica, the road deteriorated significantly. Outside Lima, on a terrible road they had been told was "fine," they were unable to reach their accommodations before nightfall. Now traveling through the night, they "pursued [their] way with Caution" through the dark woods. The "clouds oercast the sky," obscuring the road, and their carriage lurched into large holes in the road, one of which "threw the Driver from his seat between the horses, but he fortunately received no injury." Entirely lost, they spent a few anxious hours wandering through a dark landscape occasionally lit by the moon. At one point, they "perceived a light at some distance and supposing it to be a House," but "death to our hopes! it proved to be a large stump burning in the woods." Several more times they ran across this method of deforestation, but they finally emerged from the woods at an inn where they "rec'd a most cordial welcome, a comfortable dish of tea." This episode sounds dramatic, and indeed it is, but the point of the episode, to any contemporary observer, would doubtless have been just how much progress the region had seen by 1808: cast into an apparently remote and trackless wilderness, Murray's party was in fact only a few hours away from a "comfortable dish of tea."[30]

The small but steady traffic to Niagara and westward by travelers and emigrants helped create a travel infrastructure across New York State. By 1810, there were at least 118 separate places of accommodation at fifty-six different locations along the 325-mile road from Albany to Niagara, an average of about one every six miles.[31] Under perfect conditions, a traveler would never have to spend a night under the stars. Those traversing the state could purchase commercially printed "way bills" that detailed the names and locations of these inns, suggesting a small market but a highly suggestive market niche: there were enough travelers to support such a product. But in 1808 or 1810, this was not a journey casually undertaken: when Mary Murray traveled to Niagara in 1808, it took her eleven days to get there.[32] Another traveler, a member of South Carolina's Drayton family, was less inclined to dawdle, taking only eight days in 1810.[33]

Another market had arisen for Niagara-related items: by 1810, there was a large body of travel literature and reproductions of paintings and prints. This body of art and literature shaped the hopes and expectations of those adventurers who actually made the journey. Both Murray and Drayton, for example, already had high expectations about what they would see and experience once they had arrived. Murray's "great" expectations were not disappointed as they "seem'd as nothing compared with the awful the sublime reality." For her, the sight of the falls "sets all language at defiance, and fills the wrapt beholder with mute amazement." But for the Drayton traveler the hype did not meet the reality: "accounts much exaggerated," he groused, "painters not correct in the representation of the horse-shoe falls."[34]

Although by 1810 the number of travelers actually able to reach the falls was small, visitors had already had an impact on the area around the falls. For example, there was an ever-increasing number of inns, so much so that in 1808 Mary Murray, who wanted to see as much of the area as possible, was able to move daily from inn to inn, repeatedly crossing the border. In one case, she decided that she did not like the look of the inn she found at Black Rock on the American side, near the mouth of the Niagara at Lake Erie, so on the same day crossed back over to the Canadian side to find accommodations near Fort Erie.[35] Part of the reason for this bounty of small inns was the Niagara frontier's special status. Lying between American and British law, it was the perfect location for smuggling, an occupation that had been given a huge boost by the Embargo of 1807.[36] But as more legitimate visitors came, this existing infrastructure was changing to appeal to them.

Efforts were also being made to domesticate the falls themselves. Both Murray and Drayton, for example, noted that a ladder had been constructed to allow visitors access under the sheet of water. Originally made of notched logs and installed in 1795, it had been "improved" in 1805, although not enough to inspire much confidence in those who saw it. One visitor found it "so old and crazy as almost to make me give over the attempt . . . this ladder, which is eighty feet in length . . . [is] spliced and bound together in several places with grape vines."[37] Another called the splice a "bread & cheese" repair, and declined to use it.[38] Murray, perhaps sensibly, wasn't allowed to go down it by her brother, who felt a parental responsibility toward her; the Drayton traveler, though, descended the "32 or 3 rung" ladder placed "at some distance north from the falls" and from there "continued over rock, sharp & rugged, & winding along the bottom of the canyon for nearly a mile to the falls." Once under the falls, he found that "the prospect is really grand & awful." This small improvement was the first in what would eventually result in a huge reshaping of the entire region for tourist consumption.[39]

The future character of the area on the Canadian side would be determined by those early traveler-related ventures. There, access to the Niagara River's water power was barred by a sixty-six-foot-wide military use zone. The United States side had no such restriction, and as a result water-powered manufacturing was a very early and prominent feature. By 1807 a water-powered mill had already been set up there; more would follow.[40]

Although the greatest use of the Niagara would be for manufacturing, others could already see profits from the steady traffic of travelers. In 1805, Judge Peter Porter and a partner purchased prime properties on the United States side, overlooks that gave spectacular views of the falls. In 1807 Porter told a traveler, Christian Shultz, that he intended "as soon as possible" to "build a house near the best view of the falls," with the goal of keeping "a genteel tavern for the accommodation of the curious." Shultz had already observed that he was "much surprised" that "some enterprising person" had not yet built "a convenient house" for the accommodation of the "no inconsiderable number of ladies" visiting the Falls. Porter told Shultz that he also intended to remedy the precarious descent by building a stairs "sufficiently safe and easy for ladies to descend to the foot of the falls." It's revealing that as early as 1807 Porter was seeking to build something "genteel": he accurately perceived the tourist market that was developing even then. But Porter's plans were slow to be realized, and, in any case, all such ventures were shut down by the War of 1812.[41]

More than any other in the United States, the Niagara region took the brunt of the war. The area was the site of most of the major land battles, and several of the largest—Chippewa and Lundy's Lane—were fought quite near the falls. Tourism to the falls, naturally, came to a complete halt, and destruction was widespread, including the burning of Lewiston, the sacking of several farms, and the razing of Buffalo, at that time still a small village. Yet soon after the Treaty of Paris ended the war, the area of conflict in and of itself became a tourist destination. When Mrs. John Heard came to the region in 1815, she came to look at the battlefields at Chippewa, Lundy's Lane, and Queenstown. They offered a grisly kind of thrill: even four or five years after the war, tourists reported that the bones of soldiers still poked from the earth where they had fallen. It would be some years until they were given a proper burial.[42] Mrs. Heard reacted to the still-ravaged region with a curious mix of dismay and fascination. Buffalo was destroyed: "ruin & devastation mark its walls—not a house (only one excepted & that owned by a widow woman) remaining." Many of the bridges were destroyed, and the town of Chippewa had "not a house or barn but what was burnt—or the inside destroyed so as to render them uninhabitable." But she noted the tourist value of these sights: they were, she wrote, "well worth travelling five hundred miles to witness."[43]

What is striking is how rapidly this picture changed. Although Mrs. Heard found that wartime neglect of the roads had made them even more impassible, "enough to dislocate every limb," and the inns to be in even worse shape—one had "a great share of dirt—a large number of *bugs* & as many *fleas*," at another "bugs and fleas by the bushel"—peace quickly brought prosperity and a rapid expansion to the entire region.[44] The treaty that ended the war finally and conclusively established the United States–Canadian border, which had been left unresolved from the American Revolution. The settling of relations between the United States and Great Britain also allowed for a rapid expansion of trade. And the one true victory for the United States—the destruction and displacement of the most powerful Indian nations of the Old Northwest—meant that emigration could now flow uninhibited westward. There was an immediate influx of travelers, emigrants, businessmen, and, in their wake, tourists. With them came substantial improvements in the travel infrastructure. As early as 1817, one traveler in Saratoga excitedly surveyed his options: he could "move in no direction from this spot without having something interesting in view to invite . . . attention. In less than ten days I could be at Boston, New York, under the walls of Quebeck or in view of the Falls of Niagara."[45]

The most decisive transportation improvement was the Erie Canal. Begun in 1817, it would eventually offer for the first time highly reliable, smooth, and rapid transit from Buffalo to Albany. The very fact of its construction had a significant impact on the travel infrastructure of New York State long before it was completed in 1825, creating huge improvements in the roads, bridges, and ferries needed to move construction supplies and crews.[46] The canal happened to run almost entirely along the Niagara leg of the Fashionable Tour, linking Albany with Buffalo. The impact of the canal and roads associated with it meant that travelers now could cover the distance from Albany or Saratoga to Niagara significantly faster than the Ball family had a decade before. With better roads and increased traffic, both tourist and commercial, new coach and mail lines were set up to run on regular schedules, replacing most of the ad hoc arrangements Isaac Ball and his party had been obliged to work out in 1806. These improvements created a virtuous circle on these heavily traveled routes: traveling technology begat more travelers; as more travelers used the routes, even more improvements were built.

The canal itself was an early tourist site. By 1818, Jonathan Pintard wrote that it "seems to challenge the admiration of every visitor."[47] For these travelers it was an inexpressible luxury to travel smoothly on a stable platform, a canal boat. To capitalize on this, as early as 1820 passenger vessels began operating on newly completed sections of the canal even before its full length was opened. These boats, richly furnished and ornately decorated, were specifically designed to attract tourists.[48] By 1822 a line of seven packet boats in central New York connected Little Falls and Lyons, thirty miles from Rochester. They were coordinated with post coaches from Albany to Little Falls (the connection with Lyons was more haphazard). One newspaper article noted that the cost of four cents a mile or four dollars in all, board included, was not only cheaper than the cost of a stage journey but that the trip involved "no risk of life or limb, and no fatigue or dust attending." The sole sacrifice, though, was speed: boats were not fast when compared to coaches, in dry weather anyway. Early in the operation of the canal they made the stately progress of only thirty miles a day, somewhat less than two miles an hour, although many saw traveling with your sleeping quarters as a decisive advantage. By 1825, the speed had increased: travelers could expect to reach three and a half miles per hour.[49]

Canal boats quickly became much more ornate. One 1823 traveler described the boat he took on one part of his journey, the *Magnet*, as "elegant." Although it was one of the smaller canal boats, it still weighed six tons. Another part of his journey was on the *Mount Holley*, a forty-ton boat that drew only eight inches of water but was richly furnished with "elegant accommodations." These boats sought, and found, an upscale market. Rival packet lines began competing for business, currying favor wherever they could. The Utica and Schenectady Packet Boat Company built elegant boats named after political figures, such as the *De Witt Clinton* (named after the governor of New York), launched July 1823, and the *Stephen Van Rensselaer* (named after the local "patroon"—the hereditary heir of huge tracts of land about Albany—who was then a congressman in the House of Representatives), launched in 1824.[50]

Enthusiasm about canal travel ran high in certain quarters. Horatio

Spafford, the writer of the New York *Gazetteer*, published a canal guide-book in 1824, described in its opening paragraphs as *A Small Directory for the Pocket, embracing the vast extent of the lines of natural and artificial navigation in this State*. It was directed "no less . . . [to] tourists and travellers than . . . men of business."[51] Travelers would find canal travel "very pleasant, cheap, and expeditious," proclaimed Spafford, finding the food "wholesome and rich." They would "find the time pleasantly employed, in conversation, and the variety of incidents, new topics, stories, and constantly varying scenery."[52]

Despite Spafford's boosterism, general opinion about canal travel was mixed. Some found that "constantly varying scenery" quite dull. Further, Gideon Davison opined that "of the sources of gratification to the tourist, during the canal passage, that of novelty is perhaps the greatest. To the man of pleasure, it will be considered, perhaps, too little diversified with incident to be repeated."[53] David Hillhouse, a wealthy southern planter, agreed with him: he found traveling on a packet boat "quiet and monotonous" because it "affords so little opportunity of looking upon the country around." He equated it to "sitting all day in an excellent tavern hall, except that I am progressing in my journey," although he did concede that "this mode of travelling accommodates the ladies very well. They can read and sew, and sleep and chew, without the apprehension of having run-away horses, or bursting [steamboat] boilers."[54] Theodore Dwight, however, was enthusiastic, finding in it a unique form of genteel entertainment and praising "the novelty of the mode of traveling adopted on the Erie Canal, as well as the magnificence of the work itself." In addition, the "interesting objects and scenes along its course" have drawn "vast numbers" of tourists. And "a large proportion" of these travelers, he contended, "are strangers of wealth and taste."[55]

But although the canal boats were large by the standards of the day, conditions were nonetheless very cramped. Even when all of the party were genteel, tensions arose from the closeness of company. Henry Gilpin found it distracting: "If a gentleman who is very busily engaged in discoursing on state banks & stocks & guarantees and discounts would but hold his tongue I think I could spend half an hour very pleasantly in epistolizing you," he wrote his father from the canal.[56] Small cabins contributed to the overall discomfort, which was exacerbated by the summer heat. Elizabeth Pierce, writing from her uncle's home in Hunter, New York, wrote her father describing the scene during a river journey in late August of 1824. The boat, she wrote, "was really crowded." Once it came time to sleep, the rooms were so cramped they presented "a ludicrous spectacle," crowded with "ladies, servants & children . . . strewed about in all directions." The men had the luxury of going on the deck: "Many of them shouldered their matresses [*sic*] & located themselves on deck to enjoy the luxury of a little fresh air," but in her cabin the overall discomfort, combined with the noise made by, among others, "the french with the servant & children . . . making a free use of their colloquial facilities" meant it "was long before we were all tranquillized."[57]

What is striking about the passenger trade on the canal is not that it existed—experience from the Hudson River lines showed how ready competitors and entrepreneurs were to enter the business—but how quickly it happened. Thriving lines were operating mere months after the first canal stretches were in operation. But the presence of expensively outfitted boats suggests not only high profits but high expectations, expectations that the construction of yet more such boats clearly indicates were being met. Customers used them, and canal traffic would thrive until the building of a railroad across New York in the 1840s. The construction of the Erie Canal fed travelers and, later, tourists into Niagara.

Owners of land near the falls were extremely aware of the changes at Saratoga, including entrepreneurs like Peter B. Porter, a U.S. congressman from 1806 to 1812, and his brother Augustus, who traveled regularly to New York City through Saratoga. There, and elsewhere in the Hudson Valley, they saw the dramatic impact of tourist profits. Another stimulus came from the tourists themselves, who pressed these entrepreneurs about their future plans, urged and suggested improvements, and in their own way helped create the next generation of tourist infrastructure.

Niagara, however, lagged several years behind Saratoga. When John Duncan traveled to Niagara in October of 1817, he, like all writers of this period, noted the complete lack of good accommodation at the falls. He stayed at the same shabby inns that had sheltered earlier travelers. Although they had even then fallen short of prewar standards, they were now in shocking contrast to the accommodations that tourists had often just experienced at Saratoga Springs, Ballston Spa, or the major cities of America and Canada. The quality of all the infrastructure around the falls had to be upgraded before a steady and sustainable tourism could be brought there. Nonetheless, Duncan saw a region that, despite its wartime devastation, was rapidly revitalizing. Buffalo had been rebuilt and was now housing about six hundred people, and the only signs of its former destruction he could find were a bullet-riddled tavern sign and the ruins of a brick house. He described the "wondrous changes" that "time . . . that silent but most innovating of reformers" had wrought, and he presciently looked to the future, envisioning that "in a few years . . . the noise of the cataracts may be drowned in the busy hum of men; and the smoke of clustering towns, or more crowded cities, obscure on the horizon the clouds of spray."[58]

Duncan also wrote of an increasingly frequent experience for visitors to the falls: disappointment. The outpouring of fulsomely complimentary literature about the falls instilled expectations in many that could never be met. Overall, Duncan's expectations had been raised to such an extent that his first glimpse of the falls caused "disappointment," which he claimed was "a very common feeling when strangers first visit these cataracts." The outpouring of travel literature describing the sublimity of the scene had "fatigued . . . all the parts of speech, and degrees of comparison" in describing them. As for attempting to describe the falls, they had "been so frequently described, and the whole vocabulary of sublimity so completely exhausted in the service," that he entirely avoided it.[59]

The transformation of the region would be driven by a number of entrepreneurs. One of the most significant and fascinating to emerge during this period was William Forsyth. He almost singlehandedly transformed the Canadian side of the falls into a tourism machine, in the process of which he became quite wealthy. Forsyth's father, a Loyalist during the American Revolution, had moved to Stamford Township in Upper Canada in the early 1780s. There, in 1789, at the age of twenty-eight, William was tried for a felony, acquitted, but then immediately rearrested for a capital offense. The next day he escaped from the jail but was recaptured while trying to cross into the United States. Despite this record, he somehow escaped all punishment.[60]

Perhaps understandably, Forsyth's local reputation was not good: a neighbor is quoted as calling him "a man of uncouth behavior." Forsyth fought in the militia during the war, but his record there was mixed. His commander later recalled that he caused "some displeasure and trouble to my Officers by leaving his duty and going home at nights," but he also fought well at the battle of Beaver Dams. Overall, though, the commander reported that "Forsyth is a man not generally liked." And there were persistent rumors that he had profited greatly during the war through smuggling. This was entirely likely, for having grown up in a border region famous for just that he undoubtedly already had long experience before the war and its broad opportunities for profits. This may explain how he was able to raise the capital to purchase a prime tract of land just above the falls on the Canadian side right after the end of the War of 1812. In short order he built an inn on it, the first on either side of the border that was adjacent to the falls. Forsyth's land encompassed what was considered to be the premier viewing spot of the falls, a large overhang known as Table Rock.[61]

Although his inn received mixed reviews, its prime location inevitably drew large numbers of visitors.[62] When Catharine Maria Sedgwick, later to become a well-known writer, visited it in 1821, she counted the number of guests listed in his register from August 1815 to June 1816, estimating that the number of guests for this ten-month period was "upwards of 1400." This is an especially significant number: not only was there no travel for ¾ of the year, but the region, as we know from Mrs. John Heard, was also still visibly suffering from the aftereffects of the war.[63] Forsyth used his profits to create other improvements intended both to increase his revenues and to help tame the falls for tourists. Around 1818, for example, he erected a covered stairway down to the gorge and charged a shilling for its use.[64] And, as Lt. Francis Hall, a British officer, discovered in 1819, the footpath leading from the walkway to the base of the falls, formerly uneven, slippery, and treacherous, had been made more level. These improvements increased the value of Forsyth's property, but, as with so many things with him, there was a cloud over the whole affair: they had been constructed without permission on the sixty-six-foot easement adjacent to the river reserved for military use. After he was called to account for this trespassing, Forsythe did try to lease that land from the executive council of the province, but permission was denied. Although he had angered too many prominent persons, he was not so out of favor that action was taken against him either to remove the stairway or to force him to operate it for free.[65]

At the same time, on the American side, entrepreneurs were effecting

changes that would create a tourist-safe environment. In 1817, a bridge was
built by Peter B. Porter across the river to Goat Island, just above the falls,
and although it was swept away by ice in the winter of 1817–18, it was rebuilt in 1819.[66] Tourists could cross the bridge or, if they were feeling particularly adventuresome, pay for a fast boat ride down the river to the
island.[67] Once there, they could pass the time at a billiard hall and drinking
room run by Porter, or they could wander the island. One remarkably popular activity seems to have been cutting names into trees. One young traveler from New York proudly did so, but he had to search for some time to
find one that wasn't already covered with graffiti. He eventually found
"room on a small one" and in his journal described precisely where that
was, presumably for a future traveler to witness.[68] (One such future traveler, in 1826, would note that "a number of trees . . . have been cut to death
in recording the full names or initials of . . . [those] who have visited this
charming spot . . . almost every tree . . . has some . . . memento of some
visitor's employment.")[69] Porter's improvements would soon be copied
on the Canadian side, as Francis Hall predicted in 1819: "In a few years
travellers will find a finger post, 'To the Falls' Tea Gardens,' with cakes, and
refreshments, set out on the Table Rock."[70]

"The Falls of Niagara," John Pintard wrote his daughter in 1818, "has become a fashionable place of resort."[71] To complete the experience, William
Forsyth began to create a block of property where he would build Niagara's first genteel hotel. He started in 1820, when he expanded his holdings upriver by purchasing the property of his neighbor, William Dickson,
whose farm lay at and just above the falls. Forsyth now owned about four
hundred prime acres straddling the Canadian access to the falls. He exploited this monopoly by charging visitors for access to the magnificent
view from Table Rock. He then began building Niagara's first tourist
hotel. Completing it in time for the 1822 season, he named it The Pavilion,
perhaps in emulation of the hotel at Saratoga Springs of the same name.
Its design also echoed its cousins at the springs. For example, it had long
piazzas on either side from which guests could gaze upon the falls. And, in
time, it would have long side wings, just like most of the Saratoga Hotels
and the Sans Souci in Ballston. This imposing, white, three-story structure
became its own best advertisement, perched just atop the best tourist view
possible, clearly visible from the American side.[72]

By the mid-1820s, Niagara had become fully integrated into the tourist region of New York. Tourism in the Hudson Valley provided a model for the entrepreneurs of Niagara and at the same time became a conduit through which visitors passed to the great falls beyond. In the decades to follow, as the journey to Niagara became ever faster, the falls would come to equal and later eclipse the Hudson region as the destination of choice for American tourists.

ᵅᔆ 6 ᔆᵃ

Tourism and Literature

James Fenimore Cooper and Others

D URING THE SUMMER and fall of 1825, the same year that
Thomas Cole made his seminal journey up the Hudson, James
Fenimore Cooper's career hit a rocky patch. *The Pioneers* had been
as big a success as he had hoped for when it was published in 1823. The following year, his next book, *The Pilot*, was also a success. When the editor
and poet William Cullen Bryant first met Cooper in April 1824, he described him as "a little giddy."[1] At that point, Cooper's next book, *Lionel
Lincoln*, was well under way; it was completed several months later. A Revolutionary War tale, *Lincoln* was a follow-up to *The Pilot*. Cooper hoped
that they would be the beginning of a thirteen-novel cycle in honor of the
fiftieth anniversary of the Revolution. But *Lincoln* was a commercial and
critical failure, in part because of Cooper's ambiguity about the nature of
the Rebel cause: the "firmest patriot of the tale," a modern critic has noted,
was "an insane fanatic for whom the cause of liberty is a perverse metaphor
for his private past," spent as an inmate of a British asylum.[2]

Cooper worried that success was shallow, and he feared it would soon
disappear. The failure of *Lincoln* filled him with terror that he was now in
an irreversible decline, one that would once again force him on the charity
of his in-laws. And so he returned to formula. As with *The Pioneers*, he
would work in fashionable and identifiable tourist sites described in a picturesque style, along with dramatic, romantic figures. He would write a
book as close to Walter Scott as he could. Most important, the book would
have a nostalgic vision, like *The Pioneers*, in a setting stripped of the "improvements" of the present day.

Tourism was to be pivotal in the creation of this new book. Cooper's critical moment of inspiration came during a Hudson River trip he took in the summer of 1824.[3] In July of that year he was visited by four friends from Britain, a group that included the future prime minister and fourteenth Earl of Derby, Edward Stanley. The Britons had decided that they would follow the route of the Fashionable Tour and invited Cooper to join them. Although Cooper was eager to go with them, he decided that his New York obligations meant that he could only travel with them part of the way. Further, he had an honorary dinner to attend and would not be able to leave immediately.[4]

His guests, though, wanted to get on the road immediately, and the next day, July 27, they headed north from New York. They traveled to the Hudson Highlands, Pine Orchard, Kaaterskill Falls, and Saratoga Springs, places Cooper had visited the year before.[5] The morning after the honorary dinner, Cooper took the steamboat north and caught up with them somewhere along the Hudson, perhaps in Albany but most likely at Ballston Spa or Saratoga Springs.[6]

There the party decided "upon a little excursion to Lake George," with a stop at "the Glens Falls." The falls, plate number 6 of the *Hudson River Port Folio*, was a site Timothy Dwight described in enthusiastic detail. Cooper, well aware of Dwight, would have been eager to see them.[7] They arrived at the falls on a day in early August. Glens Falls was a jumbled cascade of the Hudson River, formed by "a regular series of capacious steps . . . of an imposing extent, and of incomparable beauty," in the words of the *Hudson River Port Folio*.[8] The turbulence of the water and the intermittently soft nature of the limestone outcropping forming the falls had created a number of caverns beneath them. Early in the century, a substantial bridge had been thrown across the river there, using a small island in the river's center as the location for a tollhouse. A staircase had been built down from the tollhouse to the river, and visitors could pay to visit the caverns.[9] Cooper and company descended into the caverns. In the journal that Stanley kept on the trip, he described Cooper as being "much struck with the scenery which he had not before seen; and [he] exclaimed, 'I must place one of my old Indians here.'" This cavern would become the site of a crucial scene in *The Last of the Mohicans*.[10]

Cooper and his friends then journeyed northward, to Caldwell on the shores of Lake George. The was a popular side trip for visitors to Saratoga

Springs or Ballston Spa; as early as 1802 a tavern had been built at the northern end of the lake, at Bolton Landing. The first accommodations at what would become the village of Caldwell were built around 1818, when James Caldwell, the owner of most of the land in the area, converted his home to an inn.[11] Dwight had praised the lake's scenery, and the area was a modestly successful attraction by the early 1820s.[12] Cooper's party made side trips to the ruins of Fort William Henry and Fort George, which the Hurons had successfully besieged while aiding the French during the French and Indian War—an incident that was much repeated in popular histories of the war. Cooper would work that episode, too, into *Mohicans*. The party also probably took a day trip to Fort Ticonderoga using the new steamboat that was plying the lake. Cooper returned to New York by mid-August; among other reasons, he (like the entire city) was eagerly awaiting the arrival of the Marquis de Lafayette, who was about to arrive in New York to begin a widely anticipated last tour of the United States. The idea for *Mohicans* remained dormant as Cooper completed *Lionel Lincoln*, which was published in February 1825.[13]

Cooper began writing *Mohicans* sometime before *Lincoln* was published, but as the failure of the latter became clear in the months after its publication, he quickened his pace. He worked on it through the summer of 1825 and was proofing the manuscript in September and October, just as Thomas Cole's first paintings were being exhibited. Publishing was delayed as Charles Wiley, his New York publisher, suffered a series of health and financial problems, and Cooper transferred printing to the Philadelphia firm of Carey and Lea. Finally, in early February 1826, *The Last of the Mohicans* appeared in the bookstores of America.[14]

Cooper and the Tourist Audience

Cooper was careful to make the landscape he had traveled with his friends central to the plot of *Mohicans*. Indeed, it was emphasized much more than in *The Pioneers*. Throughout, he stressed that the book's events were being conducted across tourist sites, and he regularly hinted that these were places that his readers knew. Ballston Spa, for example, was worked into the narrative. After a dramatic episode where the Munro sisters and Heywood are rescued from certain death at the hands of the Hurons, Hawkeye leads the shaken survivors a short distance, down "the precipitous sides of that hill . . . [at] whose summit had so nearly proved the scene of their massacre," across "a babbling brook . . . [to] a narrow dell, under the shade of a few water elms . . . but a few rods" from where they had been. Cooper is describing the very route that tourists would have used to enter Ballston Spa—even if, by the 1820s, they would be walking alongside a proper road. Continuing the narrative, Hawkeye and his native friends then begin "throwing aside the dried leaves, and opening the blue clay" to uncover "a clear and sparkling spring of bright, glancing water."[15] Hawkeye tells the former captives that he knew that their capturers would head for this place—that "the Mingoes would push for this springs, for the knaves well know the vartue of its waters!" Heywood drinks from it, and he experiences what many tourists must have after drinking the intensely mineralized water: he "threw it aside with grimaces of discontent." But Hawkeye laughs, and says, "Ah! you want the flavour that one gets by habit . . . but I have come to my taste, and now I crave it." To make sure that his readers know that this mineral spring is truly the one they have come to experience themselves, Cooper gives them a few obvious clues: this "solitary and silent spring" is the very one, with "its sister fountains," that "within fifty years, the wealth, beauty, and talents, of a hemisphere" would "assemble in throngs, in pursuit of health and pleasure."[16] As if that were not specific enough, in the 1831 edition he added a footnote directly identifying it as Ballston Spa, "one of the two principal watering places in America." The locations did not go unnoticed by the reading public, either. One review noted that "our modern fashionables, who take their summer's tour to Lake George and the Springs of Saratoga," would, by reading *Mohicans*, "form some faint idea of the different conditions of things" in earlier times. It claimed that "our author" had "chosen . . . a place . . . admirably adapted" to his story, one "abounding with romantic scenery of the wildest and most picturesque character."[17]

Another memorable episode is set in the caves under Glens Falls. After an attack from the Hurons, a number of the European characters, including Cooper's Scott-esque pair of heroines, Alice and Cora Munro, take refuge in the caverns beneath Glens Falls, along with Chingachgook and Uncas. What follows is a passage that is so eloquent that one critic has called it an "ecstatic description," and, like the Kaaterskill Falls passage in *The Pioneers*, it emanates from the mouth of Hawkeye. As they hide in the caves, Hawkeye is asked, "We are then on an island?" To which he replies, "Ay! there are the falls on two sides of us, and the river above and below." The falls, he continue, go by "no rule at all":

> Sometimes it leaps, sometimes it tumbles; there, it skips; here, it shoots; in one place 't is white as snow, and in another 't is green as grass; hereabouts, it pitches into deep hollows, that rumble and quake the 'arth. . . . The whole design of the river seems disconcerted. First it runs smoothly, as if meaning to go down the descent as things were ordered; then it angles about and faces the shore; nor are there places wanting where it looks backward, as if unwilling to leave the wilderness, to mingle with the salt! . . . After the water has suffered to have its will, for a time, like a headstrong man, it is gathered together by the hand that made it, and a few rods below you may see it all, flowing on steadily towards the sea, as was foreordained from the first foundation of the 'arth! [18]

The similarities of this passage to the description of Kaaterskill Falls and the view from the escarpment in *The Pioneers* is striking. Both descriptions are nothing less than painterly. One contemporary reviewer, writing in the *North American Review*, called Cooper's style "highly picturesque," as he painted "upon the grand scale, and with a bold outline," depicting "huge rocks, and overhanging woods, and tumbling cataracts, [and] with a great mist." [19] Cooper's description of Glens Falls is very much like Cole's depiction of Kaaterskill Falls: it created an idealized picture removed of all the modern-day tourist clutter. And as for *Mohicans*, it was an immediate success: Cooper's formula had once again worked.

Tourism and the Gift Book

Cooper was a part of a strong literary current. Tourism became a common literary motif of the mid-1820s, as new authors, in particular, wrote stories featuring tourism in an effort to give their writing a fashionable edge. Tourism's appeal deeply shaped some of America's most popular publications.

One of the most influential magazines in American literary history was

The Atlantic Souvenir, first published in late 1825. The *Souvenir* was the first of an entirely new genre in the United States, the literary annual. It was what was called a gift book: an elaborately decorated, expensively bound, and beautifully illustrated consumer item, the first product explicitly created for the Christmas gift-giving season in the United States. The *Souvenir* was a huge success, and by the next Christmas a number of imitators had sprung up to copy it.

Within several years, gift books had become the single most widely sold and distributed publications of the day. But beyond their significance as a consumer product, they had a profound impact on American literature: gift books introduced American fiction to the wider American public. In the process, they launched the careers of the authors who are today widely seen as constituting the core of the first flowering of American letters, authors such as Edgar Allen Poe and Nathaniel Hawthorne, to name a few.[20]

Given this illustrious pedigree, it is striking that so much of the very first gift book was devoted to stories that had tourist motifs or that used tourism as a theme. In all, something between 70 to 105 of the edition's 353 pages were related to tourism, depending on how one categorizes them.[21] These stories used Hudson Valley tourism to indicate high fashion, class, and style. Perhaps the story that used it to the greatest effect was by James Kirke Paulding, one of the Knickerbockers and a close associate of Washington Irving. His "Tale of Mystery" took up fifty pages. It tells of the exploits of a group of tourists ("gay butterflies of fashion") and is set in the Hudson River portion of the "fashionable tour." It is highly specific as to time ("in the merry month of June"), accommodations (the Hudson River Steam Navigation Company's steamboat *Chancellor Kent*), and even reading matter: one "young squire" describes a nearby highland's "heights and distances, with book in hand," a book later identified as "friend Spafford" (Horatio Spafford's widely popular 1813 *Gazetteer of the State of New York*).[22] "All who have gone on the picturesque tour," declares one of the tourists, a writer, know that one Hudson River landmark, the Sugar Loaf, is "one of the most striking objects after passing Anthony's Nose." Paulding's name- and place-dropping was his way of connecting to a traveling readership, precisely as Cooper had done.

Paulding was an established author, and he would go on to have a long career as a humorist and, later, a propagandist for slavery. Also published in the first *Atlantic Souvenir* was an author whose fame was about to surpass

Paulding's: Catharine Maria Sedgwick, whose first novel was a great success and who would become one of the decade's most popular writers. Her contribution to the *Souvenir* was "The Catholic Iroquois," a story set in and around Niagara Falls. Its main character was "a gentleman, on his way from Niagara to Montreal," clearly a tourist on the northern leg of the Fashionable Tour. Although the bulk of the story would center on the Iroquois, Sedgwick's choice of a tourist to introduce the story highlights how pervasive a stock character had become.[23] This presence of tourism in this first gift book continued through another three stories and several poems. In later years the fervor would cool, particularly as tourism itself began to become more common, but every annual for the next few years would contain at least one travel-related story.

In the meantime, the summer of 1825 would mark the strongest tourist season to date, and it would bring about the first competition between tourist guidebooks in America, as two new authors joined in literary battle with Gideon Minor Davison, the writer of the first such guide. These three guides would direct a new wave of travelers to the most fashionable destinations of the day.

❦ 7 ❧

The First Tourist Guidebook War

H AD GIDEON Minor Davison's 1822 tourist guide, *The Fashionable Tour*, not faced any competition, it would have been just a novelty and curiosity, destined to land into the dustbin of history. For three years, it was just about that.[1] But the tourist fad in literature led others to Davison's guide, and by 1825 two competitors had appeared. Like the authors of travel and tourism-related fiction, the new guidebook authors hoped to create writing careers for themselves. Each author defined his book to appeal to distinct aspects of the market, thus revealing the growing factions that were already appearing among tourists.

Gideon Davison had published the first edition of *The Fashionable Tour* as much to promote Saratoga as to further his own career as a publisher. Although the number printed was limited and Davison's means of distribution haphazard—there were no advertisements for it in the major newspapers[2]—we know that the book was highly influential for the two other guidebook authors of the 1820s, as they borrowed both the format and significant passages of the book.

Both of the new guides were published in time for the 1825 tourism season, and both were written by authors who were roughly the same age as Davison. But these authors came from far more privileged stations than the Saratoga printer, and each in his way tried to target his text toward his own class: the traveling gentry. Each took a different slant, and as a result their texts reflected different aspects of gentry attitudes toward tourism. And both of these two young writers saw tourist-related writing as a way to further nascent literary careers, indicating the scope and popularity of tourism by the mid-1820s.

Theodore Dwight, the first of these two new authors, had lived a life far removed from the hard printer's work of Gideon Davison's experience. Dwight was the nephew of the late famed travel writer Timothy Dwight, which made him an exemplar of a particular wealthy, conservative New England tradition.[3] He was raised in Connecticut and at the age of fourteen entered Yale, where he studied under his uncle, whom he revered. Like his uncle, he had initially intended to continue his studies in theology after his graduation from Yale in 1814. Later accounts held that he was disabled by disease, perhaps scarlet fever, and he was unable to continue. But if that is the case, he recovered quickly; by September of 1815 he was teaching school in Northampton, Massachusetts.[4] He never returned to college. For the next several years he had a continuing struggle with his health, which at least once, in 1816, forced him to return to his parents' home in Hartford.[5] Apparently still teaching in Northampton, in the summer of 1818 he found employment as an agent for John Trumbull's subscription printing of a facsimile of the Declaration of Independence. He traveled from New York to Boston and eventually made his way out to Ballston and Saratoga Springs in search of subscribers.[6] He probably became ill again in early 1820, and that summer he traveled to Europe, visiting Switzerland, Italy, Germany, and Holland in a vigorous pursuit of health.[7]

Dwight returned to the United States in 1821 and moved to New York City, where he began working at the offices of his father's newspaper, the *Daily Advertiser*.[8] At the same time, he began the heroic process of turning his uncle's voluminous correspondence into the four volumes of *Travels in New England*, which was published from 1822 through 1824. He was also compiling his own travel notes into a manuscript, which appeared in 1824 as *A Journal of a Tour in Italy, in the Year 1821*.[9] The book was a beautiful product, profusely illustrated with Dwight's sketches and maps, so it must have been very expensive to produce and to buy. It was never reprinted.[10]

The same summer it was published, he traveled to the Springs. Although his family had long made Ballston Spa its destination, in 1824 he went instead to Saratoga Springs, where he spent a long weekend in mid-August. The spa's new popularity was evident. He counted as many as 1500 genteel visitors, concluding, as he wrote his brother William, that "since you saw Saratoga last . . . I will venture to state in general terms that the number of visitors has considerably increased." He marveled at the two new grand hotels that had been built, the Pavilion and the United States Hotel, which "have been *completed*, to say the least." It had only been five years since he had last visited, and all of these changes had left him "a little melancholy," since in the throngs he looked "in vain for anything better than a half-way acquaintance or a homely old face or two." In all of the forced gaiety of this tourist scene, he found this group, assembled "for the purpose of being gay," to be "insufferably dull."[11]

Nonetheless, it was probably at Saratoga that he came into contact with an item that sparked his interest: Gideon Davison's little guidebook, *The Fashionable Tour*. From it, he got an inspiration: he would create his own guidebook, but this one informed by his own opinions and observations and those of his uncle. On returning to New York, he began writing. Dwight's debt to Davison is both explicit—he mentions Davison's book as one readers could refer to for "more details"—and implicit, as the book has several sections clearly borrowed from or indebted to Davison.[12] Over the next year he completed the book, and it was published as *The Northern Traveller* in the early summer of 1825.[13]

Dwight's vision for his guide was that it would become *the* definitive work—"a complete Traveller's Guide," in the words of the preface—for genteel voyagers along the Fashionable Tour. In his preface, he outlined the inadequacies of existing guides. And although he allowed that "several valuable works" had been useful for compiling his book and might be useful for some travelers, he also denigrated them, claiming that none were fully adequate for the needs of the "vast numbers" of "strangers of wealth and taste" who were now "travelling on the northern fashionable routes." He criticized some as being "too prolix for the convenience of a traveller"; others, he wrote, "contain much other matter, or have become antiquated by time; and others are confined to a few subjects."[14] A few pages later, he lists those works, and he includes Davison's *Fashionable Tour.*[15] This was a clear criticism of what was the only other existing guidebook for the Fashionable Tour route Dwight was proposing to describe. Nevertheless, he admired his rival's book enough to appropriate significant chunks of it into his own.[16]

As an author, Dwight assumed the role of a genteel man of wealth and taste and discrimination. Given his background and education, this was obviously not much of a stretch. But he did not always write out of his

own experiences. For example, he touted Ballston Springs as the ideal destination for the genteel traveler rather than new, gauche Saratoga. Ballston
had a "variety of scenery in [its] neighbourhood . . . sufficient to attract
many of those who resort to this place of health and pleasure . . . walking
and riding will be found much more agreeable here then [*sic*] at Saratoga."[17] Saratoga, by comparison, was a dusty outpost: "clusters of frail
board buildings . . . spring up among the stumps of trees lately felled in
the skirts of the pine forest . . . show[ing] what an unnatural surplus of
population the place contains during the brief period that fashion here
maintains her court."[18] Here Dwight was upholding the ideals of his uncle
(who, of course, never got to see the new Saratoga), along with those of
old-line gentry travelers including, probably, his father. Yet when he came
to Saratoga for his 1824 visit, he himself remained at there for the bulk of
his visit. Perhaps even Theodore Dwight found Ballston Spa too staid.[19]

Dwight's view of the institution of tourism was conflicted. On the one
hand, the large numbers of new travelers made his book possible. On the
other, the new, cheaper, more accessible infrastructure of tourism had
created a disquieting level of class mixing, pushing gentry together with
non-gentry. Dwight's intended readers, these neophyte but upper-class
travelers, were about to be plunged for the first time from their carefully
controlled homes into the chaotic new world of travel.

One glaring example can be found at the point of first contact that
tourists had with New York City, the consistently chaotic ferry boat landing at the foot of Courtland Street, where the ferries from New Jersey and
the Hudson River landed their throngs. "Here commenced," wrote a Mr.
Sipple in 1821, "another sea of confusion if possible more terrible than any
heretofore." The Sipples, husband, wife, and daughter, had just landed in
the city. They had come from their home in Milton, Delaware, and were
going to Saratoga for their health, a "business of more importance than
pleasure." Their day had already been ruined by an unwelcome fellow traveler with whom they had been forced to share a coach as they rode to the
New York-bound ferry. This sailor "with more tongue then [*sic*] wit" had
been "stimulating too high." In all, they found him "very disagreeable."
Now, at the ferry landing, there was even more unpleasantness: they were
accosted by a mob of porters who had charged aboard the boat the moment it landed. "They are the greatest impositioners of any I have met,"
raged Sipple; without permission, they "lay hold of your trunk and start

not knowing where it is to go too [*sic*] . . . you must either follow them or lay hold on them to keep them back until you know where to go your self." The Sipples, pious and prim, would later find much at Saratoga that challenged their mores and standards.[20]

Dwight wrote his text to help such travelers. It gently steered them away from unpleasantness and constantly referred to what persons of "taste and leisure" would prefer. And it suggested ways that one could protect oneself from the undignified situations that might arise during travel. At the ferry landing, for example, Dwight advised that "a traveller is too often pressed upon by impertinent fellows, who recommend their own vessels, and urge him to take passage in them." Protection could be found through the kind of brusque, aristocratic hauteur not normally necessary in small-town environments from which many of his readers would have come: "The only way to treat them," he counseled, is "without reply."[21]

Dwight felt that the real meaning of tourism was becoming lost in the crowds. For him, it was the society one met while traveling that mattered, not the scenery. As a consequence, he lavished much more attention on the people a traveler would meet at tourist sites. His depiction of the new Catskill Mountain House at Pine Orchard is typical: It "is the resort of so much company during the pleasant seasons of the year, that the attractions of its scenery are redoubled by the presence of agreeable and refined society. Individuals of taste and leisure, and still more, parties of travellers, will thus often enjoy a gratification which is rarely to be found in a place naturally so wild and difficult of access."[22] Dwight's continued focus on social contacts was carried through in his description of Ballston Spa. There, "scarcely any thing can communicate sensations of more complete desertion before the company have arrived, or after they have retired."[23]

Even the most widely acknowledged sublime site, Niagara Falls, got relatively short shrift: "The height of the fall on this side is 174 feet perpendicular; and this height the vast sheet of foam preserves unbroken, quite round the Grand Crescent, a distance it is estimated of 700 yards. . . . The fall on the American side is neither so high, so wide, nor so unbroken, yet, if compared with any thing else but the Crescent, would be regarded with emotions of indescribable sublimity. The breadth is 900 feet, the height 160, and about two thirds the distance to the bottom the sheet is broken by projecting rocks."[24] After allowing a few "emotions of indescribable sublimity," Dwight marched on: facts, statistics, and analysis overwhelmed any transports of emotion. In all, Dwight parted with his uncle, who often concentrated on the scenery. But his uncle traveled in a time before mass tourism.

What made Dwight's project ironic from its inception was that if it were successful it would bring in masses of people, thus destroying that exclusive society he so championed. And, in fact, that would be the case. Later, he would be distinctly uncomfortable with the frivolities of travel and of tourists, particularly in his 1827 *Sketches of Scenery and Manners in the United States* where he railed against the "numerous travellers for pleasure" who were interested "only by their present gratification."[25]

If the review in the *New-York Evening Post* is any indication (it called the book "very crude"), the reception of Dwight's guidebook was rather cool. But it is hard to gauge how accurate a barometer of public response this was, since the *Post* was a rival to Dwight's father's newspaper, the *New-York Commercial Advertiser*. Perhaps stronger evidence was that the *Northern Traveller* was published in a second, modestly expanded edition the following year, 1826. The *Post* acidly noted that this time Dwight had taken "much care" to "exclude the errors and supply the omissions of the previous one." Unlike the first edition, this one contained several engraved maps, another sign that the first edition had found its market and made its profit. The *Post* was snide about the maps, arguing that they "only serve to enhance the price without adding much to the utility" and were "useful but would be much more so if all the roads were distinctly marked upon them . . . in many cases [they are] not correct." However, the revised edition of Dwight's guidebook sold enough that the book became a perennial: new editions continued to emerge well into the early 1840s.[26]

Gideon Minor Davison, Dwight's rival and inspiration, also produced a book in 1825, a new edition of *The Fashionable Tour*. This edition dropped the misleading subtitle of the first edition, "in the summer of 1821," which had implied, incorrectly, that it was an account of a particular journey. The physical contrast between the first 1822 edition and the 1825 edition demonstrates the book's success, since the second edition was a more expensively produced product. It was bound with paper of higher quality, the page edges were neatly trimmed, and it used a nicely rendered engraving of Saratoga's newest and largest hotel, the United States, as its frontispiece. Its type was set in a looser format on slightly larger paper. The newly

upscale appearance of the 1825 edition showed that Davison wanted to increase its appeal to the fashionable patrons who frequented his bookstore.
Note that the first two editions were essentially unchanged in language
and content.[27] That it did reach that audience can be seen in the newspaper
advertisements purchased in early June of 1825 by a New York bookstore
that carried the book, exposure that the 1822 edition had not gotten.[28]

Davison's first audience had been the travelers who frequented his
bookstore in Saratoga Springs. But with wider distribution, the guide
could reach beyond that rarified crowd, to people like Davison, people
who were only now learning of the existence of tourism. This was a rising
class, with high hopes of raising their status. Tourism, with its sheen of
prosperity and fashion, was one way to do that.

For example, the aesthetic sensibility of Davison's guidebook was deli-
cately tuned. Like most of his intended audience, he had not been given a
fine education, nor had he been trained in the nuances of the sublime.
That, and his lack of social status, meant he could not claim credibility as a
spokesman of radical aesthetic notions. He could, however, embrace the
new, muted romantic sensibility of the Early Republic, and so he dedicated
a full eight pages to reprinting a story describing the exhumation of the
body of a British Revolutionary War major, John André, who had been ex-
ecuted during the hysteria surrounding the discovery of Benedict Arnold's
betrayal, an execution that many in retrospect were beginning to see as un-
just. That story, extensively reported in American newspapers, played on
an antebellum sense of pathos and romantic loss.[29]

Although this kind of gloomy romanticism was fast becoming mainstream within his reading public, his text remained mildly conservative on
aesthetic notions, and he approached even the picturesque gingerly. Therefore, Cohoes Falls was declared to be "an unusual scene of subliminity and
grandeur" where one could be overwhelmed by the "striking contrast of the
torrent, with the solitude of the scenery." But Davison suggested that this
moving scene be viewed from a pleasantly safe vantage, from the bridge
spanning the falls, where the reader would find "a fine view of the falls and
the romantick scenery around." To help hone these emotions, he added—
created?—a story attributed to "old tradition," of a Mohawk chief's plunge
over the falls (see chapter 3).[30]

In parallel with this new world of aesthetic thought, the guidebook offered directions to the new world of tourist travel. With its explicit instruc-

tions about where to find the Fashionable Tour, it opened up (to anyone who who could pay) places that had been previously restricted to the rich and fashionable. Davison's text offered regular reassurances to his newly genteel travelers that they would be welcome at these exclusive places. For example, about Pine Orchard, Davison wrote that it was "a place for which two years past, has attracted the attention of all classes of men." This was a striking assertion: nowhere in the contemporary accounts by genteel travelers to Pine Orchard (at least in its first years of operation) were there complaints or even comments about the presence of the lower classes. In the close quarters of the early Mountain House, there certainly would have been complaints if members of "all classes" had been present. In fact, Pine Orchard remained distinctly genteel in its first years; it would only be much later that lower classes came there.[31] Taken in its entirety, Davison's guidebook can be seen as a manual for social advancement, with its modest education on aesthetic issues, its instruction on how the newly wealthy could become genteel travelers, and its reassurances that, once there, one would be welcomed.

The third guidebook of 1825 was produced by a writer who did have solid aesthetic credentials. Where Theodore Dwight reflected the concerns of the conservative neophyte traveler and Gideon Davison those of entrepreneurs, strivers, and social climbers, Henry Dilworth Gilpin's text was aimed at those who wanted to be a part of the cultural avant garde. He wrote for romantics, a small but growing set of privileged, educated Americans who took their cues from the decades-old Romantic movement of Europe. Gilpin suggests throughout his guide that these aesthetic travelers are cut from this cloth.

Gilpin came from a very privileged background. He was born in 1801 into a wealthy family of Philadelphia Quakers who had retained close family connections in England. The Gilpin family had made their fortune through a series of paper mills on the Brandywine Creek in Wilmington, Delaware, along with other extensive business interests. Henry Gilpin's father, Joshua, visited England in 1799, where he met Mary Dilworth, daughter of a wealthy Lancaster industrialist. In 1800 he returned to marry her, and Henry, their first child, was born there in 1801. Joshua Gilpin and his family soon returned to the United States. Henry, though, was sent to school in England, where he remained for the remainder of his youth. On his return to the United States, he entered the University of Pennsylvania, where he graduated in 1819. After a tenure reading law in Philadelphia, in 1822 he was admitted to the bar.[32]

Gilpin's family was well connected to the artistic elite of England. His British relatives included the Reverend William Gilpin, the renowned author of definitive works about the picturesque, and the famous painter Benjamin West. Consequently, Henry Gilpin was well exposed to the ideas of the picturesque and the sublime, along with the romantic ideals exemplified by Lord Byron or Percy Bysshe Shelley. Gilpin read widely throughout his life and was well versed in the Greek and Latin classics; he could also read French, Spanish, and Italian. He became an avid reader of the popular literature of the day, including the works of Irving and Scott, whose books he devoured as soon as they arrived in America.[33]

In 1822, he was appointed secretary and legal counsel to one of the Gilpin family's businesses, the Chesapeake and Delaware Canal Company. Philadelphia was a major publishing center in the 1820s (although its status would decline as New York's grew), and through his social connections he associated with the leading members of that community, including the city's leading printer and publisher, Matthew Carey. And he met other top American publishers, such as George Ticknor, with whom he spent time during a trip to Boston. Gilpin was impressed that Ticknor had met Lord Byron.[34]

At some point in late 1824 or early 1825, Gilpin decided to write his first book. But rather than choosing to write a novel, he opted to write a tourist guidebook of the Fashionable Tour. He came to this decision at roughly the same time as Theodore Dwight, demonstrating the sudden appeal of tourism. (Unfortunately, his letters for that crucial year are lost, so we cannot know precisely what motivated him to try this genre.) It is clear from the format of the text and from several episodes in it, however, that Gilpin not only knew of Davison's book but took the liberty of appropriating certain ideas and stories from it. But where Davison rarely broke from his carefully moderate and informative format, a style of writing clearly not influenced by the romantic movement, Gilpin evidently decided that he would write an aesthete's guidebook, one that would bring an artistic sensibility to his subject and direct sensitive travelers to the correct sites.

The Northern Tour: Being a Guide to Saratoga, Lake George, Niagara, Canada, Boston, &c. &c. had originally been intended to be in bookstores by July of 1825 at the latest, but an unseasonably warm spring pushed his publisher, Matthew Carey, to move up the schedule; as Gilpin wrote his mother in late May, they were "hurrying the printing of the book, as this hot weather fills the town with strangers." Soon after, the book was being advertised in New York bookstores.[35]

Gilpin's guidebook took a looser approach than Davison's, which not only had been based much more closely on the format of the gazetteer but also had appropriated its dry and formal tone. Gilpin generally kept to that utilitarian model in that he provided capsule texts describing locations along a particular route, including useful and necessary information such as ferry schedules. But, unlike both Davison and Dwight, Gilpin allowed himself poetic flights amounting to an unabashed celebration of the American sublime, combining prosaic needs with an aesthete's eye toward the scenic wonders before him. At the Hudson Highlands, for example, Davison inserted several pages from Dr. Samuel Mitchill's widely read geology of the region. Gilpin, while acknowledging the geological theories of the site, quickly moved past them. The geology, he decided, was "decidedly primitive." Apparently, the Hudson "forced a passage through it . . . this ridge [was] the great southern boundary of a vast lake." Some conjecture, he wrote, that the valley had been formed by an explosive rupture of the ridge; others suggested erosion. In the end, he decided, it really didn't matter: "Whatever charms such an investigation may present to them, the gay traveller would rather dwell on their majestic beauties, and contemplate their romantic forms and every-varying shades, than perplex himself with theories the truth of which can never be determined."[36] Gilpin eagerly presented himself as educated but quickly moved past that to a much more entertaining stance: he is a fashionable aesthetic, a "gay traveller" who "contemplates . . . romantic forms and ever-varying shades." At Cohoes Falls, Gilpin appropriated Gideon Davison's "Indian over the falls" story. But Gilpin heavily embellished it with a high romantic gloss by adding a female victim and the shambling wreck of a male survivor. And while Davison presented his story directly, as if it were fact, Gilpin added a Washington Irving–esque introduction ("In speaking of this circumstance, old Vander Donck relates the following anecdote . . ."), a knowing wink to his audience's taste in literature.

Even at Niagara, a place that did not need such embellishment, Gilpin truly lost his head and was transported in romantic ecstasy as words momentarily failed him: "To describe the scene which then bursts upon our view, would be as hopeless for the pen as it has ever proved for the pencil. . . ." Fortunately, he was able to pick up his fallen pen and forge on somehow:

> In vain we might bid the reader to imagine the vast body of water, whirling and fretting and foaming among the rapids above—the deep and death-like stillness with which it approaches the precipice, then, gathering all its mighty force, the plunge which it makes into the abyss below—the vapour clouds, rolling above in every fantastic form—the rainbow, now glowing, now fading away, on their varying surface—and, above all, the ceaseless roar, which diffuses through the mind a feeling of ungovernable awe.
>
>> Lo! where it comes like an eternity,
>> As if to sweep down all things in its track!
>> Charming the eye with dread—a matchless cataract; . . .
>
> A scene like this is not to be described—it is only to be felt. As it stands alone in the history of nature, with nothing to equal or resemble it, so, while we rest upon its verge, will the breast glow with sensations before unknown, and swell with emotions before unfelt. We gaze with mute wonder on the scene before us, and forget, in the contemplation of nature's mighty works, the world that is around us, and the busy insignificance of man.[37]

A verse from Byron, and Gilpin is dizzy with romanticism; he grasps the sublime.

Gilpin was not immune to the allure of showing off his erudition—even at the cost of coherence. At Kaaterskill Falls, for example, he inserted, in Italian, a lengthy quote from Dante's *Inferno*. The quote was, on some level, appropriate—it did describe a descent into a valley—but it was deeply odd: the narrator in Dante's passage is outrunning a minotaur, something that happened only very rarely in upstate New York—no tourist accounts of such events survive, at any rate. But while describing the view from atop the falls, Gilpin deployed a slightly more logical quote: paragraphs from James Fenimore Cooper's *The Pioneers* describing a dramatic view in the area near the falls. [38]

But it is odder still that Gilpin uses this passage here, because its placement implies that it describes the view from the top of Kaaterskill Falls. In fact, view described is located several miles from there. This clue leads to an interesting insight about Gilpin's writing: although he had traveled widely to Europe and elsewhere, he had not actually visited most of the sites covered in his book at the time he wrote it. And he would not visit them, his correspondence reveals, until late June of 1825—nearly two months after the guide's publication, when he traveled to New York City, the Hudson River Valley, and points north. Some sites, such as Kaaterskill Falls, he did not visit until long after the 1820s. [39] Of course, this prompts the obvious question: how was he able to write a guidebook about these places? Charitably, we can describe his book as at best a product of inspired research. He used a body of facts drawn from existing gazetteers, tourist accounts, and Davison's guide, sources that kept him from straying too far into the realm of fiction. Unlike many, Gilpin was usually able to disguise the most obvious borrowings, although the source of a few of his details— for example, Davison's book for the story of the Mohawk Indian at Cohoes Falls—is obvious.

Gilpin's most important contribution to this first decade of guidebook literature was that he was the first advocate for undertaking American tourism explicitly as an act of patriotism. In the preface, he claimed that a "large portion of the citizens of the United States" had in the past wanted to "pass the summer and autumnal months in a tour through the northern section of the Union." He noted with satisfaction that this had been at the expense of travel to Europe. Although he did argue that this kind of travel would broaden the mind, he argued that a tourist in Europe would find only "customs, which have blended the rudeness and ignorance of past ages with the splendor and refinement of modern times," archaic governments, "in every form except that alone which we have learned to prize," and just plain old decadence: "civilization, here carried to the highest point of luxury, there depressed as low as human nature can endure." In all, "ambition and national pride" had destroyed "extended regions." In the aftermath of the Napoleonic Wars, not all of this was so far from the truth. [40] But in America, "our own country," one finds "a fairer and a nobler scene."

It "offers to other nations her example . . . [and] seeks not to aggrandize herself by interfering in their views, or pursuing the delusions of a false ambition." American travelers are best off at home: "There are few . . . who will not prefer it to more distant lands."[41]

Gilpin's promotion of tourism as a noble act of patriotism would become a constant refrain in later guidebooks and elsewhere. He gave his audience a parochial reassurance that home-based amusements were not more than merely as respectable as those of Europe; they were, in fact, morally superior. He was a part of the same cultural movement that championed American paintings, promoted the books of American writers, and felt that American virtue deserved to triumph over European (particularly British) decadence.

The appearance of these three works signaled the new world of tourism. It did not go unnoticed: the *United States Literary Gazette* expressed puzzlement that the publication of Davison's book "makes three little volumes, which we have seen within a few weeks, all of which have for their object to give short and instructive descriptions of the various places now become the resorts of those who travel for pleasure or for health."[42] Although it would take several years for the next round of tourist books to appear, the emergence of these books is a prime indicator of the sudden literary prominence of tourism. Their examples would set the tone for American tourist guides for decades to come. In the end, perhaps ironically, the writings of Gilpin and Davison, both initially directed at an elite reader, helped to further popularize tourism, since the broad distribution of their guides helped and convinced thousands more to travel. Tourism was definitely spreading to a much wider audience than ever before.

8

Tourism's Broader Audience

NATHANIEL P. WILLIS'S "The Vacation," published in the 1828 *Atlantic Souvenir*, begins predictably enough. The narrator is a wealthy young man just freed from the bonds of study at Yale. Standing in the yard of the college, "twirling my empty purse round my forefinger," he is the image of leisure and fecklessness. Why not a diversion? Why not a trip to Saratoga and Niagara?

This young man is sophisticated, indeed dripping with high fashion: "Every body has seen New Haven," he tells us, "and the same indefinite person knows that in the 'garniture of June,' it is like a scholar's dream of Arcadia." He is a refined aesthete, as we can tell from his description of a still, moonlit Long Island Sound as seen from the deck of a steamboat chugging to New York: "Had I fallen upon a fairy revel? or is the eye unsealed, and the hidden leaf unfolded by joy?" Later, he sees the Palisades, and he declares them "a feast for Werther," Goethe's famous hero. And he is wealthy: only after "a week or two" at Saratoga Springs, the most expensive resort in the country, do his funds begin to run low.[1]

The creator of this indolent, fashionable, aesthetic, and well-funded student traveler was Nathaniel Parker Willis. The firstborn son of a large, established New England family, Willis had been given as good an education as New England could offer: Boston Latin School, Phillips Academy, and then Yale. His father was the publisher of the *Boston Recorder*, a pious newspaper, and was a respectable member of the Boston community.

But the Willis family was large, and his father earned only a modest wage: they were by no means wealthy. So Nathaniel had to find his own financial way from the moment he left home, but his education, charm, and social adroitness marked him as gentry. At Yale, he insinuated his way into a group of wealthy students, and it was not long before he moved with the best of New Haven's society. Even before his graduation, he had published a set of well-received poems, and his social standing went up accordingly. His sparkling personality and skill with the pen gave him an entrée after graduation into an elite circle of writers and poets in New York City. He embodied the idea of high class without having a significant amount of money in his pocket.

So parts of this story of the wealthy student traveler were fantasy. But large elements of "The Vacation" were based on fact. We know, for example, that Willis accompanied his wealthy friends on a six-week tourist trip in the summer of 1827. We do not know, however, how he could have afforded it. Perhaps they loaned him the money; more likely, they simply paid his way. Willis was fun company, something that was always valuable. However he swung it, he took in all the Fashionable Tour sites, including Niagara Falls, the Erie Canal, and, of course, Saratoga.[2]

Willis's fictional narrator came from the best of classes, but Willis ended his story with the astounding assertion that "every one is at home at the Springs. . . . There is no unnecessary etiquette . . . acquaintances made there are considered par parenthése, and may be cut, or continued, elsewhere." There is, he asserts, a remarkable degree of intermingling: "The 'blood of the Howards,' and the nouveau riche, meet at the same table. . . . The city belle and the dark-eyed Jewess float together in the dance."[3] This is not the typical antebellum society. Willis is describing a world that is loose and free-form, one that allows entrée to nearly anyone who can meet the financial challenges of life at the springs. According to him, this society is surprisingly open—excluding, of course, that little matter of money.[4]

There are clues as to why Willis would present such a picture: he was someone who had made a shift himself, successfully crossing an invisible boundary. But there might have been more going on than just Willis's own story: by the late 1820s tourism was being sold to the middle class. This was not a concerted campaign like a promotion for a new commercial product. Instead, its campaign-like feeling came from the aggregated efforts of dozens of opportunistic entrepreneurs, writers, and playwrights, all seeking an audience for their products and finding it among the small but emerging middle class.

For example, in 1828 the Bowery Theater commissioned a tourism-related play. It hoped to duplicate the success the nearby Park Theater had had in 1827 with a spectacle that depicted a trip to Paris and London. The Bowery was becoming a middle-class theater, while the Park had always been the city's most exclusive. This fact, the separation of theaters by class, represented a big change in the New York theater world. Prior to the 1820s, all classes of society met at the theater. The less affluent would sit in the gallery at the top; just in front of the stage, and often exposed to the hurled insults of the gallery (both physical, such as fruit pits, and verbal) was the pit, filled with the middling classes. Held back from this melee and protected from the gallery by the tiers above them were the uppermost classes, safe in their boxes. This sorting was not accomplished through the explicit exclusion of a particular class; rather, ticket and box rental prices were set to segregate the different segments of society). But by the late 1820s, in cities with more than one viable theater, theaters had begun to differentiate themselves. New York, with its sizable theater district, exploding population, and large numbers of enthusiastic theatergoers, began to develop these class-sorted theaters. By 1828 this difference was most pronounced in three particular theaters: at the high end was the Park Theater; for the middling classes there was the Bowery, and at the lower end, the Chatham.[5] This gives us a clear signal of the shift in emphasis in the marketing of tourism. The high-class Park had mounted a spectacle directed to the perennial ideal holiday of the wealthiest tourists, a voyage to Europe. Just a year later, the middle-class Bowery presented a play for new middle-class aspirations, the trip to Niagara.

To write it, the Bowery's management pulled William Dunlap, an old warhorse, out of retirement. Although Dunlap was a famous New York author and a drama and art critic, he was not exactly the hot young playwright of the moment: it had been thirty years since he had written for the stage.[6] But he did have name recognition. One critic applauded the Bowery's choice of an American, "a native dramaturge," rather than "servilely receiving" one of the "mawkish, and, frequently, ill-suited, effusions of London play-wrights."[7] At any rate, from the evidence of the text, it is obvious that Dunlap had fun writing it. For example, he was forthright in the introduction to the printed edition of the play as to its durability or significance: "The following Farce . . . makes no pretensions to . . . higher character." In reality, the play was just window dressing. The real

star of the show was a large moving diorama that would be unveiled about
halfway through the night's entertainment. Painted on it were images of
the Fashionable Tour route from New York to the Catskills based on those
from William Guy Wall's *Hudson River Port Folio*. These "admirable
sketches," a critical admirer wrote in describing the diorama, "have been
for a long time familiar to the lovers of the fine arts."[8] Other backdrops depicted scenes of the Catskill escarpment, Albany, the Erie Canal, and Niagara Falls. The idea of having this diorama as the star of the night had been
pioneered by the Park Theater's show of the year before, which had featured one depicting the sights of Paris and London.[9] As Dunlop put it, the
play was just something to keep "the audience, or spectators, in good humour while the scenery and machinery was in preparation."[10]

It was tailored for its audience, filled with in-jokes and asides that
would have been hilarious to the theatergoers of the day.[11] The play was
presented as a spectacle typical for its time. Advertisements for it promised
a number of special effects, such as lightning and fog, while the diorama
was unfurled. Animated representations of riverboats plied the waters of
the Hudson and "tricks, such as the motion of the steamboat's works" and
"the hoisting up the sails of one of the river-craft, &c. greatly assist[ed] the
illusion," one critic reported.[12] Finally, at the play's climax, "sublime effects" involving Niagara, to be rendered "with all its terrific grandeur,"
were promised. All of it must have pleased the crowd immeasurably. It
opened on a Friday night in late November 1828 as "A Trip to Niagara: or,
Travellers in America."[13]

The characters were stock figures: drunken, clueless Irishmen; upstart
African Americans; a meddling but lovelorn maid; a snooty Frenchman;
and a haplessly arrogant but ignorant British aristocrat. Two acts, laden
with mistaken identities, low farce, and some chest-beating patriotism,
would pass before the diorama itself would be unveiled. By the end of the
second act, the principal characters had been maneuvered aboard a Hudson River steamboat. Then, at last, the diorama was deployed: as they
posed on board the stationary ship, the scenery was cranked past, signify-
ing their upriver journey.[14]

The diorama stopped when the steamboat "reached" the village of
Catskill. There, everyone debarked. The backdrop was changed, and the
new scene opened to exclamations of wonder at the stunning view from
the escarpment above the village. It is there that Dunlap engineered a colli-

sion between his characters and James Fenimore Cooper's most famous invention, Leatherstocking. That these characters were readily recognizable to the Bowery's audience signifies just how quickly and thoroughly Cooper had penetrated the middle-class consciousness.

Leatherstocking takes only a small bit of prompting to deliver a slightly modified version of his famous soliloquy describing the vista from atop the escarpment.[15] And once he delivers it, the scene shifts. Now we're at the Kaaterskill Falls, and an exchange occurs involving Leatherstocking, Amelia, a well-intentioned young British tourist, and Wentworth, her snooty brother. "On that spot," Leatherstocking claims, "I once saved a beautiful woman, like you, from the spring of a painter." Amelia is confused: "A painter?" Yes, just that, Leatherstocking continues. "I shot him. . . . She didn't see the creater [creature], and he didn't see me—I leveld [*sic*] just over her shoulder and hit him between the eyes." Both Amelia and her brother are astounded, but her brother continues, "Poor devil— but it served him right. . . . I always had a bad opinion of those vagabond sketching blades." Leatherstocking then points to his outfit and proudly notes, "I wore the creater's skin ever since." Amelia finally gets it: "O—a panther! Now I understand."[16] This bit of farce, hanging as it does on the wretched wordplay arising from Leatherstocking's accent, nonetheless works in some sly artistic references. Dunlap alludes not only to Thomas Cole, whose paintings by now had been widely seen and appreciated by this middle-class New York audience, but also, more obliquely, to William Guy Wall. The play ran to appreciative audiences for several weeks, which was a typical good run for the time: the New York theater audience was easily sated, and innovation was essential to keep their attention. The diorama was resurrected twice more in the year or two following before it was, apparently, retired forever or possibly sent on the road.[17]

What Dunlap's play meant to theatergoers is unknowable, although critics received it quite favorably. But beyond its entertainment value for the crowds that came to see it, this may have been their first exposure to a number of new ideas. They were, for example, given a primer in how to be a tourist: the characters take a steamboat, negotiate among the rival porters at the steamboat landing, use inns, travel, meet new people, and so on. The play was also an advertisement for the specific sites the characters visited: they were never afraid to name where they'd stayed, mentioning, among others, Forsyth's Hotel at Niagara.

Beyond these advertisements for place, it was also a broadcaster of ideas such as the notion of the sublime: as the characters openly appreciated the scenery, they usually rhapsodized over its sublime nature.[18] But Dunlap must have known that these ideas were inherently unsettling, so he wrote his text to bridge the gap between the traditional and the sublime. He wanted to create a kind of "tourist sublime," a safe intermediary between the uncontrollable sensations of the purely sublime and the safety of a human-ordered landscape.

For example, the traditional view tended to see beauty only where nature had been harnessed for human use. A corollary held that only savages could appreciate a wild, uncut forest. The philosophy of the sublime, on the other hand, urged its adherents to look on a wild scene with wonder, terror, and excitement. No character in the play is a devotée of the sublime in that sense. But one character does present himself as a "savage"—Leatherstocking, the white man who lives as an Indian. At his entrance, Amelia, who sees him first, is confused. "Is he an Indian?" she asks her brother. "A wild and noble figure. An Indian?" He straddles the line between "civilized" and "savage." And in his role as "savage," he is the champion of an unspoiled wilderness. Of Niagara, he declares, "What has housen [*sic*] and bridges to do among the wonders of heaven? They spoil all—they spoil all!"[19] Dunlap could have had, say, an actual Indian character deliver these sentiments, but by having Leatherstocking utter the words, he was doing something else. Leatherstocking was deployed as an inherently sympathetic figure, the hero of two wildly successful books (with more to come). By allowing him to express these sentiments, Dunlap is undercutting the idea that only savages could be pleased with wilderness: Leatherstocking is an ambassador for the sublime. However, Dunlap makes clear that even if Leatherstocking is presenting an acceptable vision of nature, he is not, on the whole, a role model for his travelers—it is not de rigueur for fashionable tourists to dismember panthers. Dunlap wants them to take only a small portion of his attitudes with them. Leatherstocking is presented as a relic of the past, a colorful figure who is, in the words of Amelia, a "strange being," fit only for the wild woods. By the end of the play, Dunlap has sent him off, in Amelia's words, "away to the prairie, the woods, and the grave."[20]

Outside the theater, sublime images were beginning to show up in a number of other settings. One prime example is the decoration and marketing of Staffordshire china, one of the most popular consumer products of the late 1820s. Before the Revolution, china and tableware from England had been available in America as luxury goods. After the war, a few specialty items, such as statuettes of Washington and Franklin, were specifically targeted at the American market. But they were expensive luxuries due to the high tariffs between the countries and the costs associated with the regular disruptions in trade. After the War of 1812, though, trade relations were regularized, and a wide variety of newly inexpensive British-made goods, including Staffordshire china, became available in the United States.

Staffordshire potters had long been mass-producing china and had become extremely efficient in finding and adapting techniques to lower costs and increase production. One of these processes, transfer-ware printing, bypassed one of the slowest and least efficient steps, the hand decoration of pottery. Transfer printing allowed for quickly manufactured, mass-produced pottery with standardized images. The images themselves were generally taken from best-selling etchings or engravings, images chosen for their popularity and as a way to differentiate the product for different market sectors. Now that they could sell large quantities of their product in the United States, Staffordshire potters began making a wide range of items specifically for that market. They created lines of china differentiated by cost, by the quality of the images, and by the quality of the production. They were so successful that by 1830 Staffordshire was omnipresent in all classes of American homes.

A significant part of the marketing was based on the images that had been chosen. The main subjects for the American trade generally depicted American places or scenes, ranging from institutions such as the Hartford Home for the Deaf and Dumb to scenery such as Passaic Falls. But a significant proportion of the non-institutional images came from places located along the Fashionable Tour.[21] Transfer-printed ware used images from every variety of popular engraving, but the most widely reproduced images were those of William Guy Wall. His watercolors, as rendered in the *Hudson River Port Folio*, became standards of the Staffordshire market, with nearly every British manufacturer distributing wares with reproductions of his prints.[22] There are several possible reasons for this. Perhaps one factor was his clarity of line, since the transfer ware process did not allow for great subtleties of style. Another was the success of the *Port Folio*, one of the earliest comprehensive folios of American views. In any case, the weakness of the copyright laws meant that these images were free to the producers. And their wide reproduction indicates their popularity among American consumers.

But the *Port Folio* was not the only source for scenes. British manufacturers rummaged through every engraving and image they could find, and eventually they would depict every other major site along the Fashionable Tour, including the most touted scenic sites of the Hudson, the Erie Canal, Niagara Falls, and parts of Canada. Even Ballston Springs, not particularly renowned for its scenic value, was depicted. By the mid-1830s, probably the single most popular Fashionable Tour site depicted was the Catskill Mountain House. Many of the pieces were from a widely reproduced 1830 engraving based on an 1828 Thomas Cole painting, *View of the Catskill Mountain House*.[23]

This emphasis on Fashionable Tour sites shows how thoroughly ingrained these images had become in the American mind as *the* American scenery. And their iconic status demonstrates how thoroughly established Hudson Valley had become as the locus of American tourism. The widespread presence of images of these formerly exclusive sites on every middle-class table must have been galling to the elites for whom the sites had originally been built. In fact, there is strong evidence that shows how shopworn Hudson Valley tourism had become among the fashionable elite by the late 1820s. In a review of a travel book in the premier literary journal in the United States, the *North American Review*, an anonymous reviewer wrote, "It would be difficult at this time to write a new thing on . . . the Hudson river." Likewise, none of the other major sites of the Fashionable Tour could be described without resorting to cliché. Nor, the reviewer went on, could anything new be written of about any "nook and corner of the United States, within reach of stage-coaches, steamboats, or even pedestrian enterprises. . . . We [now] have standard descriptions of all these wonders of nature and of art, under their present aspects; and until they exhibit new features, inquirers may safely be left to existing authorities for information."[24] There was a true saturation of materials about this one section of American scenery. But on another level, what this commentator was noting was that these places had been made, by the relentless marketing of their images, almost commonplace. Their prevalence in the marketplace meant that they were no longer special, unique, or, most important for the tourist elite, exclusive: they had lost their cultural cachet.

The consequences would play out in several ways. One would be the emergence of a set of highly skeptical writers whose works would begin the process of demystifying tourism and its sites. Another was the beginning of the trend by the elite to seek out more exclusive destinations.

❧ 9 ❧

Skeptics

EVEN AS TOURISM crested in the late 1820s, it raised the hackles of critics. Skeptics saw tourism from a variety of negative angles: some felt it exemplified the commercial and consumerist changes the United States was experiencing in the 1820s, changes that would come to shape American culture profoundly; others viewed tourism as typical of the worst of their times, artificial, manufactured, superficial. And one observer, the Virginian Anne Royall, saw what was happening in the Hudson Valley as typical of the superficiality of the North and wrote about it in negative contrast to the genteel and aristocratic travel culture of the South. Although their writings and commentaries fought against the rising tide of praise by tourism's many boosters and although they had relatively limited reach, they were able to influence the very audience that had made tourism possible.

Catharine Maria Sedgwick and Tourism

In her earliest published works, Catharine Maria Sedgwick appeared to embrace tourism. But she was about to change course radically, to turn her back on it entirely. Just a year after her tourism-related story appeared in the 1824 *Atlantic Souvenir*, she published a book that starkly criticized tourism as emblematic of the speed, commercialism, and superficiality of her times.

Sedgwick was born into a prominent and staunchly Federalist family in Stockbridge, Massachusetts, in 1789. She was related, through her mother, to both Timothy and Theodore Dwight, and she shared much of that family's sensibility and political inclinations. She was given an elementary school education at various schools nearby, but found the education she received at home to be much more valuable. Through it, she was able to gain a fair grounding in the classics of New England religious thought. This early education was conservative, with one foot still in the old Puritan sensibilities that frowned on such things as theater or fiction. But the times were changing, and, like most of her contemporaries, Sedgwick began reading and appreciating novels and fiction. She only began writing in her late twenties, and by her early thirties she had completed several keenly observed sketches of her hometown. The encouragement of her brothers inspired her to begin her first novel.[1]

Her personal experience with tourism occurred in the early summer of 1821. While still writing her first book, she made a long summer journey with her family on one variation of the Fashionable Tour route. That trip took her from Stockbridge to Lebanon Springs and then on to Albany, up the Hudson River, over to Niagara Falls, and from there to Montreal and Quebec. They returned via Lake Champlain and the Hudson, bypassing the springs. All the time she was traveling, she wrote long letters home, and after she returned she compiled them into a travel journal of some length. The journal was circulated among the nontraveling members of her family and her friends, as often happened with travel letters. In a way, she had created her own version of the now-common travel book.[2]

Sedgwick, thirty-three years old when she went on this trip, was just on the edge of celebrity. When her first book, *A New-England Tale*, was published in 1822, it was an immediate success, with long, appreciative reviews in the major literary magazines of the day; it became a best-seller.[3] When she published her next book, *Redwood*, in 1824, the only element of the new tourist culture was the fact that her main character, Henry Redwood, a slave owner from Virginia, is traveling in southern Vermont at the outset of the book.[4]

In her next book, though, she would make a strong and definitive statement about tourism, its uses and abuses, and what she felt should be the ultimate meaning of American scenery. For her, tourism had come to symbolize all that was wrong with the society of her time. This placed her in the growing rank of skeptics concerned about the impact of this new and unnerving fad.

The Travellers: A Tale Designed for Young People (1825) was directly and deeply influenced by Sedgwick's experiences in the tourist culture.[5] It was her didactic effort against the corrupting effects of city life on the education and moral life of youth. For her, tourists and tourism were exemplars of the moral cavity she saw developing at the center of her society. Sedgwick did allow that some kinds of tourism could be useful, but only if conducted properly. Her ideal tourist had a diverse, solid, and comprehensive education in aesthetics, combined with a sense of spirituality that connected natural beauty with godly power.

In *The Travellers*, Sedgwick imagined a prosperous and well-educated urban nuclear family, the Sackvilles. The book starts with Mr. Sackville's announcement of a decision to his children: he is going to remove his family, with his wife's permission, from the city. He has purchased a "fine estate" in a small country town. Edward, eight, and Julia, ten, have qualms: Edward worries that he will be bored; he envisions a future filled with school lessons. The country, he worries, offers no chance for recreation, particularly the theater, his favorite entertainment. His sister, too, wonders how she will survive without her charming French dancing teacher. But their mother reassures them. Not only will they have "clever children in the neighborhood" to play with, but nature's "far more beautiful spectacles" will easily replace the theater and the other (implicitly corrupting) attractions of the city.

Of course, she is proven correct, and in time the children learn to entertain themselves. But an even better transformation happens after a year in the country: they are no longer little urbanites. "Return to town, now, mother!" exclaims Edward in horror. "It is impossible." But Sedgwick keeps them in the country for another year before allowing them to travel from this cocoon; only now are the children properly inculcated with education and aesthetics. The urbanity that had clouded their vision has now been purged through country living and a proper aesthetic education.[6] Informed of their trip, the children look forward to travel with "the anticipation of unbounded delight," the kind of sensation-seeking excusable only in youth. Their parents, naturally, are much more reserved and look forward to the trip with "rational expectations of pleasure." Sedgwick's careful modulation of language here is telling.[7]

"We are well aware that young people do not like to be harangued about scenery," Sedgwick writes once her characters are on the boat heading up the Hudson, "therefore . . . we shall resist every temptation to describe its beautiful features." One main reason for her restraint came from the understanding that readers of all ages were by this time already saturated with travel description. Another was that she expected most of them to have been travelers themselves on the Hudson; its features, she writes, are "as well known and loved as the familiar face of a friend." Sedgwick also acknowledges the proliferation of visual representations of the Hudson and Mohawk Rivers when little Julia says that the scenery is "a perfect picture, mother, all the way." She is speaking more than metaphorically.[8]

Sedgwick's child travelers are ideal picturesque travelers who appreciate and understand aesthetic beauty: "They came to a spot which Julia insisted could not be surpassed," writes Sedgwick. "She begged her mother to make a sketch there." Their mother sets up her sketch pad and is counseled by the children, in some detail, on the framing and composition of the picture. Their superior education makes them able to appreciate and even criticize the artistic possibilities best found in nature.[9]

Of course, like most children's books, this is aimed as much at their parents, if not more so. For example, after some small adventures, the party arrives at Niagara Falls. The falls themselves are given a breathless description ("the sublime falls—the various hues of the mass of waters—the snowy whiteness, and the deep bright green"), but the main point of seeing them is conveyed by Mrs. Sackville, who, after an extended spiritual moment, intones that the sight is "the spirit of God moving on the face of the waters." Seeing the falls, she declares, "exalts our affections above language." Now Sedgwick can deliver a Unitarian-derived message: "this temple," declares Mrs. Sackville, "does not need a preacher."[10]

Sedgwick's treatment of Niagara reveals the heart of her resentments about tourism. In her eyes, the typical tourist's response was a form of sacrilege: tourism had divorced the dramatic power of the falls from the intensely spiritual feeling one should feel in the presence of so powerful a manifestation of God's presence. Without that intensely spiritual response, travel was worse than worthless; it was a kind of pornography, a cheap and shallow form of sensation-seeking.

She illustrates this with an episode set at the edge of the falls. The young Edward asks his father about a group of tourists they had encountered earlier in the day, a "party of city shop-keepers" with whom they had shared lunch: "I heard one of the ladies say, 'I have been so disappointed in my journey.' I dropped my knife and fork and exclaimed, 'Disappointed, madam? does not the fall look as high as you expected?' 'Oh, child,' she replied, laughing, 'I was not speaking of the fall; but I find it is quite too early in the season to travel in the country. I have not seen a roast pig or a broiled chicken since I left the city.'" His father delivers his verdict: "I think, my dear, she is a vulgar woman, who travels because others do; and is naturally disappointed in not meeting with the only circumstances that could give her pleasure."[11] Although this is clearly a condemnation, Sedgwick does offer an explanation for the woman's insensitivity: as a "shop keeper," she could not have had access to the kind of education that has made our little travelers so sensitive.

But what of those whose wealth and privilege allowed them the luxury of that kind of education? Edward continues, asking about a wealthy woman they had encountered: "There's Mrs. Hilton, papa, who, I am sure, is not vulgar—at least she is as rich as Croesus—and I heard her say to a gentleman, that if she could have remained at the Springs, and then could have gone home and said she had been to the Falls, she should have been glad; for she was sure no one came here but for the name of it." His father replies, "Mrs. Hilton is of the class of the vulgar rich, among whom vulgarity is quite as obvious, and much more disgusting, than with the vulgar poor," [replied his father.][12] This Mrs. Hilton, one of the wealthy, had access to the same education and enlightenment that the children did, and she should have taken advantage of it. For Sedgwick, her lapse in good taste and betrayal of her class was inexcusable.

The first episode with the village shopkeepers was based on an encounter Sedgwick had on her 1821 trip, while the figure of the crudely wealthy woman apparently was entirely fiction.[13] Nonetheless, it is revealing that she chose women to exemplify these transgressions: she felt, as many had come to believe, that it was the duty of women to educate themselves, not only morally but aesthetically.

Sedgwick's view that the shallow world of tourism was, in effect, a kind of sacrilege was one aspect of a small but growing criticism of the entire tourist experience.[14] And although this book was not in and of itself influential, it neatly encapsulates a new and growing set of concerns on the part of people like Sedgwick about the brash, new, money-oriented, ostentatious tourist culture of the 1820s.

Theodore Dwight's "Rational Traveller"

Another New Englander to voice concerns about tourism was none other than Theodore Dwight. Although he had written one of the first tourist guidebooks, he was always careful to set himself apart from the scrum of writers about tourism as well as from tourists themselves. He presumed that his readers shared his attitudes, that they would want to distance themselves from the "ordinary" tourist. He wanted his guide to be a handbook for those of the gentry and for those who wanted to be of the gentry: he wanted it to be a kind of handbook for aspiring aristocrats. And so, when describing the route from Saratoga back to Boston, he declared that "*The most interesting route* that can be chosen by a man of taste, from the springs to Boston, is through Vermont to the White Mountains"; later, summing up the journey, he stated that "Too much cannot be said to the traveller in favour of this delightful region, if he be a man of taste, as all that he especially loves in the varying face of nature is here and presented to view." Dwight's calls for what a "man of taste" would appreciate were his way of alerting his readers what they should appreciate if they wanted to be truly genteel.[15]

Dwight felt that ignorance was to be expected from the lower classes. What worried him most, though, was what was happening among his more affluent contemporaries: in particular, he deeply distrusted Romanticism. Romanticism, he felt, was a fad, an insincere mantle too easily worn by the somewhat educated, by callow members of his social world. (In a later work, he would write, "Instead of wishing to see the world through a fancied medium, the rational traveller wishes to view it as it is.")[16] One of the elements of his suspicion came from the sense that a romantic did not need knowledge based on discipline or instruction: the romantic's reliance on emotion would obviate any true understanding of the thing seen. Of course, it is difficult to fight the attitudes of thousands, but perhaps he could do his part through the medium he had already chosen, the book. His guide had been a first step, but to complete the job he needed to expand its reach and influence. To do that, he determined to corner the market in guides: he decided to close down one of his rivals.

Recall that when Dwight first published the *Northern Traveller* in 1825, there were only two other competitors on the market: Gideon Davison's *Fashionable Tour* and Henry D. Gilpin's *Northern Tour*. Davison's book had been easy for Dwight to dismiss: it was published by a rough-handed printer with ink under his fingernails. But Gilpin was another matter. With his impeccable artistic education and lofty family credentials, he stood as Dwight's major rival for that crucial gentry audience. And his guidebook was a handbook for romantics, loaded with emotion, poetry, sensationalism, the sublime. It stood in direct opposition to Dwight's ideals.

But it turned out that Gilpin, unlike Dwight, had no intention of making a franchise of his guidebook. His restless literary intelligence had moved on to take up the editorship of the *Atlantic Souvenir*.[17] Consequently, at some point, probably in 1826, Dwight came to an understanding with Gilpin and purchased the rights to the *Northern Tour*.[18] And when Dwight published a new edition of his own guidebook in 1828, it was renamed to reflect this: it was now *The Northern Traveller (Combined with the Northern Tour)*.[19]

Although Dwight had presumably spent good money for Gilpin's title, he included virtually nothing from Gilpin in the new edition. Gone was Gilpin's florid romanticism, his high-flown poetic quotations, his personality. The only content Dwight incorporated from his old rival was some information about ancillary routes: Gilpin's descriptions of the New England cities, for example, or his lengthy description of Pennsylvania's coal mines (then tourist attractions). So why did Dwight bother? With the purchase of the *Northern Tour*, Dwight was able to fulfill two objectives: not only would he close out half of his competition in the Hudson Valley guidebook market, he also could eliminate that detested romantic text from his tourist world.

Moving rapidly beyond Gilpin, Dwight started on his next book. In 1829 he published *Sketches of Scenery and Manners in the United States*.[20] This curious work interspersed chapters of descriptive travel literature with philosophical essays that explained, for example, Dwight's educational ideas about the need for "Infant Schools." The overall point of it, however, was to press forward Dwight's campaign to reform the crass new tourism.

The book's final essay was called "Travelling to Good Purpose." Here, Dwight directly attacked the emerging tourist culture. Only "some individuals . . . among the numerous travellers for pleasure" traveled with anything resembling "a method." Of the rest, they travel only "by their present gratification." The result of this was that the majority of tourists return home "with . . . nothing distinct, interesting, or useful."[21] These numerous shallow and facile travelers undermined the important educational impact that traveling should have had. In fact, this kind of tourist represented an outright danger, not only to those who indulged in it but, by implication, to the community to which they returned: "the wild, the extravagant, and the uninstructed" brought home with them "little more than their own ignorance and the prejudices or vices of others." For the rest of their lives, he argued, they would display "their deficiencies and circumscribed opinions in an unfavorable relief." If, on the other hand, one traveled "to good purpose," it would be immediately evident "to the sagacious and attentive observer." A model Dwight traveler would become a good citizen and stalwart of the community; an incautious traveler, though, would become, at best, an embarrassment.[22]

Dwight's rejection of romanticism led him to envision a traveler who could sit outside of contemporary trends and culture. His ideal traveler would therefore be self-contained, lacking the need for external validation, and able to operate in any environment. With this attitude, Dwight argued, that traveler could remain properly aloof during those now inescapable times when he was forced to travel amid his lessers, something that had become increasingly common as tourism expanded in popularity. Like a millionaire on a modern subway, Dwight's self-contained traveler would bring with him a self-created zone of separation. In essence, Dwight was directing his readers to become deliberate nontourists, travelers who rejected not only the rosy architecture of romanticism but, by implication, the shallow commercialism Dwight associated with trend.

When this ideal traveler returned home his energies would not be spent in ostentatious self-glorification of his new-found experience and knowledge; instead, his time would be "chiefly directed to reviewing and arranging the knowledge he has acquired and considering how he may apply it in the most advantageous manner." If he had traveled overseas, he would return and "in his grounds, his furniture, and his dress" there would be "no prominent trait of foreign fashions . . . he does not plead fashion as an excuse for folly." [23] Freed from the burden and vanity of fashion, he would be liberated from the need for outward display and conspicuous consumption: he would have broken loose from the emerging consumer culture of the day. [24]

Dwight directed his attack mainly at the affectations of his own class, as Catharine Maria Sedgwick did. Romanticism was a rich person's luxury, and Dwight wanted reform to begin at the top, he wanted to create travelers who would lead by example. In his own small way, Dwight helped begin attitudes that would eventually lead the most wealthy away from ordinary tourism and toward the creation of hidden resorts and exclusive havens.

James Kirke Paulding's Parody

A more oblique attack on the romantic tourist came in the form of a parody from the decade's premier satirist. James Kirke Paulding had entered the 1820s as one of the country's most popular authors, having originally gained fame as one of the Knickerbockers and as a collaborator with Washington Irving in the first *Salmagundi* series. Socially, Paulding was a conservative who described himself as "a Dutchman. . . . I hate all interlopers, and reverence Old customs." (In 1820s New York, being a "Dutchman" signaled a resistance to change.) [25] He lived in Hyde Park, New York, near the Fashionable Tour route, and so would have been able to see tourism at first hand.[26] In 1828, Paulding published *The New Mirror for Travellers: and a Guide to the Springs*.[27] Although *The New Mirror* was a parody, it actually contained enough useful information that a traveler could use it as a guidebook. It was filled with the kind of humorous tweaks that kept Paulding a popular writer throughout the 1820s. But his main targets were tourists.

Paulding held that the current vogue for American scenery was mere romantic pretense and, ultimately, sheer hypocrisy. What was lost, Paulding felt, was any feeling for the Hudson's real scenery. "There is . . . a pleasant little ride . . . due north of Saratoga," he writes, "along an excellent road, skirted on one band by rich meadows, on the other by a rugged, rocky hill" where "on a fine afternoon towards sunset . . . the slanting beams of the sun leave the east side of the hills enveloped in cooling shades." He basks in these "charms of nature," a pleasant respite "after revelling in those of art at the springs." But he comes to his senses: "What are we talking about? we have forgot ourselves. Such matters are unworthy our book and those to whom it is addressed." The springs are what matters, not these foolish things of nature, for "who indeed would waste his time in loitering about these ignoble scenes, unsaid and unsung by names of fashionable note, when they can walk back and forth the long piazzas at the springs?"[28] The region's true scenery had become enslaved to the commercialism of tourism. Kaaterskill Falls, for example, "want nothing but a little more water to be wonderfully sublime." With "the proper application of half a dollar," by payment to the mill owner, the illusion would be complete.

He was not opposed to the representations of scenery that had made the Hudson so popular. He argued that "the drawing-rooms of the wealthy" should be graced by illustrations of them by Thomas Cole and William Guy Wall. But he had little praise for the new tourist infrastructure atop the escarpment. Fashionable people, he argued, climbed the mountain primarily to build an appetite: "It is amazing what a glorious propensity to eating is generated by the keen air" of mountains. "The stomach expands with the majesty and expansion of the prospect, and the worthy landlord at the Pine Orchard . . . has assured us that he has known a sickly young lady, who was travelling for an appetite, discussing venison for breakfast like an alderman."[29]

Finally, over many pages, Paulding dissects the manners and morals of the springs. In chapters directed to single women, married women, single men, and married men, he offers "rules" for each group which, in aggregate, provides a vision of life at the springs as facile, superficial, obsessed with appearance yet solipsistic. He ends The *New Mirror* at the Springs, because, as he argues, "there is nothing beyond" it: it is the "*ultima Thule*" of the fashionable world."[30]

Like Dwight, Paulding argued that the artificiality of tourism had obscured the essential goodness of the place. Unlike Dwight, though, he had no solution; like most good satirists, he was content merely to criticize. Nonetheless, his observations had more than a kernel of truth.

Anne Royall: Unlikely Southern Elitist

One other critic of tourism came at it from a unique perspective. Anne Royall came out stridently against the vulgar show she identified with Saratoga and Ballston, arguing that true genteel tourism could only be found in the South. Royall's key argument was based on class: she felt that the class boundaries that had built America were being undermined by the mixing she saw at the northern tourist sites. True, pure tourism, she felt, existed only at the elite gathering spots of the South, specifically at the springs in Virginia she had known for decades.

Royall, however, was a highly unlikely advocate for this kind of elitism. She was born in 1769 to a poor Virginia family. When she was a teenager, she and her mother moved to Sweet Springs, Virginia, where they served as housekeepers for William Royall, a wealthy farmer and Revolutionary War veteran. Young Anne caught William's eye and earned a privileged position in his household. He allowed her to read from his extensive library and made her into something of a companion, and when she was twenty-seven he scandalized his family by marrying her (he was in his fifties). William Royall's nephew by marriage, James Roane, was particularly upset: his son had been promised Royall's estate during the veteran's long bachelorhood. Royall, though, had become increasingly disillusioned with Roane, whom he perceived to be a bit of a parasite. His original will, properly filed, had left his estate to Roane's son. However, after about ten years of marriage to Anne, he scribbled out a will that left the bulk of his estate to her. But he never properly recorded it or had it witnessed: instead, he shoved it into a desk drawer and forgot about it. William Royall died in 1812, his life shortened by alcoholism.[31]

Anne claimed the estate under the revised will, but Royall's nephew immediately sued to break it, and a titanic legal battle ensued. In the meanwhile, Anne was left without any access to the estate's income, and she began to slide into poverty. In 1817, the revised will was rejected by the court. She appealed but decided in the interim to move to Alabama. In June 1819 the decision was returned and it brought both parties disastrous news: the court ruled that neither of William Royall's wills was valid and was declared to have died intestate. Anne was held liable even for court costs. Soon after, her former relatives filed a series of other lawsuits against her related to the estate. The only thing keeping Anne, now laden with legal expenses, from complete destitution was a small widow's dower protected from legal action.[32]

For the next four years, she used that dower to travel around Alabama. On her travels she wrote what she saw, and these reflections, compiled in some thirty-one long letters sent to her lawyer, would later form the basis of her first book. At the same time, she also pursued the possibility of gaining a fraction of a pension for her husband's Revolutionary War service, something other widows had gained. However, since she was married after the war, she was initially unsuccessful. Eventually, she concluded that she would have to go to Washington, D.C., to lobby her congressman for a pension. As she did, she decided, she would record her travels in a book. By the time she left, she had settled on a title: *Sketches of History, Life, and Manners in the United States*.

As she sought her widow's pension in Washington, she gathered gossip and recorded her experiences. She met with the highest officials in government, including John Quincy Adams, then secretary of state, and wrote cutting and perceptive profiles of them. She also came up with an interesting funding mechanism: she sold pre-publication subscriptions of *Sketches*; indeed, she was even able to sell one to Adams. Her resourcefulness included gaining an interview with the Marquis de Lafayette, during his triumphant anniversary tour. By January 1825, she had earned enough from subscriptions to journey northward to Baltimore, Philadelphia, and New York.

In New York, she was able to get money from the Masons because of her husband's long membership in the organization, but otherwise the city generally viewed her with a cold eye. She met with newspaper publishers including Theodore Dwight, the father of the guidebook author and editor of the *New-York Daily Advertiser*, and Charles King of the *New York American*, but her assertive manner led both men to consider her entirely too unfeminine. But she gained an ally in Mordecai Noah, the editor of the *National Advocate*, a flamboyant Sephardic Jew and onetime sheriff of New York who must have seen in Royall a kindred spirit. However, for every friend she made, her persona and style alienated another. Nevertheless, the friends she did make were loyal to a remarkable degree, and she was able to complete her travels through New England recording interviews with, among others, Daniel Webster (which did not go well);

Jedidiah Morse, the geographer (which did); and the historian Hannah Adams, a distant cousin of the presidents.[33]

In May 1826, *Sketches of History, Life, and Manners* was printed in New Haven, Connecticut. Although per convention it was credited anonymously to "A Traveller," Anne Royall had no intention of hiding her identity. In what may be the first book tour in American letters, she took as many copies as she could transport and, having arranged for her publishers to send her regular shipments at the cities she was to visit, set out once again. Her first stop was the New York City office of Theodore Dwight. Her visit there was brief and not pleasant. The ensuing review of her book was, at best, tepid: It "contains nothing remarkable. The style is easy. . . . It is new to us to be criticized by travellers from that point of the compass."[34] Royall did not sell many books in New York. But she got a much more genial reception in Boston and sold out the entire stock she had taken there; more copies were duly ordered. From Boston, Royall continued to Albany, where she interviewed the governor, and then she went on to Saratoga and Ballston Springs. There, she was received with equal measures of indifference and hostility. Soon after, she returned to Alabama to write her next book.

Royall never forgot a slight. With remarkable speed she produced *The Black Book*, which, she claimed, recorded "the black deeds of evil doers"; when it was published in 1828, she revenged herself against all of the calumnies that had been heaped on her. She also gave us a rare contrarian view of the people and life at the springs. Saratoga, she wrote, was a grasping, crowded, overhyped town that had seen more fashionable days, one that worked to extract every cent from the visitor while offering little more than a name in return. For example, she found the food at her boarding house, Reed's, "shocking; and the flies, in swarms, covered every dish for half an hour, at least, before the boarders were called to sit down. As for fly-fans, there is not one at the springs."[35] She found the entertainment tedious, consisting mainly of "riding, walking and balls; some walk fast, some walk slow."[36]

She was particularly cutting about some of the people she encountered. One was her nemesis, Theodore Dwight, vacationing with his family at Aldridge's at Ballston Spa. "Mr. D. is about fifty years of age," she wrote, "a stout heavy-made man . . . his forehead is high and smooth, but the venom of his eye would guillotine a whole world; it is a small redish [*sic*] black eye, and glistens with a nameless malignity." His wife she found "hagard [*sic*] and wrinkled, and looked much the oldest," and his daughter was "a stout, coarse, hard featured old maid" who "looked as old as her father, and not half so handsome."[37]

Royall also gives us the only surviving description of the guidebook author Gideon Minor Davison. He was "a gloomy Presbyterian . . . a stout man, of young appearance, young complexion and a malignant black eye; cold and forbidding in his manners . . . a sour grum [*sic*] looking man, about as well polished as a Missouri Bear."[38] She was particularly contemptuous of the writeups that Davison worked so hard to place in newspapers around the country. These dispatches from Saratoga had been quite effective, but Royall skewered them mercilessly. "It is amusing to observe how the Editor of the place, puffs in the season of the springs," she sneered. Of the "one thousand visitors" Davison claimed were at the Springs, Royall saw only a few. She had expected to have a good market for her books, "a fine harvest I thought for my travels," but when she arrived, "lo! The thousand dwindled to about 60 or 70 of all sorts and sizes."[39]

Probably her most telling criticisms came when she discussed the character and class of the tourists at the Spa. These criticisms speak volumes of the differences between the Virginia Springs, which had remained an exclusive resort limited primarily to the wealthy and powerful from across the South, and Saratoga, which had begun to be flooded with persons of all classes:

> The society at these springs, is very different. . . . [At the Virginia Springs,] the people come in their own carriages, bring their own servants, come early and stay late, usually from six to eight weeks. They are people of the first respectability, and associate together. . . . But at Saratoga, the different boarding houses separates the company. At the Virginia . . . Springs, no country people come. . . . Here they come in shoals, and fairly eclipse the fashionables; in fact they are the fashionables in relation to numbers and dress, and though they do not add legitimately to society, they make up a part, and no small one, of the puffs in Mr. [Davison's] paper. This description of people are little advantage to the springs, as they never stay over one night, and very few of them eat a meal's victuals.[40]

Royall's criticism of class mixing at Saratoga Springs reveals her deep investment in the class system. She had fought tooth and nail for many long years first to gain and then to defend her class standing. During her years of poverty after she was dispossessed of her husband's estate, she had nothing but her fierce dignity to sustain her, and she was as deeply sensitive to slights, real or perceived, as anyone could be.

Anne Royall was perhaps the most articulate observer of the difference between the northern and southern resorts. Where southern resorts controlled access through remoteness and cost, the northern resorts' relative openness and accessibility made them open to a much broader class of people. This level of access would, in time, cause serious problems for the northern resorts.

What About the Tourists Themselves?

What is striking about the literary criticism of tourism that the writings of Dwight and Royall exemplify is that very few tourists recorded similar views. Perhaps part of the reason was that travelers tended to write their journals and letters for those left back home or for posterity, and they may have felt it would be churlish to criticize such unique opportunities. As a result, surviving descriptions from the 1820s tended toward wide-eyed enthusiasm.

There are some exceptions, however. Francis Dallam, whose story appears in the introduction, is an excellent example. Dallam's first trip to Saratoga Springs was in 1827. It was also his last, apparently. It produced a welter of criticisms, of the water ("I think [it is] inferior to Bedford," he declared, comparing it to that produced by the Virginia Springs), the crowds ("the company is large about 700 . . . all strangers and many of them foreigners"), and the general level of posturing ("too much fashion and extravagance for me").[41]

Another southerner, David Hillhouse, basically liked the springs but was explicit about its shortcomings. "How," he asked rhetorically in his journal of a trip there in 1826, "are so many visitors accommodated?" His answer? "Poorly." At the meals, "there is such a jostling of elbows; so great crying for help; so much over-reaching for supplies; so great dissatisfaction with what is received; such hurry and bustling by waiters and visitors, as makes eating a laborious business, rather than a pleasurable recreation." He remarks on the smell of this jostled company: "The headed atmosphere in such a crowded walk occasions a most overwhelming exhalation of emetics, colognes, cordials, oils and ottoes [fragrant oil] with which the ladies, and the ladies' gentlemen, are most abundantly besmear'd."

Hillhouse was not thrilled with his accommodations, either. In the evening he was ushered "into a small room, 8 feet by 12, furnished with a window, chair, wash-stand, &c. In this there may be a creaking bedstead, and a narrow straw bed, which, though evidently not itself on skids or wheels, is constantly sliding about, to the certain discomfiture of the occupant. To aid the general comfort, these beds upon perpetual *moving steads*, are placed against a very thin partition, adjoining a public entry." All of this "may, and must be borne, for *fashionable*," although " 'Twould any of my friends learn more of this fashionable resort, 'twould be last to visit it."[42]

The concerns and complains of the skeptics all contained several similar themes. The once-exclusive tourist world had become cheapened, invaded by the less educated, less sensitive, or crass. In order for tourism to survive, these critics implied, it would have to recreate itself in a new image. These complaints would soon be echoed by others, and the late 1820s would see a series of efforts to form this new, more exclusive world.

Too Popular?

Tourism's popularity first began to crest in the mid-1820s, just after the thousands of new tourists appeared at what had formerly been exclusive terrain. The earliest tourists, now swamped by these arrivistes, worried that a cheapened and debased tourism had emerged, assisted by the very technology that had made tourism so much more accessible than before. For them, the tourist routes had become too popular, and what had once been a genial, quiet, and exclusive pursuit had become, like so much else in the changing society of the 1820s, scruffy, plebian, or even dangerous. In response, they sought to recreate the exclusivity that had once been their refuge. Although these earliest efforts would not be successful, they were indicators for what was to come.

One prime source of elite dissatisfaction were the conditions they encountered on steamboats after the collapse of the North River's monopoly

in 1824. Under the monopoly, Hudson River steamboats had been relatively quiet and controlled: the North River line set standards of conduct
that were more or less enforced, and the company's high fares had made
steamboat travel a real luxury. As we have seen, however, after 1824, a number of new companies sprang up overnight, and steamboat travel became
uncontrollably open and chaotic. Steamboat lines vied for passengers at
the piers, particularly at the main terminals at the foot of Courtland Street
on the Hudson River. There, a number of writers and diarists complained,
arriving and departing passengers mixed with a motley assortment of
porters, hucksters, pickpockets, sightseers, and well-wishers, creating, in
the words of one shocked new arrival, "a sea of confusion if possible more
terrible than any heretofore." Theodore Dwight's guide had counseled passengers to maintain their aloofness when they got there, but clearly the situation was no longer genteel.[43]

Suddenly thievery became a problem on the steamboats. Although by
modern standards it was minor, its very appearance was a cause for alarm.
"In the hurry and opposition" engendered by the collapse of the Hudson
River steamboat monopoly in the early summer of 1824, the *Saratoga Sentinel* reported that "it may be well for passengers to keep a sharp eye on
their baggage." It then described how a Hudson River steamboat passenger from Troy lost track of his trunk, which contained, among other
things, more than five thousand dollars in "notes and drafts." Several days
later, he spotted a porter carrying that same trunk onto the Brooklyn ferry.
Alerting the police, he regained his trunk and they arrested the thief, who
had "a large amount of [stolen] property."[44] David Hillhouse, a passenger
in 1825, mentioned that "there were a great many passengers — of course in
the number were those of almost every character," among which were "a
few rogues, who under the guise of gentlemen, contrived to pilfer a portion away of hats and baggage of several gentlemen passengers." The
crowded boat made it "uncomfortable to all but the ladies who have of
course, and of right, exclusive privileges."[45]

In the years to come, the tourist routes became, at least by the standards
of the time, hotbeds of crime. Prior to 1825, there had been remarkably little theft or any other crime at Saratoga or Ballston. From 1804 (the first
year of publication) until 1824, the newspapers carried only a single report
of thefts or confidence jobs: a stolen pocketbook in 1812. After 1824,
though, a veritable crime wave began at the springs. In 1825, for example,

pickpockets were reported to be operating in the community, and visitors were warned to watch their wallets. And in the years after that, several wallets or watches would disappear each season. This new wave of crime was not limited to Saratoga. Where previously the steamboats had been relatively safe modes of transportation, the lower fares and increased crowding of passengers gave new opportunities for criminals.[46]

This situation did not go unanswered. The first such attempt was made by the North River Steam Company itself. Hoping to trade on its reputation for decorum, it sought out a market niche as the gentry steamboat line. But enough of the expected passengers did not flock to North River boats, so the line's efforts to maintain high standards (and high fares) failed: eventually, the company went bankrupt.

Another effort was made in 1827 by the Stevens family of Hoboken, New Jersey. Their company was very well established: John Stevens, the founder, had been one of the first American steamboat experimenters, having worked for a time on early prototypes in the 1790s with Chancellor Livingston. After Fulton's success, Stevens appropriated a number of his advances and created a line of his own operating out of New Jersey. He stayed out of the Hudson market as long as the North River line operated, but on its demise in 1826, he and his sons leapt into the gap.[47] In 1827, they entered the fight with an elegant new flagship, the *Albany*, one of the most advanced boats of its time.

The *Albany* would eventually be paired with another boat, the *New Philadelphia*, and the two boats would work as a team, one leaving Albany at the moment the other left New York. Both were designed to be as fast and attractive as possible. They were day boats, which meant that they had to be beautiful. Night boats were utilitarian, attractive only to the traveler on a budget, as they saved the cost of a night's lodging; day boats, on the other hand, offered, in the words of an advertisement, the "gratification of viewing the beautiful and sublime scenery of the Hudson"—and companies charged accordingly. They did not offer sleeping quarters and were better furnished and elegantly decorated.[48]

The *Albany* cost the Stevenses $65,000. Of that, the furnishings were a significant expense, nearly $10,000. But one of the most striking expenditures the Stevenses made was more than $4,000 to commission original art, a gallery of paintings, for the boat's main salon. This extravagance is even more striking given that the Stevenses had never been art collectors;

no member of the family is ever recorded offering any other artistic commission in this period. The resulting gallery was of a quality and size almost unknown outside America's major cities.[49]

Twelve large paintings, each 22 by 46 inches in size, were hung in the main cabin. These represented the cream of American art: anyone familiar with the art world would have been deeply impressed with the collection. And, as in all galleries of the day, the paintings were not hung randomly. They were intended to converse with each other, providing a didactic journey with moral lessons and opportunities for discussion. But beyond their artistic significance, half of the twelve paintings were chosen specifically to please a tourist audience.[50]

The two paintings most obviously intended for this audience were by Thomas Cole. At that moment, Cole was a star only in the New York art world. His inclusion means that the Stevenses were being advised by someone conversant in the new dialogue he had introduced into American painting, someone who knew of the excitement being generated by Cole's works. The works themselves were significant: *Landscape View near the Falls of the Kauterskill* was his last major view of Kaaterskill Falls, while *Scene from the Last of the Mohicans* was his first painting illustrating themes from Cooper's writing.[51] Less explicitly linked but still heavily influenced by the tourist-influenced celebration of American scenery was Thomas Doughty's *Lake Scene at Sunrise, Composition*, while the connection between Robert Weir's *Landscape of Lake George* and Hudson tourism is obvious.[52]

Tourism's influence on the Stevenses' choice of the last two paintings is much less obvious, as both took Napoleonic themes. One was a copy of David's *Bonaparte Crossing the Alps*, while another depicted Point Breeze, the Bordentown, New Jersey, estate of Napoleon Bonaparte's exiled brother, Joseph.[53] He had fled to the United States after the Hundred Days in 1815. Calling himself the "Comte de Survilliers," after a property he had purchased adjacent to his former estate near Paris, he purchased Point Breeze and settled into a velvet exile. He was extravagantly wealthy thanks to the money and jewels he had managed to smuggle out of France, and he remodeled his estate into one of America's most magnificent. Hundreds of paintings graced the walls, including pieces by da Vinci, Velasquez, Rubens, and Canaletto, and it was sumptuously furnished. After it burned in 1820—most of the paintings and furnishings were saved by the local townspeople—he rebuilt in an even grander style. Its glories were an object of curiosity, and it became a tourist site in its own right. Staffordshire plates depicting Point Breeze were sold in the United States; engravings of it appeared in magazines and journals.[54]

Bonaparte was also an essential figure in Hudson Valley tourism. Nearly every summer after his arrival in America, he traveled northward to take the waters at Saratoga. After a stay of a week or more, he would then voyage onward to Niagara. Each year, his passage through New York City would be noted in the local newspapers, and his arrival would be announced in Saratoga's local newspaper. His presence at the tourist hotels or aboard steamboats was reported in travelers' diaries.[55]

Joseph Bonaparte, then, was the ideal tourist. His participation on the American tourist circuit validated it in the eyes of traveling Americans. The Napoleonic paintings aboard the *Albany* subtly reminded passengers of that fact, and if the Stevenses were lucky enough to have Joseph himself aboard, so much the better: the paintings would have pleased him immeasurably. His presence on the boat, in addition to burnishing its reputation, would have been good for business.

Predictably, passage on the *Albany* was costly. A ticket on it was more than 30 percent more expensive than its competitors (four dollars to their three). The intent was to create a premium trip for discerning travelers, one that would neatly segregate gentry from nongentry. The art gallery itself was to be the main tool to separate refined, discerning, and sensitive travelers from the others. Such a traveler would be willing to pay more for the experience. But that effort was a failure. After only one season, the company was forced to drop its fare to two dollars to match its competitors. Meals, formerly included, now cost fifty cents each. But even these fares couldn't hold, and in 1829 it was forced to drop them once again, to a dollar. But its competitors had also cut fares: some day line journeys now were only fifty cents.[56]

The drop in fares ultimately undermined the *Albany*'s charter intent. With passage on it as cheap as any other, the steamboat's staterooms became crowded, as on the other boats, with the "lesser" classes. The gentry were disgusted: they were once again surrounded, in the words of the New York editor William Leete Stone, by "the would-be ultra-genteels."[57]

The crowds, the crime, the sheer pressure of tourists: underlying all of this were concerns about the large numbers of unknown people among the travelers. The dangers were obvious: how could a genteel traveler know which one of these fashionably dressed strangers was a bona fide member of genteel society? Which one was the dangerous stranger? Without the comfortable markers of gentility, without the traditional safeguards of a tightly knit society, a confidence man (or woman) could easily infiltrate this relatively open society and take advantage of vulnerable members. Or, perhaps worse yet, their reckless children would make difficult marriage outside their class.

Fears of the power of charming but unscrupulous adventurers over vulnerable young women were not new. This theme had long run through much of the popular literature of the time, including classics such as Susanna Rowson's widely republished 1794 book, *Charlotte Temple*. But these stories relied on drawing-room or other meetings, all in places where the adventurer generally required some kind of intermediary to gain access to society. In the early years of the springs, when the ties between the springs and gentry sites like New York were quite close, the danger from imposters was checked by these traditional safeguards. Tourism undermined them, and the danger (real or perceived) by the 1820s had increased. American society had grown so large and diffuse that pretenders could more readily infiltrate it.

This was a society that relied on sincerity. Many of the neophyte tourists of this era were all too naïve. Some tourists would have been at least somewhat on their guard: the social cues—dress, accent, bearing—of the most obviously threatening persons would have been immediately noted. But what if a criminal passed the most obvious tests? Tourists could be quite trusting, if approached properly. For example, consider the experience of the Sipples (mentioned in chapter 7). When this tourist couple first arrived in New York from their small Delaware town on a July morning in 1828, they encountered the chaos of huckster capitalism, those porters Mr. Sipple called "the greatest impositioners of any I have met." As Sipple was chasing down his bags, he was approached by a kindly man, someone who had the genteel manners needed for a successful approach. "A gentleman by the name of W. J. Cadwell had placed one of his cards in my hand and solicited us to take board with him during our stay in N York," wrote Mr. Sipple. He thanked him but explained that they were headed for Albany at the first opportunity. But could he point the way to the Hudson steamboat landing? Cadwell offered to accompany him there; on the way, coincidentally, they passed his boarding house. Sipple was impressed: "I found [it] to be one of the first rate boarding houses in the City." At the office of the steamboat line, Cadwell helped Sipple buy tickets for the afternoon boat: "He assisted me in striving to procure burths [*sic*]," Sipple wrote, "but the greater part of them [were] taken." A crowded boat was distasteful to Sipple, so he decided to stay the weekend at Cadwell's. Later that day a chance acquaintance helped them book passage on a rival line, and they opted to leave for Saratoga immediately. But Sipple trusted Cadwell enough to return to his "house" (inn) later on during his trip.[58]

How much manipulation, subtle or otherwise, had Cadwell used to persuade Sipple to lodge with him? "He assisted me," Sipple wrote, "to procure burths." How much did Cadwell "assist" Sipple? Were, in fact, "the greater part of them . . . taken?" We will never know; Cadwell operated under the rules of genteel conduct. He had successfully won Sipple over amid that distinctly ungenteel sea of "impositioners." In the end, nothing happened beyond Cadwell's securing a tenant. But had Cadwell been more malicious, Sipple's ingenuousness could have had unfortunate results. As Theodore Dwight had noted in 1826, many travelers were disconcerted by this brutal scrum of confusion at the steamboat landing.[59]

For antebellum society, the situations that were created in tourist venues were the leading edge of what would come to be perceived of as an epidemic of crime.[60] And although street crime was a serious concern, probably the most disturbing type of crime came not from the easily identified thug but rather from the smooth and calculated confidence man.[61]

How real this threat was is unknown. Probably, like so many societal terrors, the actual threat was far less than was imagined. Few truly wealthy, well-connected persons eloped or broke the bonds of society or were swindled by confidence men or women. But societal terrors are created in response to real situations. Tales of insincere adventurers, whether male or female, helped to shape a heightened awareness of the potential risks. Lying more deeply than that fear was a sense of uncontrollable change. For those who had been traveling to the springs for ten or twenty years, the evidence would have been right before their eyes: a sea of unfamiliar faces, each one a possible threat, each one a possible bona fide member of their society. This uncertainty led many to become obsessed with a search for the truly authentic and the attempt to devise some foolproof mechanism to detect those who operated under false pretenses. These concerns are the beginnings of what would become societal obsessions that would consume antebellum society in the 1830s, 1840s, and 1850s: the fear of the imposter, the terror of the confidence man, and the quest for the authentically sincere.[62] As for the steamboats, the gentry would continue to ride them: there was no alternative. For the moment, they would have to just put up with it.

❧ 10 ☙

The Next Big Thing

T HE CUMULATIVE DISCONTENT with the Hudson Valley route—its overexposure, the rising crime, the large number of "would-be ultra-genteels"—meant that some began to look for new fields for tourism, for places that could deliver the promise of unspoiled, yet readily accessible nature.

One way to measure this development is to look at the tourist guidebooks. Gideon Minor Davison's *Fashionable Tour*, for example, was the first description of that pioneering tourist circuit. In the original 1822 edition, it described a route from New York up to Saratoga, out to Niagara, and back via Quebec to Burlington, Vermont, and through western Massachusetts to Boston.[1] The 1825 edition's route was virtually identical, although among its additions was a description of Mt. Holyoke, near Northampton, Massachusetts, where a new mountain house had been built. This and other descriptions neither expanded the route of the Fashionable Tour nor changed its basic itinerary. But in the 1828 edition Davison substantially added to the itinerary: he devoted several pages to the White Mountains of New Hampshire, focusing particularly on the area around Franconia Notch. Theodore Dwight, too, added a White Mountain section to his 1828 guidebook, and he devoted even more pages to it than Davison. He also included not only a twenty-one page essay on them in his 1829 *Sketches of Scenery and Manners* but also a four-page appendix.[2]

The White Mountains are a spectacularly scenic mountain range in northern New Hampshire. As they are the home of Mount Washington, the highest mountain on the eastern seaboard, they were well known, at least as unusual landscape features, in early America. And although there had been some literary attention paid to them in travel literature prior to the mid-1820s, relatively little had been written about visiting them. Getting to them was a problem: the roads were good enough for trade, but it was a long and difficult journey from the main routes of travel.

As the highest peak, Mount Washington had a built-in attraction. It had first been climbed by an European in the mid–seventeenth century, and a few others came there to repeat that feat over the years. Those travelers who came to the mountain in the first years of the nineteenth century stayed at an inn built by Ethan Crawford located in the Franconia Notch, a dramatic site where the White Mountains are cleft by a narrow valley. There, sheer mountainsides rise high above the fast-running Saco River. With the light but steady traffic of climbers, Crawford hoped to increase his patronage. In the summer of 1818, he cut the first trail to the top of Mount Washington, a trail that began, naturally enough, at his inn. He then began to lead small groups of adventurers to the mountain's summit. More attention was focused on the mountains when Timothy Dwight praised them in his 1821 *Travels in New York and New England*, but their remoteness meant that they were not widely thought of as a tourist destination before 1826.[3]

That year, a catastrophe put the White Mountains on the tourist map. An intense summer drought dried out the lands on either side of the Franconia Notch homestead of the Willey family. Sudden heavy midsummer rains loosened the soil high above their home, and late one night a landslide roared down the mountain. The family, hearing this and realizing their fate, fled the home. Had they stayed in place, though, they would have survived: the building itself was spared because it stood on an outcropping that parted the flood. The landslide killed the parents, their five children, and two hired hands.[4]

The Willey disaster and the wide publicity it gained caused a relative flood of tourists to descend on the White Mountains. Thomas Cole, for example, would come in 1827 through the advice of a patron, Daniel Wadsworth. And although he would not paint the mountains for a number of years, he would write after an 1828 visit that the area was suffused with a "wild grandeur." The spectacular view was made especially poignant in his mind by the Willey family home, a "little patch of green in the gloomy desolation" that "very naturally recalled to mind the horrors of the night" when the family died. Dwight spent pages reflecting on the pathos of the scene and the ancillary damage the landslide caused to places he had fished and visited years earlier; he was overwhelmed by "feelings of sublimity" that became "painful," "feelings that we should not choose to experience for a long time, at least without some intermission."[5] Also visiting that summer were Henry David Thoreau, Ralph Waldo Emerson, Nathaniel Hawthorne, Daniel Webster, and Washington Irving, among others. Although the growth in tourists was dramatic compared to earlier years, for the remainder of the 1820s the numbers going to the White Mountains remained just a fraction of those who came to the Hudson.[6]

But the White Mountains were perfectly positioned for the next wave of tourism. They were simultaneously wild and untamed (Cole wrote of an "unbroken silence reigning through the whole region") and yet accessible enough that when it came time to leave, Cole had to walk only six miles to catch a coach back to Boston.[7] Accommodations within the Notch remained rude even well into the 1830s, but they were available, and continued to improve: Crawford, eventually added a bowling alley, a dance floor, and a petting zoo to his always rustic inn.[8] Like the Hudson, the area would get its own cultural infrastructure: for example, Hawthorne would romanticize and immortalize the Willey story in "The Ambitious Guest" in 1835.

What we see with the White Mountains is an example of how tourism thrives on fashion. Destinations shift according to the whims of fashion, and high fashion shifted from the Hudson to the Whites. In another decade, it would turn away from the Whites. The White Mountains were the perfect next step after the Hudson, since reaching them involved just enough additional time and expense to cut down the number of visitors. Once those barriers had fallen, the hot light of fashionable tourism would shine elsewhere.

This does not mean that the Hudson had lost all cachet. Far from it: new methods would be invented to make it ever more exclusive. Still, it was an unceasing struggle to achieve that, to maintain business while making improvements. The tourist infrastructure of the Hudson would be regularly improved, and each step of that sort, though appealing to the gentry's desire for ease of travel, would have the less desirable result of making Hudson Valley resorts more accessible to crowds of non-elite visitors.

Saratoga, though, did not sink into obscurity. It found a number of ways to bring new people to the resort, and for a certain set it did not lose its cachet for quite some time. New attractions were found to maintain excitement and interest. For example, New York had long been resistant to legalized horse racing, but promoters from Saratoga eventually convinced the state legislature to allow them to open a race track there in 1847.[9] And gambling, first tried in the early 1830s, would become enshrined in permanent quarters by the end of the 1840s. These steps drew a new generation of tourists to Saratoga, particularly those from the South. New hotels were built, reaching new heights of cost and exclusivity. Over the next century and a half, Saratoga's exclusive status would wax and wane, fading for a decade or two before coming back as exclusive as ever.[10]

Coda: The Future of Tourism

From the early 1830s, we can catch a glimpse into the future of tourism. By the late 1820s, the Saratoga experience had been successfully sold as a nearly complete package of transport and entertainment. The hotels were there, waiting, ready; the steamboats whisked travelers northward and then home; and the mystique of the place awaited.

But all of this still had a glimmer of its roots in the aristocratic pursuit of traveling leisure, with its ideal of an unlimited amount of time and money. A new kind of tourism would soon develop in the Hudson Valley, a tourism that was born from the needs of those who work for a living and from their desires to do as the aristocracy had done for generations. This tourism was fast, slick, brief, dependent on the most modern of technologies, and it was brief: people rarely, if ever, took more than two weeks off.

One of the best descriptions of this new kind of tourism is found in an article—an editorial, really—that was printed in the *American Railroad Journal and Advocate of Internal Improvement* in June 1833. "Go to Saratoga!" it exhorted those who had had an "an arduous and we trust a profitable, spring business." Even for those "who think they cannot afford it," the article insisted on travel to the spa. Why? Technology had transformed the journey into something almost anyone can afford.

Beyond the unseemly questions of money, there were still those of time. The article resoundingly demolished any such qualms for those who thought they were too busy for recreation: "And as for the *time*. . . . If *time* is an object to you, adopt the following plan: Rise early each morning and be industrious through the week until Friday at 3 P.M.; then get ready for the 5 o'clock boat . . . which will land you in Albany next morning, in time for the *first* or half past six o'clock train of cars to Schenectady. . . . From Schenectady to Saratoga, through Ballston, the distance is 22 miles, which is performed by horse power in two hours with great ease." Once at the Springs, the article continued, stay at Saratoga until Monday morning. If a visitor left at noon he could be back to Albany by late afternoon and in New York Tuesday morning, ready for the work week. Each way, the trip would take seventeen hours, a short, fast visit to the springs.[11]

This article distilled a decade's worth of tourist experience. Most tourists did not stay at the springs for more than a few days; here, we see that taken to an extreme. This ultimate commodification of the Hudson tourist experience is specifically tailored to middle-class sensibilities: a bit of play, but little work lost. A weekend retreat, but a return in time for most of a week's work. Later in the article, there is the suggestion that a very busy traveler could take an even more stripped-down journey. By staying just long enough at the springs to gulp "a half dozen glasses of . . . water," a traveler could leave on a Friday and be back by Sunday. No need, the writer assures us, for the reverent gaze: the leisurely aristocratic journey has been reduced to its most essential elements, to an easily digested commodity to be consumed as quickly as possible.

Notes

Introduction

1. Dallam (1787–1857) served as collector of taxes for the city of Baltimore from 1820 through 1835. From an old family of Harford County, Maryland, he and his brother, Richard, lived in Nashville, Tennessee, from 1804 to 1810, where he was listed in the 1810 U.S. Census with nine slaves. He moved back to Baltimore that year. The 1820 U.S. Census lists Dallam in Baltimore (p. 412) with his wife, three children (with three more to come), three slaves, and one "free colored" female under fourteen years of age. The Dallam Papers (Ms. 1250), Maryland Historical Society, Baltimore, Maryland, contain evidence of his rent income in letters from Paco Smith and the 1819–25 Francis Dallum Notebook, which lists expenses and records various grants he made.

2. His friend was a "Wm. Wendeall" (probably a phonetic rendering; Dallam's spelling was always idiosyncratic). Slaves were very rarely, if ever, mentioned in slave owners' travel diaries, and Dallam was typical in that he did not mention traveling with one. However, it would have been characteristic for a man of Dallam's class from the South to travel with a slave or servant of some sort. Francis J. Dallam (1787–1857) Travel Diary, 1827, Dallam Papers, ms.1250, box 2, Maryland Historical Society.

3. See chapter 9 for a description of his reactions to Saratoga. Ironically, he was rather disappointed in what he found.

4. Dallam Diary, 2 August 1827. Dallam was a member of the Maryland House of Representatives in 1813 and 1814; see *A Biographical Dictionary of the Maryland Legislature, 1635–1789*, vol. 1 (Baltimore: Johns Hopkins University Press, 1979). He was Baltimore's collector of taxes from at least 1827 through 1833, with listings as such in *Matchett's Baltimore Director* [sic] *for 1827*, 70, 91 (accessible at http://aomol.net/000001/000491/html/index.html), and subsequent directories. Although Dallam had not traveled much for leisure in his lifetime—he had traveled widely for business and to relocate—two letters in the Dallam Papers from 1826 (July 29, July 31) from Sarah P. Dallam (wife) to F. J. Dallam show that he went to Bedford Springs, Pennsylvania, that year. There is no other evidence of leisure travel in the papers from 1815 to 1833.

5. For example, only 452 visitors were recorded visiting Newport, Rhode Island, one of America's only Colonial-era resorts, from 1767 to 1775. Carl Bridenbaugh, "Colonial Newport as a Summer Resort," *Rhode Island Historical Society Collections* 26 (1933): 23. For examples of aristocratic nontravelers, see the pri-

163

vate diary of Charles Carroll of Carrollton, 1792–1802, ms. 209, Maryland Historical Society. Carroll rarely spent more than a week away from his plantation, and he took no major trips. Henry D. Gilpin took his first tourist trip in 1825, despite his years spent in England at school and his extraordinarily lucrative holdings in Delaware and Pennsylvania; he would not travel as a tourist again until 1835. Box 59, Gilpin Family Papers, Historical Society of Delaware, Wilmington, Delaware; see chapter 7 as well. Another Philadelphia resident, J. Fisher Leaming, a Quaker businessman, took no vacations from 1813 to 1833 despite a great deal of traveling. Leaming Family Papers, Historical Society of Pennsylvania, Philadelphia, Pennsylvania. The number of truly frequent travelers even into the antebellum era is quite small in surviving collections compared to those who took one or two trips in their lifetime. Examples of frequent travelers include William Elliott, who took northern trips from his South Carolina home a number of times from 1806 to 1839. Ms. Collection 1009, Elliott and Gonzalez Family Papers, Southern Historical Collection, Chapel Hill, North Carolina. An analysis of a later period that is probably still relevant for this era is Jane Pease, "A Note on Patterns of Conspicuous Consumption Among Seaboard Planters, 1820–1860," *Journal of Southern History* 35, no. 3 (August 1969): 391–92. Pease describes the Grand Tour of Europe as a rare event, occasionally used to "finish" a young man or to present a daughter to society.

6. David Jaffee has argued that the "traditional" resistance to consumption was in fact a part of a general resistance after the Revolution to what was seen as British excess, a resistance that was in part broken down by the omnipresence of consumer goods by midcentury. Jaffee, "Peddlers of Progress and the Transformation of the Rural North, 1760–1860," *Journal of American History* 78, no. 2 (September 1991): 511–35. Countering his argument is a school of thought exemplified by the work of T. H. Breen, who contends that consumerism had long been a part of American society; see note 13.

7. Rationales for tourism proved to be amazingly malleable: For some, tourism was a way to a genuine appreciation of nature, sometimes seen as a route to God himself. For others it was a form of patriotism, while still others argued that travel was a way of advancing one's education. Such advocates either rejected the notion that tourism was consumption or argued that only through rigorous discipline could a tourist steer clear of the sin of consumerism.

8. Class in Colonial and Early Republic America is difficult to define. Throughout this study, I will use the word *gentry* to denote not only those with significant amounts of money but also those with longstanding power. Merchants, wealthy lawyers, successful businessmen fall into this category. They tended to be the leaders of their communities in a pattern stretching back a hundred years or more. But in the 1810s and 1820s a new class of wealthy persons emerged. These usurpers were seen by the old order as gauche and uncultivated, and they represented a significant threat to the traditional conduits of power. Standing behind this new group was a small but rising upper middle class, the true threat to traditional power.

9. Although by no means a definitive measure, the vast majority of tourist narratives in my research come from New Yorkers. The second largest group was comprised of travelers from the South (an admittedly large region), mainly

slave-owning aristocrats. Much smaller numbers came from Philadelphia and Baltimore, the country's largest cities after New York. Conspicuously missing, though, is Boston. A comprehensive search through all of the major Boston-area archives reveals that Bostonians (and New Englanders in general) rarely participated in the tourism of the 1820s. This might be a sampling error: their travel journals or letters may not have survived. On the other hand, perhaps Bostonians did not see leisure travel as necessary, important, or perhaps even moral.

10. The age when tourism has been identified as beginning has been steadily drifting backward in the decades since the subject began to be studied with any rigor. From Daniel Boorstein's *The Image*, which postulated that tourism—cheapened, coarse, popular—started only after the jet allowed cheap mass travel to Europe, to Marguerite S. Shaffer's 2001 *See America First*, the threshold of where tourism began has most often been placed not long after the Civil War. It is clear, however, that this later tourism was modeled on the practices of a much earlier time. See Boorstein, *The Image: A Guide to Pseudo-Events in America* (New York: Harper and Row, 1964), originally published as *The Image, or What Happened to the American Dream* (New York: Atheneum, 1962); and Shaffer, *See America First: Tourism and National Identity, 1880–1940* (Washington, D.C.: Smithsonian Institution, 2001).

11. See, for example, Thomas A. Chambers, *Drinking the Waters: Creating an American Leisure Class at Nineteenth-Century Mineral Springs* (Washington, D.C.: Smithsonian Institution Press, 2002); and Charlene M. Boyer Lewis, *Ladies and Gentlemen on Display: Planter Society at the Virginia Springs, 1790–1860* (Charlottesville: University of Virginia Press, 2001). There is also some debate as to the frequency of travel among wealthy southern families: until relatively recently it was widely held that they traveled a great deal, and some still argue the point. In general, it is safe to assert that by the 1850s a large number of these families left home regularly. But there is little evidence to point to large numbers of southerners leaving home for the entire summer or for long periods as a regular activity before that time: rather, what emerges is that this was an evolving activity, with few leaving for long periods at the turn of the nineteenth century, many more doing so by the 1830s, and relatively large numbers doing so by the 1850s. Finally, members of the southern gentry were relatively few, especially compared to the northern gentry, and thus the raw number of southern travelers would always be low. Given their wealth and ostentation, though, those who did travel were much more visible and likely to be noticed by others.

12. See, among others, John Sears, *Sacred Places: American Tourist Attractions in the Nineteenth Century* (New York: Oxford University Press, 1989); Dona Brown, *Inventing New England: Regional Tourism in the Nineteenth Century* (Washington, D.C.: Smithsonian Institution Press, 1995); and Eric Purchase, *Out of Nowhere: Disaster and Tourism in the White Mountains* (Baltimore: Johns Hopkins University Press, 1999).

13. In my view, tourism was a direct outgrowth of a consumer revolution that blossomed in the 1820s and 1830s, a line of thought associated with a group of writers including Stephen Nissenbaum, *The Battle for Christmas* (New York:

Alfred A. Knopf, 1996); Richard Bushman, *The Refinement of America: Persons, Houses, Cities* (New York: Alfred A. Knopf, 1992); Stuart Blumin, *The Emergence of the Middle Class: Social Experience in the American City, 1760–1900* (New York: Cambridge University Press, 1989), and "Hypothesis of Middle-Class Formation in Nineteenth-Century America: A Critique and Some Proposals," *American Historical Review* 90, no. 2 (April 1985): 299–338; and, to some extent, Charles Sellers, *The Market Revolution: Jacksonian America, 1815–1846* (New York: Oxford University Press, 1991). Note, however, that I do not agree with much of Sellers's argument that it was only in the 1820s that a broad capitalist culture arrived in the United States; the work of more recent historians convincingly places the origins of that culture much earlier, at some point in the eighteenth century. These include T. H. Breen, " 'Baubles of Britain': The American and Consumer Revolutions of the Eighteenth Century," *Past and Present* 119 (1988): 73–104, and *The Marketplace of Revolution: How Consumer Politics Shaped American Independence* (New York: Oxford University Press, 2004); Timothy Shannon, "Dressing for Success on the Mohawk Frontier: Hendrick, William Johnson, and the Indian Fashion," *William and Mary Quarterly*, 3rd ser., 53, no. 1 (January 1996): 13–42; and Gloria Main and Jackson Main, "Economic Growth and the Standard of Living in Southern New England, 1640–1774," *Journal of Economic History* 48, no. 1 (1988): 27–46. This is in contrast to a group of historians who argue for a much later consumer revolution, include William Leach, *Land of Desire* (New York: Pantheon Books, 1993); and Richard Butsch, "Introduction: Leisure and Hegemony in America," in *For Fun and Profit: The Transformation of Leisure into Consumption*, ed. Richard Butsch (Philadelphia: Temple University Press, 1990), 3–27, with whom I differ. Tourism was an expression of a phenomenon of the 1820s, the huge societal expansion of an already existing set of consumer attitudes. Perhaps the best recent summation of current thinking in this matter is Daniel Walker Howe, *What Hath God Wrought: The Transformation of America, 1815–1848* (New York: Oxford University Press, 2007).

1. Laying the Foundation

1. Nancy Goyne Evans, "The Sans Souci, a Fashionable Resort Hotel in Ballston Spa," *Winterthur Portfolio* 6 (1970): 111. See also Sue C. Patrick, "Low, Nicholas," *American National Biography*, vol. 14 (New York: Oxford University Press, 1999).

2. Henry Sigerist, "The Early Medical History of Saratoga Springs," *Bulletin of the History of Medicine* 13 (1943): 540–41. Ballston Spa should not be confused with the village of Ballston, which is several miles away from the springs. In this book, "Ballston" or "Ballston Springs" invariably refers to Ballston Spa. Eliphalet Ball, for whom the town was named, brought his parishioners to Ballston from Bedford, New York, in 1770. Hugh Bradley lists several of the many differing phonetic renderings of the Mohawk name for Saratoga in *Such Was Saratoga* (New York: Doubleday, 1940), 2–3. See also Timothy Dwight, *Travels in New England and New York* (1822; repr., with notes and edited by Barbara Miller Solomon, Cambridge, MA: Belknap Press, 1969), 3:293.

3. Evans, "Sans Souci," 111.

4. Quoted in ibid., 111.

5. Timothy Dwight, *Travels*, 3:293.

6. The house became known as the Aldridge House in 1795; it would function as a hotel until 1846. It is the only one of the early hotels still extant; it has since become Brookside, the Saratoga County History Center. The piazza was so popular that it became a standard feature of nearly all the major resort hotels of the antebellum era. A description of its early character can be found in Nathaniel B. Sylvester, *History of Saratoga County, New York: With Illustrations and Biographical Sketches* (Philadelphia: Everts & Ensign, 1878), ch. 30.

7. The map showing the streets of the village is at the New York Public Library Manuscript Room; see the "Nicholas Low Map," Map Case. An accounting of Low's land leases and sales is in the Nicholas Low Land Book No. 2, apparently a post-1819 copy (since it refers to the canal at Ballston). For information about Low and Saratoga, see Evans, "Sans Souci," 111–12; Washington Irving, *Journals and Notebooks*, ed. Nathalia Wright (Madison: University of Wisconsin Press, 1969), 1:7n20; and Robert Ernst, "Nicholas Low: Merchant and Speculator in Post-Revolutionary New York," *New York History* 75, no. 4 (October 1994): 371.

8. Quoted in Jedidiah Morse, *The American Universal Geography*, 5th ed. (Boston: Thomas & Andrews, 1805), 492–95.

9. James Read to Susan Read, 9 August 1797, Read-Eckard Letters, box 36, folder 1, Historical Society of Delaware.

10. James Read to Susan Read, 18 August 1797, Read-Eckard Letters.

11. Abigail May, 26 May 1800 (Morn), Abigail May Journal, Goddard-May Papers, Schlesinger Library, Radcliffe Institute, Harvard University. The New York State Historical Society in Cooperstown, New York, has three different transcriptions of this journal, all of which alter the text in some manner, whether by adding a paragraph structure, changing the orthography, or adding modern punctuation.

12. Sylvester, *History of Saratoga County*, ch. 30.

13. Abigail May Journal, 1 June 1800.

14. John Russell, ed., *Memoirs, Journal, and Correspondence of Thomas Moore* (London: Longman, 1853), 1:167–68.

15. Low annually visited his northern and eastern New York land holdings; he definitely came to Ballston in 1802 but probably came other years as well. Ernst, "Nicholas Low," 369.

16. Evans, "Sans Souci," 112–13.

17. Irving, *Journals*, 1:7.

18. For a list of "published sources [that] suggest the hotel was the first of its size anywhere in the United States," see Evans, "Sans Souci," 114n9.

19. John Melish claimed that the hotel cost somewhere between $30,000 to $60,000 to build. Melish, *Travels Through the United States of America in the Years 1806 & 1807, and 1809, 1810, & 1811* (London: George Cowie and Co., 1818), 552. Cited in Henry Dilworth Gilpin, *A Northern Tour: Being a Guide to Saratoga, Lake George, Niagara, Canada, Boston, &c. &c.* (Philadelphia: Carey & Lea, 1825), and quoted in Evans, "Sans Souci," 113. This figure is at best apoc-

ryphal (it is probably far too high), but it does adequately communicate the sense of awe the structure conveyed.

20. Evans, "Sans Souci," 114–15.

21. Ibid., 117.

22. For the most complete account of the early British spa industry, see Phyllis Hembry, *The English Spa, 1560–1815: A History* (London: Athlone Press, 1990).

23. Marshall Scott Legan, "Hydropathy in America: A Nineteenth Century Panacea," *Bulletin of the History of Medicine* 45 (1971): 267–80; and Sigerist, "Early Medical History of Saratoga Springs," 540–84.

24. Carl Bridenbaugh, "Baths and Watering Places of Colonial America," *William and Mary Quarterly*, 3rd ser., 3, no. 2 (April 1946): 151–81.

25. Abigail May Journal, 24 May 1800 (Morn).

26. She expressed quiet despair at several points, including, for example, a summary of potential cures, sighing at the end that "my hand shall lay down as gentle in the dust, as if we had been in unison all our lives"; several days later she noted that "two long years my sad heart has brooded over this poor limb." Abigail May Journal, 17 June 1800, 22 June 1800.

27. Ibid., 15 June 1800.

28. Classical thought was expressed by, for example, Hippocrates, while English cold-water therapy is exemplified by a 1715 London tract by Sir John Floyer and Edward Baynard, *Psychrolousia, or the History of Cold Bathing* (London, 1702). The first known work published in America extolling these virtues was John Smith, *The Curiosities of Common Water*, first published in London in 1723 and printed in Philadelphia later the same year. These ideas would be made more formal later in the nineteenth century, particularly through the works of Vincenz Priessnitz (1799–1851), who was given authority by the Austrian government in 1830 to receive patients and treat them with plain water. See Legan, "Hydropathy in America," 270–71.

29. Richard L. Bushman and Claudia L. Bushman, "The Early History of Cleanliness in America," *Journal of American History* 74, no. 4 (March 1988): 1213–38; and Jack Larkin, *The Reshaping of Everyday Life, 1790–1840* (New York: Harper, 1988), 163–66.

30. See Legan, "Hydropathy in America"; Sigerist, "Early Medical History of Saratoga Springs," and "American Spas in Historical Perspective," *Bulletin of the History of Medicine* 11 (1942): 133–47; Bridenbaugh, "Baths and Watering Places," 151–81; Jonathan Paul de Vierville, "American Healing Waters: A Chronology and Historical Survey (1513–1946) of America's Major Springs, Spas, and Health Resorts . . . ," PhD diss., University of Texas, Austin, 1992; Charlene Marie Lewis [later Charlene M. Boyer Lewis], *Ladies and Gentlemen on Display: Planter Society at the Virginia Springs, 1790–1860*" (Charlottesville: University Press of Virginia, 2001); Thomas A. Chambers, *Drinking the Waters: Creating an American Leisure Class at Nineteenth-Century Mineral Springs* (Washington, D.C.: Smithsonian Institution Press, 2002).

31. *Port Folio*, 30 October 1802, 340, a reprint from an undated piece in the *New-York Morning Chronicle*.

32. Abigail May Journal, 26 May 1800.

33. Ibid., 7 June 1800.

34. Abigail May Journal.

35. Dr. Tobias Smollett, "An Essay on the External Use of Water . . . ," reprinted with notes by Claude E. Jones in *Bulletin of the History of Medicine* 3 (1935): 37–82.

36. 3 September 1800, Thomas Handasyd Perkins Papers, Massachusetts Historical Society, Boston. A profile of Perkins can be found in Freeman Hunt, *Lives of American Merchants* (1856; repr. New York: August M. Kelley Publishers, 1969), 33–102.

37. For example, see Abigail May Journal, 18 June 1800: "I wish I could feel more encor.[agement]—but let me stop the subject—I always avoid speaking of it."

38. Ibid., 13 August 1800. A short obituary appeared in the *Boston Columbian Centinel,* 10 September 1800.

39. Dr. Adam Alexander, 29 June 1801, no. 11, subcollection 1, subseries 3.3, folder 40, Dr. Adam Alexander Journal, Alexander-Hillhouse Papers, Southern Historical Collection. See the Finding Aid for biographical information on Alexander: http://www.lib.unc.edu/mss/inv/a/Alexander_and_Hillhouse_Family.html (accessed 6 Jan 2008).

40. Evans cites revenues from the gaming house as $170 in the 1812 season. Evans, "Sans Souci," 120–21.

41. Abigail came from the prominent Boston family of Col. John May and Abigail May. The same family would later produce the writer Louisa May Alcott, whose mother, also Abigail May, was given the same name as her distant cousin, our subject here. May's journal, which runs to some sixty manuscript pages and covers the period from her departure from Boston on May 19, 1800, to her return in early September, is the single best resource describing this aspect of the day; no other existing travel journals give this much detail about the life at the springs in the period from 1790 to 1810. In fact, there are only a few other, mostly fragmentary, accounts for the crucial period from 1797 to 1803.

42. Abigail May Journal, 23 June 1800.

43. Ibid., 25 June 1800.

44. Ibid., 12 and 14 August 1800.

45. Ibid., 6 June 1800.

46. Ibid., 7 and 8 June 1800.

47. Ibid., 14 August 1800.

48. Ibid., 4 June 1800.

49. This is an expression of the phenomenon known as "liminality," a process in which people shed some of their traditional roles and mores and enjoy brief expressions of freedom in a relatively safe setting. (We will soon encounter examples of the dangers of this.) Jon Sterngass, *First Resorts: Pursuing Pleasure at Saratoga Springs, Newport, and Coney Island* (Baltimore: Johns Hopkins University Press, 2001), gives a fine analysis of this phenomenon in the context of nineteenth-century vacation areas; see esp. 121–38. Charlene M. Boyer Lewis, *Ladies and Gentlemen on Display: Planter Society at the Virginia Springs, 1790–1860* (Charlottesville: University Press of Virginia, 2002), discusses this in a Southern context.

50. Abigail May Journal, 8 June 1800.

51. Mr. and Mrs. [Caleb? and Levenia?] Sipple Diary, 26 August 1821 (referring to

Saratoga Springs): "Religion does not appear to be their object the church service and sermon is but formality. Religion & vital piety I think is a very scarce article in this Country." New-York Historical Society, New York.

52. Abigail May Journal, 9 July 1800.

53. James Read to Susan Read, 9 August 1797, Read-Eckard Letters.

54. James Hawkins to Nicholas Low, 10 February 1804, Papers of Nicholas Low (1739–1826), Library of Congress, quoted in Evans, "Sans Souci," 115. See also Abigail May Journal, 22 July 1800.

55. This was probably Frederic De Peyster, a lawyer from New York City, father of the General Frederic De Peyster. *Cyclopedia of American Biography* (New York: Press Association Compilers, Inc., 1918–1931), 2:43.

56. May apparently used an alias to disguise the identity of the young woman (perhaps a variation of "kiss me"). There are no "Kissams" in the New York City directories of the time.

57. Abigail May Journal, 9 July 1800.

58. Ibid., 22 July 1800.

59. Again, "Gilliam" may have been an alias given him by May.

60. Abigail May Journal, 22 July 1800. May renders his name as "Skuyler." Schuyler was an early investor at Ballston; see the Nicholas Low Land Book No. 2, New York Public Library.

61. 10 September 1800, Bound vol. 7, Thomas Handasyd Perkins Papers.

62. *Port Folio*, 30 October 1802, 340.

63. Richard Derby was the second son of Elias Haskett Derby, a prominent Salem merchant known as "America's first millionaire."

64. Eliza Southgate Bowne, *A Girl's Life Eighty Years Ago: Selections from the Letters of Eliza Southgate Bowne* (1887; reprinted Williamstown, MA: Corner House Publishers, Clarence Cook, ed., 1980), 128–31. See chapter 2. For a good overview of this phenomenon in later decades, see Chambers, *Drinking the Waters*.

65. Bowne, *A Girl's Life*, 140.

66. Ibid., 140.

67. Ibid., 139–40. Emphasis in original.

68. Ibid., 177–82. Bowne's term as mayor extended from 1829 to 1832.

69. Ibid., 182. Murray's father was also father of Mary and Hannah Murray, whose travel narratives are described in chapter 5. "Miss Rogers" was one of the era's most famous beauties; a portrait of her hangs in the Maryland Historical Society.

70. Thomas Law, *Ballston Springs* (New York: S. Gould, 1806).

71. Washington Irving, *Journals and Notebooks*, 1:4–8.

72. Washington Irving, *History, Tales, and Sketches* (New York: Library of America, 1983), 287–88.

73. Washington Irving, *History, Tales, and Sketches*, 286–87.

74. Ibid., 286–92.

75. William Elliott to Phoebe Waight Elliott, 13 July 1809, Elliott and Gonzales Family Papers, Southern Historical Collection.

76. August estimate: Abigail May Journal, 12 August 1800. In addition to Aldridge's and Low's inns, a few cottages were available for visitors to rent. In 1795, Benjamin Waterhouse claimed that "thousands" came to benefit from the

spas, in fact the number of visitors per year probably was on the lower end of that range—perhaps a maximum of fifteen hundred visitors per year, including locals. Quoted in Morse, *American Universal Geography*, 5th ed., 492–95.

77. Isaac Weld, *Travels Through the States of North America* (1807; repr. New York: Johnson Reprint Corp., 1968), 267–71; and Dr. Adam Alexander Journal, 23 July 1801. James Flexner asserts that an average journey up the Hudson was four days from New York to Albany. Flexner, *Steamboats Come True* (New York: Viking Press, 1944), 25. See also John Pintard, *Letters from John Pintard to His Daughter* (New York: New-York Historical Society, 1940), 1:321.

78. For a colorful account of Fitch's life and personal problems, see Flexner, *Steamboats Come True*, esp. 144–207. Note the brief description of Fitch's Delaware River company at 186–87. Fitch's quirky and self-justifying autobiography was reprinted in Frank D. Prager, ed., *The Autobiography of John Fitch* (Philadelphia: American Philosophical Society, 1976).

79. Maurice Baxter, *The Steamboat Monopoly: Gibbons v. Ogden, 1824* (New York: Alfred A. Knopf, 1972), 8.

80. Flexner notes that Fulton's boat was only later renamed the *Clermont*. Flexner, *Steamboats Come True*, 319–20.

81. The best recent biography of Fulton is Cynthia Owen Philip, *Robert Fulton: A Biography* (New York: Franklin Watts, 1985); Philip provides an extensive description of the tangled relationship between Fulton and Livingston (120ff).

82. Flexner, *Steamboats Come True*, 332; and John Morrison, *History of American Steam Navigation* (1903; repr. New York: Argosy-Antiquarian Ltd., 1967), 26.

83. The monthly wage for an agricultural worker in the Philadelphia area in 1807 was about $7, or around one-third of the monthly pay for a common laborer in the city. See Donald R. Adams Jr., "Wage Rates in the Early National Period: Philadelphia, 1785–1830," *Journal of Economic History* 28, no. 3 (September 1968): 404–26.

84. There was a series of minor accidents and collisions with other vessels which were probably deliberate, instigated by river men who rightly saw the steamboat as the beginning of the end of their traditional way of life. Philip, *Robert Fulton*, 205–6, 226.

85. Peter Benes, "Itinerant Entertainers in New England and New York, 1687–1830," in *Itinerancy in New England and New York: The Dublin Seminar for New England Folklife Annual Proceedings, 1984* (Boston: Boston University Press, 1986), 126.

86. The panorama depicted the Battle of Arcola, recently fought between Napoleon and Britain in Spain. Advertised in the *Ballston Spa Independent American*, 21 August 1810, 4, and *The Ballston Spa Advertiser*, 21 August 1810, 3. The panorama genre was invented in Scotland in the 1780s and had been institutionalized in London with the construction of a specialized exhibition building exhibition in 1794. See Ralph Hyde, *Panorama! The Art and Entertainment of the "All-Embracing" View* (London: Trefoil Press, 1988); and Thomas Lawson, "Time Bandits, Space Vampires," *Artforum International* 26, no. 2 (January 1988): 88–95. The first recorded appearance of a panorama in the United States was in 1798 at the Gardner Baker museum (predecessor of the American Museum, which was the predecessor of P. T. Barnum's famous museum). George Odell, *Annals of the New York Stage* (New York: Columbia University Press,

1927), 2:33. Wolfgang Born mistakenly claimed that it was Fulton who painted and exhibited the first U.S. panorama in 1807. Born, *American Landscape Painting: An Interpretation* (New Haven: Yale University Press, 1948), 77.

87. In New York, variations on the standard panorama had been exhibited; for example, in 1808 a new panorama had opened of an ideal commercial and manufacturing town with a mechanical foreground of moving boats, carriages, and factories. Odell, *Annals*, 2:303. One of the few surviving panoramas from this era, John Vanderlyn's 1818 *Panorama of the Palace and Gardens of Versailles*, is exhibited at the Metropolitan Museum of New York. Eleanor Heartney, "A Room With a View," *ARTNews* 88 (March 1989): 18–19.

88. *Ballston Spa Independent American*, 6 August 1811, 3. The advertisement mentions that handbills were to be distributed in the village. For a description of the formation of these "cabinets of curiosities" in America, see Andrea Stulman Dennett, *Weird and Wonderful: The Dime Museum in America* (New York: New York University Press, 1997), 1–22. They are also related to the circuses and menageries described in Richard Flint, "Entrepreneurial and Cultural Aspects of the Early-Nineteenth-Century Circus and Menagerie Business," in *Itinerancy in New England and New York*, 131–49. Either the same model of Daniel Lambert or a duplicate was being exhibited at the American Museum in New York City in July 1811, and advertised in the *New York Columbian*, 3 July 1811, 3. The figure would continue to be exhibited there for at least twenty years, as is evidenced by an 1823 catalog, "A Companion to Scudder's American Museum," in the collections of the New-York Historical Society. See also the mention in Lloyd Haberly, "The American Museum from Baker to Barnum," *New-York Historical Society Quarterly* 53, no. 3 (July 1959): 278. The figure of Lambert would become a synecdoche for all obese performers. See Odell, *Annals*, 2:537, 2:567.

89. *The Ballston Spa Advertiser*, 30 July 1811, 2. "Mr. Stewart" may have been the performer "Mr. Steward" who did "different *pas de danse* and feats of horsemanship" in New York City on June 23, 1810. "Signor Victoriani" is probably the rope-dancer "Victorian" who performed in New York City in July 1809. Odell, *Annals*, 2:325, 2:346.

90. Theater performances in the *Ballston Spa Independent American*, 6 August 1811, 3, and 13 August 1811, 3.

91. *George Barnwell*, by George Lillo, had been a hit since its premiere in 1731, and had been produced hundreds of times in England and America. The play had gone through several periods of decline and revival but would be performed regularly in America well into the nineteenth century. Odell, *Annals*, notes productions in New York City in 1800, 1801, 1804, 1805 and 1813 in the period from 1798 to 1821. *The Lying Valet* was written by David Garrick. Phyllis Dirks, *David Garrick* (Boston: Twayne Publishers, 1985), 13–17, offers a succinct summary. Both *The Lying Valet* and *Barnwell* were probably produced by a single resident troupe that set up in Ballston for the weeks these performances ran. Both plays had four or five male parts and three or four female parts (depending on the script used). This meant that the company had to have some degree of organization and coherence, and it had to expect a significant return to cover expenses. Each performance was advertised as if it were running only one night,

but probably ran more performances depending on the take. Finally, at least in the newspaper advertisements, none of the actors was billed, which meant that none of them had "star power": they took it for granted that they would be unknown as individuals to the crowds at Ballston. Hence this may be the first appearance in America of the phenomenon that has since come to be known as "summer stock."

2. *Inventing the Resort*

1. It is important to distinguish Saratoga Springs from the nearby town of Saratoga, just as Ballston Spa is now distinct from the village of Ballston. (Confusingly, a separate village of Ballston was established outside of Ballston Spa after Ballston Spa was renamed.) All are in Saratoga County.

2. Thomas Chambers, *Drinking the Waters: Creating an American Leisure Class at Nineteenth-Century Mineral Springs* (Washington, D.C.: Smithsonian Institution Press, 2002), 33–34, more fully describes the Johnson legend, its uses, and its inaccuracies. Most evidence points to Johnson's cure being effected at the nearby Lebanon Springs. Henry Sigerist, "The Early Medical History of Saratoga Springs," *Bulletin of the History of Medicine* 13 (1943). All pre-1988 literature incorrectly dates Johnson's visit as 1767. Recent books on Saratoga include Jon Sterngass, *First Resorts: Pursuing Pleasure at Saratoga Springs, Newport, and Coney Island* (Baltimore: Johns Hopkins University Press, 2001); and Theodore Corbett, *The Making of American Resorts: Saratoga Springs, Ballston Spa, Lake George* (New Brunswick, NJ: Rutgers University Press, 2001). A valuable discussion of Saratoga in a later era is found in Myra Beth Young Armstead, *Lord, Please Don't Take Me in August: African Americans in Newport and Saratoga Springs* (Urbana: University of Illinois Press, 1999). There are a number of worthwhile older works on Saratoga. The two root books are Nathaniel B. Sylvester, *History of Saratoga County, New York: With Illustrations and Biographical Sketches* (Philadelphia: Everts & Ensign, 1878); and William L. Stone, *Reminiscences of Saratoga and Ballston* (New York: R. Worthington, 1880; full text available at www.rootsweb.com/~nysarato/Stone/Contents.html (accessed 24 June 2007). There are also a number of later popular histories such as Hugh Bradley, *Such Was Saratoga* (New York: Doubleday, 1940); and George Waller, *Saratoga: Saga of an Impious Era* (Englewood Cliffs, NJ: Prentice-Hall, 1966), but they tend to repeat in a more colorful way the already documented stories of the town.

3. Mrs. Abigail Dwight (mother of Theodore Dwight, profiled in chapter 7), quoted in Stone, *Reminiscences*, ch. 3.

4. Quoted in Theodore Dwight, *Summer Tours: or Notes of a Traveller through Some of the Middle and Northern States* (New York: 1847), 110.

5. Samuel Tenney, "An Account of a Number of Medicinal Springs at Saratoga . . . ," *Memoirs of the American Academy of Arts and Sciences* 2, no. 1 (1793): 43–61; quoted in Sigerist, "Early Medical History," 543. The analysis was written in 1783 but took ten years to come to print. Another analysis was Valentine Seaman, *A Dissertation on the Mineral Waters of Saratoga* (New York: Samuel Campbell, 1793).

6. Samuel Mitchill, "Medicinal Springs of Saratoga, Report on Experiments, Description of High Rock Spring," *The Rural Magazine or Vermont Repository* 1 (September 1795): 351–53. Excerpted in Jedidiah Morse, *The American Universal Geography, or, A View of the Present State of All the Empires . . .* (Philadelphia: Matthew Carey, 1796). Morse's geography went through many editions, including abridgements such as *Geography Made Easy* (Philadelphia: Matthew Carey, 1798 and onward). It became the standard reference work for travel writers and geographers and was widely excerpted (both credited and uncredited) in numerous later works.

7. James Read to Susan Read, 19 August 1797, Read-Eckard Letters, Historical Society of Delaware.

8. Putnam's house is described in Bradley, *Such Was Saratoga*, 48–49. Hanging in front of it was a famous sign showing Putnam's relative, Gen. Israel Putnam, pulling a wolf by its ears from its den. Some discussion of this legend is found in Chambers, "Fashionable Dis-Ease," 2–3. Putnam also improved Congress Spring, Saratoga's most central spring, by drilling down when the water stopped in 1804 and building the first enclosure around it. Today the spring emerges amid a formal, late-nineteenth-century fountain.

9. Timothy Howe, *A History of the Medicinal Springs at Saratoga and Ballstown, being a brief account of the situation, composition, operation, and effects of those celebrated waters . . .* (Brattleboro, VT: 1804); quoted in Sigerist, "Early Medical History," 563–68.

10. *Port Folio*, 30 October 1802, 340.

11. This traffic scheme did not stand the test of time, and by the early 1820s the streets had either been rerouted or terminated before they reached the springs.

12. Bradley, *Such Was Saratoga*, 51–52.

13. Ibid., 52–53.

14. The thousand-person estimate is in Timothy Bigelow, *Journal of a Tour to Niagara Falls* (Boston: John Wilson and Son, 1876), 14. A more reliable figure can be derived from the capacities of the various lodging places. The Sans Souci could house 150 relatively comfortably; Aldridge, as we have seen, could put up as many as a hundred. Figures for McMaster's (later Resolved Given's, 1809) are difficult to come by, but his house by all accounts was smaller than Aldridge's, with room for perhaps 75, and White's boarding house was about the same size. Rooms in private homes were also available, but could not have exceeded 100 to 150, as the permanent population of the village was only 800 in 1805.

15. Saratoga had six newspapers from 1804 to 1818, none of which lasted for more than a few years; the longest printed for six years, to judge by the holdings of the American Antiquarian Society.

16. The lending library, started by John Cook, was first mentioned in the *Ballston Spa Independent American*, 10 January 1809, 4. However, the library quickly suffered the fate of all libraries: after some months Cook ran an advertisement announcing that he had "lost several BOOKS . . . and as it is probable boarders may have left them in some of the houses," he requested owners to return them (*Independent American*, 1 October 1808).

17. The temperance society (the Moreau and Northumberland Temperance Soci-

ety, founded by Dr. Billy J. Clark) is claimed to be the first in the nation in Saratoga-printed sources such as W. Hay, *A History of Temperance in Saratoga County* (Saratoga Springs, 1855). These assertions are repeated in Bradley, *Such Was Saratoga*, 55; Waller, *Saratoga*, 62; Armstead, *Lord, Please Don't Take Me in August*, 11; and Corbett, *Making of American Resorts*, 191. Although there is no confirmation beyond the memories of Saratogans that this was, indeed, the first such group in the United States, and the date of its creation is uncertain, it is possible that it was among the nation's first temperance societies. However, none of major works about early temperance mention it: Ian Tyrrell, *Sobering Up: From Temperance to Prohibition in Antebellum America, 1800–1860* (Westport, CT: Greenwood Press, 1979); Thomas R. Pegram, *Battling Demon Rum: The Struggle for a Dry America, 1800–1933* (Chicago: Ivan R. Dee, 1998); John Rumbarger, *Profits, Power, and Prohibition: Alcohol Reform and the Industrialization of America, 1800–1930* (Albany: State University of New York Press, 1989); and Joel Bernard, "Between Religion and Reform: American Moral Societies, 1811–1821," *Proceedings of the Massachusetts Historical Society* 105 (1994): 1–9.

18. *Ballston Spa Independent American*, 4 August 1812, 3. This was, not incidentally, paralleled by "three seasons of hardship" in the New York theater, causing a re-ordering of that entertainment world. George Odell, *Annals of the New York Stage* (New York: Columbia University Press, 1927), 2:397.

19. Mrs. John Heard, 19 July 1815, Mrs. John Heard Journal, Mrs. J. Heard Collection, Massachusetts Historical Society.

20. *Ballston Spa Independent American*, 6 August 1813; *Saratoga Patriot*, 20 July 1812, 1; and Robert Ernst, "Nicholas Low: Merchant and Speculator in Post-Revolutionary New York," *New York History* 75, no. 4 (October 1994): 371.

21. *Ballston Spa Independent American*, 3 July 1816, 3.

22. *New York Herald*, 31 July 1816, 2.

23. *Ballston Spa Independent American*, 15 May 1816, 4; 31 July 1816, 3. Both were operated by Reuben Sears; by the July advertisement, he was in partnership with James Comstock.

24. *New York Herald*, 16 June 1816, 2. For a detailed meteorological survey of 1816 and discussion of its impact on the farm economy, see Joseph Hoyt, "The Cold Summer of 1816," *Annals of the Association of American Geographers* 48, no. 1 (March 1958): 118–31. Henry Stommel and Elizabeth Stommel, *Volcano Weather: The Story of 1816, the Year Without a Summer* (Newport, RI: Seven Seas Press, 1983), details the social and economic effects.

25. William Appleton Almanac, 1816, folder 64, box 34, Appleton Family Papers, Massachusetts Historical Society.

26. For evidence of prosperity at White Sulfur Springs, Virginia, during 1816, see Chambers, "Fashionable Dis-Ease," 18.

27. "Circus," *Ballston Spa Independent American*, 13 August 1817, 3.

28. "Spa Guests," *Ballston Spa Independent American*, 10 September 1817, 3.

29. Gideon Davison in the *Saratoga Sentinel*, 2 June 1819, 3.

30. Perhaps an indication of this was the 1816 disinvestment by Nicholas Low, who sold his land holdings there. However, Low was also in declining health and would die in 1818. Ernst, "Nicholas Low," 371.

31. Barnes Frisbie, *The History of Middletown, Vermont, in Three Discourses, Delivered*

before the Citizens of that Town (1867; repr. Middletown Springs Historical Society, 1976), 24–26. Fay's wife Lydia had been born and raised in Middletown, and it is probably through her that Fay found his apprentices, who included not only Gideon but Davison's cousin, Ovid Miner. Stone, *Reminiscences*, 313–17. Biographical information also on the Printer's Cards at the American Antiquarian Society, Worcester, Massachusetts. Davison and Fay cowrote a guidebook and history of the War of 1812, Gideon M. Davison and William Fay, *Sketches of the War, Between the United States and the British Isles: Intended as a Faithful History of All the Material Events from the Time of the Declaration in 1812* (Rutland, VT: Fay and Davison, 1815).

32. Dr. John Steel, *An Analysis of the Mineral Waters of Saratoga and Ballston* (Albany: E. & E. Hosford, 1817). It widely quoted in later geographical and travel literature and was also important in spreading the reputation of Saratoga.

33. The American Antiquarian Society has a full run of the *Saratoga Sentinel*.

34. *Saratoga Sentinel*, vol. 1, no. 1, 1. Emphasis in original.

35. The phrase comes from Paul Starr, *The Creation of the Media: Political Origins of Modern Communications* (New York: Basic Books, 2004), 83. Studies of reading and literacy include William Gilmore, *Reading Becomes a Necessity of Life: Material and Cultural Life in Rural New England, 1780–1835* (Knoxville: University of Tennessee Press, 1989); and David Henkin, *City Reading: Written Words and Public Spaces in Antebellum New York* (New York: Columbia University Press, 1998).

36. For example, the catalog of the American Antiquarian Society lists eight distinct Ballston Spa and Saratoga Springs newspapers (that is, with different publishers) from 1804 to 1820. A further three represent existing papers whose names were changed. At this time the total permanent population of Saratoga County ranged from around 24,000 in 1800 to 36,000 in 1820, according to the U.S. Census. Note that this development happened long before the "penny press" phenomenon, which is more associated with the 1830s and after. For a description, see Edwin G. Burrows and Mike Wallace, *Gotham* (New York: Oxford University Press, 1999), 676–78.

37. Starr, *The Creation of the Media*, 87–92.

38. The American Antiquarian Society holds runs of the six surviving Saratoga newspapers in its collection. They date from 1804 to 1818: the Saratoga *Advertiser*, *Patriot*, *Journal*, *Courier*, *Republican*, and the *Rural Visiter* [sic] *& Saratoga Advertiser*. None of them lasted more than six or seven years; most folded after a year or two.

39. Another factor was the strength of Saratoga's springs. Ballston Spa had problems maintaining the water flow of its springs, and they lessened year by year. But the social factors were just as important, if not more so. For a description of Ballston's water problems, see Corbett, *Making of American Resorts*, 37–38.

40. Walton was a wealthy lawyer. His family had been loyalist during the Revolution, and he had been educated in England. He returned some years later and until 1808 lived in Ballston on an estate five miles from the springs, on land his family had held since before the Revolution. After living in New York for seven years, he moved to Saratoga in 1815. Corbett, *Making of American Resorts*, 16–17, 37. The Pavilion was built and run by Nathan Lewis, a master carpenter.

41. Corbett is particularly good on the parkland around the hotel. Ibid., 87, 238.

42. See the Pavilion's large display ads in *New-York Evening Post*, for example 7, 8, 9, 10, 12, 13 July 1819; the largest front-page advertisement appeared on 10 July 1819.

43. Corbett, *Making of American Resorts*, 87–89. The Pavilion burned down in 1843.

44. Chambers, "Fashionable Dis-Ease," 44–45. Samuel Mordecai to Ellen Mordecai, 3 August 1817, folder 13, subseries 1.2, Mordecai Family Papers, Southern Historical Collection. "New Lebanon Springs," *New York Evening Post*, 18 June 1823, 3. Schooley Mountain ads: *New York Evening Post*, 25 May 1820, 1; 22 June 1822, 2. Both Ballston and Saratoga touted and sold their waters; Saratoga's marketing campaign was far more successful. See also Gerard Koeppel, *Water for Gotham: A History* (Princeton: Princeton University Press, 2000), 121.

45. *Saratoga Sentinel*, 2 June 1819, 3.

46. There are very few solid figures for visitors to hotels to the southern spas at this time, but these hotels tended to be significantly smaller, and it is safe to say that the numbers were smaller as well. See Chambers, *Drinking the Waters*. As for other regions of the United States, outside the cities there were no large hotels save at Saratoga Springs; this includes New England, which would not see rural tourism for another decade or more.

47. *Saratoga Sentinel*, 11 August 1819, 3.

48. *Saratoga Sentinel*, 21 July 1819, 3.

49. For example, Davison's report from August 2, 1820 (including the line "about one thousand strangers partook of the waters of the Congress Spring on Sunday morning last") was printed verbatim in the *New-York Evening Post*, 6 August 1820, 2.

50. For a detailed overview of the society of courtship at the springs in the antebellum era, see Chambers, *Drinking the Waters*, ch. 5. He describes it as an "elite national marriage market." Corbett argues that this did not exist, that spa life was based mainly on "chivalry, the display of manners, rather than the serious business of marriage." Corbett, *Making of American Resorts*, 220–22.

51. Finding Aid, Codman Family Papers, Historic New England, Boston. Another indication of the regal status of Ogden and her circle comes from a watercolor by John Searles, *Prominent New Yorkers at the Park Theatre, Nov. 1822*, which belongs to the New-York Historical Society and is reproduced (with key) in Edward Pessen, "The Egalitarian Myth and the American Social Reality: Wealth, Mobility, and Equality in the 'Era of the Common Man,' " *American Historical Review* 76, no. 4 (October 1971): 1002, and *Riches, Class, and Power before the Civil War* (Lexington, MA: D. C. Heath, 1973), 20. It is also reproduced in Foster Rhea Dulles, *A History of Recreation* (New York: Appleton-Century-Crofts, 1965), plate following p. 106. Ogden sits prominently in a central box, her scarf dangling from the rail, surrounded by her Bayard and LeRoy relatives.

52. None of the previous letters surviving at Historic New England (formerly the Society for the Preservation of New England Antiquities) mention any suitors taken seriously by Sarah or Catharine Bayard (their author) take seriously. "The Stricken Deer," item 9, folder 321, Codman Family Papers.

53. Charles L. Ogden to David A. Ogden, 23 August 1820, item 15, folder 321, Codman Family Papers.

54. Catharine Bayard to Sarah Ogden, 30 August 1820, 23 October 1820, Codman Family Papers; and E.S.?, "To Miss S.O. on Returning to Her the *Ballston Poetry*," January 1821, item 8, folder 322, Codman Family Papers.

55. Rebecca Cornell Edwards Ogden to Sarah Ogden, n.d. 1822, item 1, folder 323, Codman Family Papers.

56. In the end, Sarah Ogden would not marry until she was thirty-seven, quite old by the standards of the day. In 1836 she met a prominent Boston widower, Charles Russell Codman. They married, and she would have four children by him in what to all accounts was a happy marriage. Sarah Ogden Codman died of consumption (probably tuberculosis) at the age of forty-three. Finding Aid, Codman Family Papers.

57. Sheldon Hanft, "Mordecai's Female Academy," *American Jewish History* 79, no. 1 (Autumn 1989): 72–93. More information about this fascinating early Jewish-American family can be found in Emily Bingham, *Mordecai: An Early American Family* (New York: Hill and Wang, 2004); Ruth Nuermberger, "Some Notes on the Mordecai Family," *Virginia Magazine of History and Biography* 49 (1941): 364–73; and William Barlow and David O. Powell, "A Dedicated Medical Student: Solomon Mordecai, 1819–1822," *Journal of the Early Republic* 7 (Winter, 1987): 377–97.

58. Description of his journey: Solomon Mordecai to Ellen Mordecai, 3 August 1817; Solomon to Ellen Mordecai, 10 July 1817. Digestive ailments: 20 July 1817, Solomon to Caroline Mordecai, all folder 13, subseries 1.2, Mordecai Family Papers.

59. Solomon to Ellen Mordecai, 10 July 1817; Solomon to Julia Mordecai, 30 July 1817 ("Saratoga—or both"), all folder 12, subseries 1.3, Mordecai Family Papers.

60. Solomon to Ellen Mordecai, 3 August 1817, Mordecai Family Papers.

61. All of the unmarried Mordecai men were frustrated by the small number of available Jewish women. His brother Moses had given up the search and become engaged to a Gentile. Now in his last summer as a bachelor, Moses was spending the season at the Virginia Springs. From there he wrote Mordecai a letter that cryptically referred to this problem faced by all of his brothers: "On your return thr NY. Phila. & Balt. do not let your investigations be confined to the works of the trowel, the chisel or the pencil—but *search out among the fairest of natures work some specimens from which your brothers & yourself may stock their cabinets*—Were I alone in the world I believe I could even furnish my own . . . it is time we should act instead of speak." Moses to Solomon Mordecai, 8 August 1817, Mordecai Family Papers. Emphasis added.

62. Solomon to Caroline Mordecai, 8 August 1817, Mordecai Family Papers.

63. Solomon to Caroline Mordecai, 10 August 1817, Mordecai Family Papers.

64. According to Chambers, by the mid-1830s some social restraints were being put on these cross-cultural and cross-class meetings by creating clubs that limited spontaneous introductions and courtship. It is uncertain how effective these measures were, however. See Chambers, *Drinking the Waters*, 138. As for Solomon Mordecai in 1817, he stayed at Saratoga for weeks more than the poor hunting would have suggested. A travel companion he had met on the Hudson River steamboat fell ill, and Solomon cancelled his inchoate plans to go on to Niagara or elsewhere and instead became a nurse to his friend. Although there

is no direct evidence linking this episode with his eventual decision to become a doctor, it is intriguing that in 1819, soon after his father sold their school for a substantial amount of money, Solomon entered the Medical School of the University of Pennsylvania, where he became an M.D. in 1822. He remained a bachelor until 1824, when he married a Gentile, Caroline Waller. Barlow and Powell, "Dedicated Medical Student," 377; and Nuermberger, "Some Notes," 369.

3. *The Revolution of Seeing*

1. This transition is described in a number of works. Two of the most influential are Perry Miller, *Errand into the Wilderness* (Cambridge: Belknap Press, 1956); and Roderick Nash, *Wilderness and the American Mind* (New Haven: Yale University Press, 1967). Others include Raymond O'Brien, *American Sublime: Landscape and Scenery of the Lower Hudson Valley* (New York: Columbia University Press, 1981); Hans Huth, *Nature and the American* (Berkeley: University of California Press, 1957); Leo Marx, *The Machine in the Garden: Technology and the Pastoral Ideal in America* (New York: Oxford University Press, 1964); and Paul Shepard, *Man in the Landscape: A Historic View of the Esthetics of Nature* (New York: Alfred Knopf, 1967).

2. Edmund Burke, *A Philosophical Enquiry into the Origin of our Ideas of the Sublime and Beautiful* (1757; repr. Oxford: Basil Blackwell, 1987).

3. Jean-Jacques Rousseau, "Discourse on the Origin of Inequality Among Men," in *The First and Second Discourses and Essays on the Origins of Languages*, trans. Victor Gourevitch (New York: Harper Collins, 1986), 140.

4. See note 14.

5. His first artistic publication was *An Essay on Prints . . .* (London: J. Robson, 1768), which earned him some fame and a school headmaster's position that allowed him time to travel around the British Islands. His notes and sketches became five completed manuscripts, and the first was published in 1782. Highly influential works on the aesthetics and theory of picturesque scenery followed: *Remarks on Forest Scenery and other Woodland Views* (1790) and *Three Essays: on Picturesque Beauty; on Picturesque Travel; and on Sketching Landscape* (1792). The Oxford English Dictionary notes Gilpin's 1768 use of the word *picturesque* as one of the earliest in a book title. (The first cited use is in Richard Steele's play *The Tender Husband* in 1703.)

6. The main biographical profiles of Gilpin are "Gilpin, William," *Dictionary of National Biography*, ed. Sir Leslie Stephen and Sidney Lee (Oxford: Oxford University Press, 1886), 7:1262–64; William D. Templeman, *The Life and Work of William Gilpin (1724–1804), Master of the Picturesque and Vicar of Boldre* (Urbana: University of Illinois Press, 1939); and Carl Paul Barbier, *William Gilpin: His Drawings, Teaching, and Theory of the Picturesque* (Oxford: Clarendon Press, 1963).

7. A good brief review of this history is found in Bruce Robertson, "The Picturesque Traveler in America," in *Views and Visions: American Landscape before 1830*, ed. Edward Nuygren and Robertson (Washington, D.C.: Corcoran Gallery, 1986), 189–90.

8. This interpretation is widely accepted. See, for example, William Gilmore, *Reading Becomes a Necessity of Life: Material and Cultural Life in Rural New England, 1780–1835* (Knoxville: University of Tennessee Press, 1989), 212 and elsewhere, which describes the United States of 1820 as still being, in many ways, an intellectual province of Great Britain. See also Oswaldo Rodrigues Roque, "The Exaltation of American Landscape Painting," in *American Paradise: The World of the Hudson River School*, ed. John Howat (New York: Metropolitan Museum of Art, 1987), 21–22. A rare dissenting voice to this consensus is J. Meredith Neil, *Toward a National Taste: America's Quest for Aesthetic Independence* (Honolulu: University Press of Hawaii, 1975), which argues that a distinct national taste had developed long before 1815, and that in painting, for example, the foundations for the Hudson River School had been laid in the first decades of the century by painters such as Benjamin West (106–39). But he does concede that "the American school of painting, prior to the 1820s, remained a potential rather than an actual development" (125).

9. The literary roots of an American picturesque movement can also be found in the work of Charles Brockden Brown, especially in *Edgar Huntly* (1799). But although Brown's works were modestly popular, they did not achieve the remarkably wide reach of Scott's, which cut across class lines and were much more widely distributed. Brown's writings also came too early; although they had some influence among the most progressive elements of the gentry, it took another generation for their ideas to have wide credence even among the gentry. For advocacy of Brown's role, see Dennis Berthold, "Charles Brockden Brown, 'Edgar Huntly,' and the Origins of the American Picturesque," *William and Mary Quarterly*, 3rd ser., 41, no. 1 (January 1984): 62–84. Bryant's *A Forest Hymn* (1824) is often cited as a part of this movement, although it comes relatively late. A brief but useful discussion of the spread of romantic thought and literature and attitudes toward it in America is Jean Matthews, *Toward a New Society: American Thought and Culture, 1800–1830* (Boston: Twayne Publishers, 1991), 120–23.

10. William B. Todd and Ann Bowden, *Sir Walter Scott: A Bibliographic History, 1796–1832* (New Castle, DE: Oak Knoll Press, 1998), 554–56. See also Emily B. Todd, "Walter Scott and the Nineteenth-Century American Literary Marketplace: Antebellum Richmond Readers and the Collected Editions of the Waverley Novels," *Papers of the Bibliographical Society of America* 93, no. 4 (1999): 495–517; David Kaser, "Waverley in America," *Papers of the Bibliographical Society of America* 51 (1957): 163–67; and David A. Randall, "Waverley in America," *Colophon*, n.s., 1 (Summer 1935): 39–55.

11. Kathryn Sutherland, "Walter Scott and Washington Irving: 'Editors of the land of Utopia.'" *Journal of American Studies* 10, no. 1 (1976): 85–90.

12. As Edward is about to meet the Highland chief, Flora's brother, he "prepared himself to meet a stern, gigantic, ferocious figure, such as Salvator would have chosen to be the central object of a group of banditti." Walter Scott, *Waverley* (1814; repr. London: Oxford University Press, 1981), 80. Further studies of this theme are in Eric G. Walter, *Scott's Fiction and the Picturesque* (Salzburg: Institut für Anglistik und Amerikanistik, Universität Salzburg, 1982); Barton Thurber, "Scott and the Sublime," and Alexander M. Ross, " 'Waverley' and the Pic-

turesque," both in *Scott and His Influence: The Papers of the Aberdeen Scott Conference, 1982* (Aberdeen: Association for Scottish Literary Studies, 1983), 87–89, 99–108.

13. For a good explanation of this dynamic, see George G. Dekker, *The Fictions of Romantic Tourism: Radcliffe, Scott, and Mary Shelley* (Stanford, CA: Stanford University Press, 2005), esp. 126–53.

14. The many instances of the use of the word "sublime" in travel accounts before 1820 include, for example, Harriet Horry's 1793 diary: "Here is one of the most sublime and grand views that can be imagined" (about the Hudson Valley near West Point; 22 July 1793, Pinckney-Lowndes Papers, 34–81, South Carolina Historical Society, Charleston, South Carolina); Mary Murray's diary: "My expectations were great, but they seem'd as nothing compared with the awful the sublime reality" (Niagara; 8 June 1808, New York Historical Society); Drayton? Journal: "The sail [up the Hudson] is really delightful. . . . But beautiful & charming as this expansive scene may appear, it is much inferior when compared with the sublime & awful view on entering the highlands . . ." (11 July 1810, Drayton? Papers, South Carolina Historical Society); and Mrs. John Heard's 1815 travel diary, describing a valley in the Berkshire Mountains in Massachusetts, Chippewa Falls, and (14 July 1815) Niagara Falls: "the imagination—if it is wrought to the highest pitch—must last—far short of the reality of this sublime & grand scene of nature" (Mrs. J. Heard Papers, Massachusetts Historical Society).

15. This is not to say that American scenery was not represented at all. For a landscape of a recognizable American site to be acceptable in the American market, it had to have several elements. Most crucially, it needed to depict signs of civilization: a farm, cleared fields, order. For example, Francis Guy of Baltimore earned modest acclaim specializing in painting the stately manor homes of his patrons. There were exceptions, most notably in the depiction of Niagara Falls. Even then, though, the paintings were never allowed to be totally wild; some recognizably Euro-American or European human figure had to be inserted. A few painters, such as Thomas Doughty of Philadelphia, did do American landscapes, but always within the ideal of the picturesque, with well-ordered renderings in carefully balanced compositions. For a discussion of these early painters in the context of the Hudson River School and the creation of an American landscape tradition, see William Gerdts, "American Landscape Painting: Critical Judgments, 1730–1845," *Art Journal* (Winter 1985): 28–59.

16. For example, the valley's Highlands had become such an attraction that in 1821 the North River Steamboat Company advertised day trips to "take an opportunity of viewing the sublime and picturesque scenery" there, returning to New York City by evening. "Steam-Boats," *New-York Evening Post*, 4 August 1821, 2.

17. There is scant literature on Wall, who left neither papers nor any other documentary information and whose death in Ireland happened at some unknown date after 1864. See Mark W. Sullivan, "Wall, William Guy," *Dictionary of American Art* (New York: MacMillan, 1996), 799; "Wall, William Guy," *Who Was Who in American Art, 1564–1975* (Madison, CT: Soundview Press, 1999), 3448–49; Donald A. Shelley, "William Guy Wall and His Watercolors for the Historic *Hudson River Portfolio*," *New-York Historical Society Quarterly* 31, no. 1

(January 1947): 25–45; and John K. Howat, "A Picturesque Site in the Catskills: The Kaaterskill Falls as Painted by William Guy Wall," *Honolulu Academy of Art Journal* 1 (1974): 17–30. Christopher Finch credits Wall and the *Port Folio* for doing "much to spread interest in landscape painting . . . [and giving] impetus to the Hudson River School." Finch, *American Watercolors* (New York: Abbeville Press, 1986), 41.

18. Aquatinting is an etching process that creates prints with delicate shading and colors, "ideally suited to the reproduction of late 18th-century British watercolors." Craig Hartley, "Aquatint," *The Grove Dictionary of Art*, ed. Jane Turner (New York: Macmillan Publishers, 1996), 2:240. James Flexner posits that John Hill commissioned the prints, but Richard J. Koke notes that Hill submitted his bills to the printer, Henry Megarey. See Flexner, *The Light of Distant Skies* (New York: Dover Publications, 1969), 186; and Koke, *A Checklist of the American Engravings of John Hill (1770–1850), Master of Aquatint* (New York: New-York Historical Society, 1961), 29.

19. Agg's story is unusual. A British author, he wrote a number of parodies and whimsies under pseudonyms between 1812 and 1817, including one piece purporting to have been by Lord Byron (who objected strongly to it). He emigrated to New York in September 1820 at the age of 36; after he penned the *Port Folio* entries, he disappears from the records. Elizabeth P. Bentley, *Passenger Arrivals at the Port of New York, 1820–1829* (Baltimore: Genealogical Publishing Co., 1999), 7.

20. *New-York Evening Post*, 9 June 1823, 2. For a complete history of the run, see Koke, *A Checklist*, 29–41. A previous work by John Hill, *Picturesque Views of American Scenery*, should also be mentioned. It never had the success of the *Port Folio*. A series of twenty aquatints from paintings by Joshua Shaw printed from 1819 to 1821, only three of the four "numbers" were printed, implying poor sales. The images chosen ranged from Washington's tomb to views of Schuylkill Falls in Pennsylvania to images of Norfolk, Fayetteville, and Boston. Koke, *A Checklist*, 14–26.

21. Richard Koke, comp., *A Catalog of the Collection, including Historical, Narrative, and Marine Art* (New York: New-York Historical Society, 1982). The New-York Historical Society has a very rare complete set of the prints.

22. This can be seen in *Hudson River Port Folio*, plates 19 ("Palisadoes"), 13 ("Hudson"), and 16 ("West Point"). In plate 15 ("View from Fishkill"), the boat is steaming southward. (Note that there are two plates numbered 15; the other is called "Hudson.")

23. Ibid., plate 1 ("Little Falls at Luzerne").

24. Ibid., plate 22 ("View near Ft. Montgomery") in 1822 edition; in the 1828 edition, it is plate 18.

25. Ibid., plate 7 ("View near Sandy Hill"), plate 3 ("View near Jessup's Landing"), and plate 7 ("View near Sandy Hill").

26. Ibid., plate 2 ("Meeting of the Hudson and Sacandaga"), plate 10 ("Fort Edward").

27. Louis Legrand Noble, *The Life and Works of Thomas Cole* (1853; Cambridge: Belknap Press, 1964), 32–33; see also Ellwood Parry III, "Thomas Cole's Early

Career: 1818–1829," in *Views and Visions: American Landscape before 1830*, ed. Edward Nygern with Bruce Robertson (Washington, D.C.: Corcoran Gallery, 1986), 161–67. Descriptions of Cole's early influences can be found in Tracie Felker, "Thomas Cole's Drawings of His 1825 Trip Up the Hudson River," *American Art Journal* 24 (1992): 60–67.

28. Ellwood Parry III determined the time frame for Cole's journey, based mainly on the fact that he already had five finished paintings from this trip ready for sale by late October. See Parry, *The Art of Thomas Cole: Ambition and Imagination* (Newark: University of Delaware Press, 1988), 24.

29. Tracie Felker, "First Impressions: Thomas Cole's Drawings of His 1825 Trip Up the Hudson River," *American Art Journal* 24, nos. 1–2 (1992): 60–67. For more on the Supreme Court ruling, see chapter 9.

30. Gideon Davison, *Fashionable Tour* (1822), 30–31. Today the Hudson is dammed at Cohoes Falls; save for a spillway, the falls are dry.

31. Felker reproduces three pages of Cole's notes (figs. 1, 2, 3), which describe the location and subject of each sketch. Felker, "First Impressions," 61–62. For more on Pine Orchard, see chapter 5.

32. Holes drilled into the rock for the supporting poles, now filled with rust, still exist at the top of the falls. One other early image of the falls, undated but probably contemporaneous with Cole's, survives: Thomas Hilson's *Platform and Hut Overlooking Cauterskill Falls*, pencil on paper, c. 1825–30, Museum of Fine Arts, Boston. As one tourist's account from 1827 describes, "the falls . . . [are] 2½ miles from the mountain house, situated in the Mountains . . . [at] the top of the falls . . . there is a Mill & house with refreshments." Francis J. Dallam Diary, 24 July 1827, Dallam Papers, ms. 1250, box 2, Maryland Historical Society, Baltimore, Maryland. The platform is mentioned in the 1824 travel account of Charles West Thomson, 2 August 1824, C. W. [Charles West] Thompson Papers, box IV, New-York Historical Society.

33. Felker, "First Impressions," 76–81; see figs. 16 (Cole's sketch no. 17), 19 (Cole's no. 19, face), 20 (Cole's no. 19, verso). The immediate surroundings at the top of the falls, with mention of the "house of the guide," are described in Henry Dilworth Gilpin, *A Northern Tour: Being a Guide to Saratoga, Lake George, Niagara, Canada, Boston, &c. &c.* (Philadelphia: Carey & Lea, 1825), 40.

34. These paintings are "unlocated." Parry, "Thomas Cole's Early Career," 169.

35. Also "unlocated" today. A copy of that painting, *View of Kaaterskill Falls* (today exhibited as *Kaaterskill Falls*), was commissioned in 1826 by Daniel Wadsworth, John Trumbull's nephew-in-law, and hangs in the Wadsworth Athenaeum in Hartford, Connecticut. Kenneth John Myers, "Selling the Sublime: The Catskills and the Social Construction of Landscape Experience in the United States, 1776–1876" (PhD diss., Yale University, 1990), 174n11.

36. *New-York Evening Post*, 22 November 1825, 2.

37. After aesthetics and politics, Cole's relations with his patrons are the most examined aspect of his life. Studies include Larry Sullivan and Mary Alice Mackay, "Another Clue to Thomas Cole," *Arts Magazine* 60, no. 5 (January 1986): 68–71; Barbara Novak, "Thomas Cole and Robert Gilmor," *Art Quarterly* 25, no. 1 (Spring 1962): 41–53; Thomas Cole, *The Correspondence of Thomas Cole and Daniel Wadsworth* (Hartford: Connecticut Historical Society, 1983);

Alan Wallach, "Thomas Cole and the Aristocracy," *Arts Magazine* 56, no. 3 (November 1981): 94–106, and "Thomas Cole: Landscape and the Course of American Empire," in *Thomas Cole: Landscape into History*, ed. William H. Truettner and Alan Wallach (New Haven: Yale University Press, 1994), esp. section 2, "Aristocratic Patronage," 34–38.

38. See, for example, Sullivan and Mackay, "Another Clue to Thomas Cole," 68–71, which details the correspondence between Cole and Daniel Wadsworth, for whom Cole would paint a number of works.

39. Davison, *Fashionable Tour* (1822), 13.

40. Parry, "Thomas Cole's Early Career," 169.

41. Davison, *Fashionable Tour* (1822), 30–31.

42. Gilpin, *Northern Tour*, 58–59.

43. The "Indian over the falls" motif was often repeated. For example, two of these stories set at Niagara Falls are found in Carl David Arfwedson, *The United States and Canada in 1832, 1833, and 1834* (1834; repr. New York: Johnson Reprint Corporation, 1969), 2:318; and in Isaac Weld Jr., *Travels through the States of North America.* . . . In each case, the victim, discovering that it was too late to prevent his slide over the falls, with "great composure" (Weld) "laid himself down quietly" (Arfwedson) in his canoe and resigned himself to his fate.

44. Alf Evers, *The Catskills: From Wilderness to Woodstock* (New York: Doubleday, 1972), 351.

45. "The falls . . . [are] fed by a small Lake . . . after going to the top of the falls . . . we then went below and walked around the sheat of water, which is small, but by raising the gate Letting the water out of the dam, the effect is very handsome." Francis Dallam, Dallam 1827 Diary, Maryland Historical Society.

46. I am deeply indebted to Kenneth Myers's analysis of *Lake* and *Falls* in "Selling the Sublime," 172–81, which outlines the subtexts discussed in this paragraph and describes Cole's fondness for pairing his paintings to create a didactic message. William Leete Stone noted the irony of the dam atop the falls, speculating that it had been "dammed up the water so as to nearly destroy the beauty of the cascade at pleasure, and when visitors come . . . [the owner] lets off the waters as a matter of favor . . . [and] duns everyone to pay for it." Stone, "Ten Days in the Country," *New-York Commercial Advertiser*, 7 September 1824.

47. Featherstonehaugh was instrumental in creating one of America's first railroads, the Mohawk and Hudson, which would be connected to another very early railroad, the Saratoga and Mohawk. Together, in 1831, they would create Saratoga's rail link to the world. Simon Baatz, "Featherstonehaugh, George William," in *American National Biography*, vol. 7, ed. John Garraty and Mark Carnes (New York: Oxford University Press, 1999), 783–85.

48. Cole's images of the falls would be reproduced in, for example, J. H. Hinton, *The History and Topography of the United States*, vol. 2 (Philadelphia: Thomas Wardle, 1832); he would also inspire imitators, such as Thomas Doughty, whose engraving of *Catskill Falls* appeared in the 1827 *Atlantic Souvenir*.

4. *Travel Literature, the Fashionable Tour, and the Spread of Tourism*

1. William Gilmore, *Reading Becomes a Necessity of Life: Material and Cultural Life in Rural New England, 1780–1835* (Knoxville: University of Tennessee Press, 1989), 192. For the post-1790 growth of travel books, see 26.

2. Roger Haydon has described the surge of British travelers writing and publishing their travels after the War of 1812. Many of these accounts were contested by Americans, and they soon began to publish and purchase their own travel accounts. Haydon, *Upstate Travels: British Views of Nineteenth-Century New York* (Syracuse, NY: Syracuse University Press, 1982), xii.

3. A study of 130 travel articles and reviews in American magazines has found that in the period from 1782 to 1810, the vast majority of articles (114, or 86%) described travel in all parts of Europe, with a strong emphasis on Grand Tour sites (64). Only 6 articles discussed New World travel in that entire period (less than half of one percent). But in the five years from 1811 to 1815, the overall frequency of travel articles increased (81 in that period), the percentage of European articles decreased (52, or 64%), and the number of articles on New World travel tripled, to 18 (22%). Furthermore, they shifted emphasis toward picturesque areas rather than the highly developed Grand Tour sites. J. Meredith Neil, *Toward a National Taste: America's Quest for Aesthetic Independence* (Honolulu: University Press of Hawaii, 1975), 247; see also ch. 9, "From Grand Tour to the Romantic Traveller," 236–66.

4. For example, William Darby's appendix on Ballston ran to seven pages. William Darby, *A Tour from the City of New York, to Detroit* (1819; repr. New York: Quadrangle Books, 1962), appendix 3.

5. "To Travellers," *New-York Evening Post*, 21 June 1820, 2. The city guide was probably *The Picture of New-York and Stranger's Guide Through the Commercial Emporium of the United States* (New York: A. T. Goodrich & Co., 1818).

6. Goodrich ads can be found in the *New-York Evening Post*, 2 June, 9 July, 14 August 1821.

7. Gideon M. Davison, *The Fashionable Tour: or, a Trip to the Springs, Niagara, Quebeck, and Boston, in the Summer of 1821* (Saratoga Springs, NY: G. M. Davison, 1822). Perhaps not coincidentally, Davison sold his guide at Goodrich's New York store.

8. There is a wide and valuable body of academic work on the Grand Tour. A concise and coherent explanation can be found in Fred Inglis, *The Delicious History of the Holiday* (New York: Routledge, 2000), esp. ch. 2. Jeremy Black, *The British Abroad: The Grand Tour in the Eighteenth Century* (New York: St. Martin's Press, 1992) provides hard data and a cogent analysis. Lynne Withey, *Grand Tours and Cook's Tours: A History of Leisure Travel, 1750–1915* (New York: William Morrow, 1997) gives a good overall survey of worldwide travel, including both the American and the European tours. Christopher Hibbert, *The Grand Tour* (London: Thames Methuen, 1987) is lively and colorful. An important earlier work is William Edward Mead, *The Grand Tour in the Eighteenth Century* (Boston: Houghton Mifflin, 1914). Explorations on the idea of nation by leisure travelers can be found in Russell Chamberlain, *The Idea of England* (London: Thames and Hudson, 1986); and Margaret R. Hunt, "Racism, Im-

perialism, and the Traveler's Gaze in Eighteenth-Century England," *Journal of British Studies* 32, no. 4 (October 1993). It is possible that the example of American tourism, with its emphasis on fast, mechanized travel, was copied just a few years later during the reemergence of Rhine River tourism, which even in times of peace was often difficult and uncomfortable.

9. Isaac Ball to John Ball Jr., 29 June, 11 July, 3 September, 13 September, and 6 October 1806, Ball Family Papers, folders 28 and 29, South Caroliniana Library, University of South Carolina, Columbia, South Carolina.

10. See, for example, the travels of John Pintard, who rarely left New York for more than a week or two. See *Letters from John Pintard to His Daughter* (New York: New-York Historical Society Collections, 1940–1941), vols. 1–4 (1816–1833). Edward Pessen found that 78 percent of the wealthiest New Yorkers remained active merchants. It was frowned upon for southern plantation owners to leave their estates for the summer, but the very presence of such complaints in the literature of the time indicates that it was a not entirely uncommon occurrence. Edward Pessen, *Riches, Class, and Power before the Civil War* (Lexington, MA: D. C. Heath, 1973), 46–75, esp. table 4-1 on 47.

11. See Mary Murray, "Journal from New York to Niagara [8 June to 7 July 1808]", 18 June 1808, New-York Historical Society. There were other places where the route of the tour appears, but all are from the post-1812 period. See, for example, Philip Stansbury, *A Pedestrian Tour of Two Thousand Three Hundred Miles in North America* (New York: J. D. Myers & W. Smith, 1822), v.; and C. C. Sebring, in *Prominent Features of a Northern Tour* (Charleston, SC: Printed for the author, 1822) described following the Fashionable Tour route (although he does not call it that) in 1822. See also Catharine Maria Sedgwick to Henry D. Sedgwick and Jane Minot Sedgwick, 22 June 1821: "We have begun the grand tour." Catharine Maria Sedgwick Papers, Massachusetts Historical Society, Boston, series III, folder 2, item 15.

12. Catherine Bayard to Sarah (Sally) Ogden (later Codman), 13 July 1818, item 3, folder 320, box 21, Codman Family Collections, Historic New England, Boston.

13. On the origins of guidebooks see Richard Gassan, "The First American Tourist Guidebooks: Authorship and the Print Culture of the 1820s," *Book History* 8 (2005), 51–74, modified portions of which appear here.

14. Davison, *Fashionable Tour* (1822), 26, 83.

15. Ibid., 10.

16. The examples in the collections of the American Antiquarian Society are 15 cm (5.9 inches) high and around 6 cm (2.5 inches) wide.

17. Davison, *Fashionable Tour* (1822), 3.

18. No real conclusions can be drawn from its bindings because at the time most books were sold in sheets (either loose or lightly stitched). Purchasers would then pay to have them bound together. Later editions of the book, and those of his later competitors, were sold already bound (rather than unbound), often with nicely decorated covers, probably because they were intended for eye-catching sale and immediate consumption.

19. For a discussion of the Knickerbockers' concern about their city and society's future, see Stephen Nissenbaum, *The Battle for Christmas* (New York: Alfred. A. Knopf, 1996), esp. 55–65.

20. A good short sketch of Irving's writing career can be found in *Washington Irving: Letters, Volume 1 (1802–23)*, ed. Ralph Aderman, Herbert Kleinfield, and Jenifer Banks (Boston: Twayne Publishers, 1978), xxiii–lvi.

21. Richard D. Rust, ed., *The Complete Works of Washington Irving* (Boston: Twayne, 1978), 29.

22. A similar goal was being pursued in painting. See chapter 5, page 87, for travelers' citing of Irving

23. Irving, *Complete Works*, 272. Irving had spent many summers at the Hudson Highlands home of a friend, Capt. Frederick Philipse. Irving writes from or about Philipse's home many times in his letters; see, for example, Irving to Henry Brevoort, 22 September 1810, *Letters*, 1:288–89; Philipse was a close member of Irving's circle of friends, which included Henry Brevoort, James K. Paulding, and Henry Ogden. *Letters*, 1:219n. There is a large literature about the various origins of the stories in the *Sketch Book*; see, for example, Walter Reichart, *Washington Irving and Germany* (Ann Arbor: University of Michigan Press, 1957), 23; and Stanley Williams, *The Life of Washington Irving* (New York: Oxford University Press, 1935).

24. Dwight's standing was lessened somewhat by his participation in the Federalist Hartford Convention (1814), which was accused, probably correctly, of having espoused a secessionist agenda for New England. In any case, the public's perception of Federalist perfidy in the face of war led to the destruction of the party.

25. Timothy Dwight, *Travels in New England and New York* (1822; repr., edited by Barbara Miller Solomon, Cambridge, MA: Belknap Press, 1969). Much more on Theodore Dwight, writer of a popular tourist guidebook, in chapter 7.

26. So many of the existing published travel accounts had been written by foreigners, mainly Britons, that a backlash had developed against them. An early example of this was an essay Irving wrote in the *Sketch Book*, "English Writers on America," a gentle criticism of their mistaken notions of Americans. The backlash heightened in the 1820s: see, for example, the lengthy and scathing review of Basil Hall's *Travels in the United States and Canada* in the *North American Review* 29, no. 4 (October 1829): 522–75.

27. For example, New York City's Delancey Street was named for the family.

28. Perhaps the best recent profile of James Fenimore Cooper is found in Alan Taylor, *William Cooper's Town* (New York: Knopf, 1996), passim. For a neat disposal of the traditional story that William Cooper had been murdered, see 363–71. However he died, it was shocking for the Cooper family.

29. For a discussion of Cooper's turn to writing, see Taylor, *William Cooper's Town*, 406–23; the success of *The Spy*, 409. Taylor notes that Cooper "wrote primarily for the middle and elite classes," that is, those who could afford to buy his books, 419.

30. James D. Wallace argues that Cooper was strongly influenced by and "exploited" the popularity of travel literature. Wallace, *Early Cooper and His Audience* (New York: Columbia University Press, 1986), 130–36.

31. James Fenimore Cooper, *The Pioneers* (1821; repr. Albany: State University of New York Press, 1980), 292.

32. James Cooper to Andrew Thomson Goodrich, 28 June 1820, in *The Letters and*

Journals of James Fenimore Cooper, ed. James F. Beard (Cambridge, MA: Harvard University Press, 1960), 1:44.

33. Dwight, *Travels*, 4:122–24. Mention of Kaaterskill Falls first appeared in Spafford's first edition of his *Gazetteer of the State of New York* (Albany: H. C. Southwick, 1813), the most highly regarded reference book for the state, which contained a very brief notice of the falls. In the second edition (1824), he expanded the description, mainly, he wrote, because he had heard "rhapsodies" about the falls—that they had been "so much admired of late." He also noted that "a house of entertainment" was "about to be erected at Pine Orchard"; beyond that, his description was vague. Horatio Spafford, *Gazetteer of the State of New York* (Albany: B. D. Packard, 1824), 245. It is not certain when Cooper first saw Kaaterskill Falls. Dwight's descriptions were quite thorough, however, and Cooper could have cribbed crucial details from him. He probably visited the falls on an 1823 tourist trip upriver, a trip that was highly influential in the writing of *Last of the Mohicans*, as we will see. James Franklin Beard, introduction to *The Last of the Mohicans* (Albany: State University of New York, 1983), xix. He almost certainly saw the falls before his 1828 departure for Europe; his journal from Switzerland that year compares Staubbach Falls to "the Cattskill Leap." James Fenimore Cooper [III], ed., *Correspondence of James Fenimore Cooper* (New Haven: Yale University Press, 1922), 1:275.

34. Cooper, *Pioneers*, 293.

35. Alf Evers, *The Catskills: From Wilderness to Woodstock* (New York: Doubleday, 1972), 332–40. See also Myers, "Selling the Sublime," 129–33. Cooper's description gives another clue that he may have relied heavily on Dwight rather than on personal information; Dwight's letter describing the falls, "Journey to Utica," was written in 1815, before industrialization and logging had taken over the valley. Dwight wrote that "the mountains on either side were steep, wild, and shaggy, covered almost everywhere with a dark forest," Timothy Dwight, *Travels*, 4:122.

36. The dam is described in Evers, *The Catskills*, 351, 362–63, 489; see also Myers, "Selling the Sublime," 176n. Its retaining walls are still visible today, just above the falls.

37. For discussions of the "authenticity" of tourists (or lack thereof) in a twentieth-century context, see, for example, Daniel Boorstin, "From Traveler to Tourist: The Lost Art of Travel in America," in *The Image: A Guide to Pseudo-Events in America* (1961: repr. New York: Vintage Books, 1987), 77–117; and Marielle Risse, "White Knee Socks Versus Photojournalist Vests: Distinguishing between Travelers and Tourists," in *Travel Culture: Essays on What Makes Us Go*, ed. Carol Traynor Williams (Westport, CT: Praeger, 1998), 41–50. For an early example, see Theodore Dwight, *Sketches of Scenery and Manners in the United States* (1829; repr. Delmar, NY: Scholars' Facsimiles, 1983), ch. 9.

38. Alan Taylor takes issue with, among others, Dorothy Waples, *The Whig Myth of James Fenimore Cooper* (Hamden, CT: Archon Books, 1968). Cooper's support for Andrew Jackson, the exemplar of the "self-made man," came mainly from parochial motivations having to do with New York politics. Many of his true feelings about the "era of common man" would be revealed in, for example, his 1828 book *Notions of the Americans*. See Taylor, *William Cooper's Town*, 419–23.

39. For a good discussion about this trend, see Robert Berkhofer Jr., *The White Man's Indian* (New York: Alfred A. Knopf, 1978), esp. 93–94.
40. See Taylor, *William Cooper's Town*, 386–423. Larzer Ziff also contextualizes Cooper as portraying essentially conservative themes in his literature. See Ziff, *Writing in the New Nation: Prose, Print, and Politics in the Early Republic* (New Haven: Yale University Press, 1991), 146–49, 203n17.

5. Expanding Tourism beyond the Springs

1. James G. Percival, *Poems* (New York: Charles Wiley, 1823), 248. Originally issued as *Clio, I & II*, 1822. The poem, titled "A Picture" (Scene—The Valley of the Catskill River north of the Catskill Mountains), begins

   > The glories of a clouded moonlit night—
   > An union of wild mountains, and dark storms
   > Gathering around their summits, or in forms
   > Majestic, moving far away in light,
   > Like pillared snow, or specters wreathed in flame—

   Only after another fifty-four lines of this storm-tossed night do we arrive at a "lonely wanderer" who, "with soul subdued, and awed," gazes upon "the flying cohorts of the storm" with an "enchanted eye." Ultimately he "can only bow before them and adore."
2. A Lover of Nature, "Catskill Mountains," *New-York Evening Post*, 9 July 1823, 2; 10 July 1823, 2. See Alf Evers, *The Catskills: From Wilderness to Woodstock* (New York: Doubleday, 1972), 351.
3. Roland Van Zandt, *The Catskill Mountain House* (New Brunswick, NJ: Rutgers University Press, 1966), 33–37. A slight modification to Van Zandt's account is necessary, since a contemporaneous letter published in *New-York Evening Post* implies that the permanent structure was already underway rather than to be built in the fall: "A temporary wooden building for the accommodation of visitors, the southern wing of which is about fifty feet long, hung with evergreens, being the ball room, has been constructed near an abrupt rocky precipice. . . . Mr. Van Bergen, with his family, are in possession, and the accommodations are good. They company are about erecting a building sixty feet in front, with a wing of the same length running back; and the house is to be three stories." See "Hudson, June 26th, 1823," in the *New-York Evening Post*, 9 July 1823, 2. Evers dates this to 1822. Evers, *The Catskills*, 352.
4. "E. Beach's Stage Line," 15 July 1823, *New-York Evening Post*, 3.
5. DeWitt Clinton Diary, 23 August 1823, New-York Historical Society. An 1823 visit by Aaron Burr is suggested in Van Zandt, *Catskill Mountain House*, 34.
6. Elias Ball to Isaac Ball from Saratoga Springs, 23 July 1823, Ball Family Papers.
7. Ibid.
8. Ibid.
9. Charles West Thomson Diary, 2 August 1824, box 4, C. W. Thompson Papers, New-York Historical Society.
10. S. Shulling Diary, 18? July 1825, Am. 1524, Historical Society of Pennsylvania,

Philadelphia, Pennsylvania. There is no record, oddly enough, of Leatherstocking impersonators on the mountain, at least in the 1820s.

11. Charles West Thomson Diary, 2 August 1824.

12. The Mountain House would be expanded over the years and would eventually become one of America's grand hotels. But it never recovered from the decline during World War II and was eventually abandoned. Badly damaged through neglect, it was destroyed in January 1963. Van Zandt, *Catskill Mountain House*, 310–40.

13. The best history of the Mt. Holyoke mountain house is David Graci, *Mt. Holyoke: An Enduring Prospect* (Holyoke, MA: Calem Publishing, 1985).

14. See Doris Elizabeth King, "The First-Class Hotel and the Age of the Common Man," *Journal of Southern History* 23, no. 2 (May 1957): 173–88. She describes the Boston Exchange Hotel, which opened in 1809 with three hundred rooms, as "the most significant and prophetic" of its time. New York hotels, she contends, had nothing to rival it until the late 1820s; Baltimore's City Hotel (Barnum's), which opened in 1826, had two hundred rooms. Saratoga's preeminence would continue through the 1820s.

15. Gideon M. Davison, *The Fashionable Tour: or, a Trip to the Springs, Niagara, Quebeck, and Boston, in the Summer of 1821* (Saratoga Springs, NY: G. M. Davison, 1822), 53; and John Melish, *Travels through the United States of America in the Years 1806 & 1807, and 1809, 1810, & 1811* (London: George Cowie and Co., 1818), 552. Ballston Spa had remained static: the Sans Souci and Aldridge's remained the principal accommodations. Although the village would grow some in the 1820s, adding another hotel, this was mainly from spillover from Saratoga Springs. These rates were not cheap: for example, a carpenter or other skilled worker in Philadelphia's shipbuilding or construction industry might earn $1.50 a day in 1820 ($45 a month), common laborers around $1 a day. Donald R. Adams Jr., "Wage Rates in the Early National Period: Philadelphia, 1785–1830," *Journal of Economic History* 28, no. 3 (September 1968); see especially the appendixes, 418–26.

16. Samuel Reznek, "The Depression of 1819–1822, a Social History," *American Historical Review* 39, no. 1 (October 1933): 28–47.

17. "Mr. Cristiani's Musical Entertainment, at the Pavilion," *Saratoga Sentinel*, 4 July 1821, 3. Cristiani had performed at least twice in New York, in 1819 and in May 1821. George Odell, *Annals of the New York Stage*, 2:541, 604.

18. "Grand Caravan," 30 July 1822, 3; "Dunlap's 'Picture of the Christ Rejected,' " 8 July 1823, 3; "Celebrated Painting of the Capuchin Chapel, by Mr. Sully," 15 July 1823, 2; "Museum of Fine Arts . . . Grand Panorama" 12 August 1823, 3; "Mr. Brown at Home," 12 August 1823, 2; and "Concert by Mr. Keene," 19 August 1823, 3. For Frederick Brown's roles, see Odell, *Annals*, 2:559–60, 3:153, 3:162.

19. "New Theatre," *Saratoga Sentinel*, 11 August 1824, 3, and advertisement, 3.

20. "W.," "Trifles Light as Air," *Saratoga Sentinel*, 11 August 1824, 3.

21. "Rapid Travelling," *Saratoga Sentinel*, 8 August 1821, 2.

22. "To the Editor," *Saratoga Sentinel*, 11 August 1824, 3.

23. S. A. [Sarah Ann] Merry to Robert D. C. Merry, 28 June 1828, letter 1, folder 79, MC 424, Bradley Family Papers, Schlesinger Library, Radcliffe Institute, Harvard University.

24. *Saratoga Sentinel*, 4 May 1824, 2; 29 June 1824, 3; and 27 July 1824, 3.

25. John Morrison, *History of American Steam Navigation* (1903; repr. New York: Argosy-Antiquarian Ltd., 1967), 51.

26. Charles West Thomson Diary, 29 July 1824.

27. Ibid., 2 and 3 August 1824. Thompson would become one of the more prolific contributors to the gift books of the 1830s through 1850s and was considered one of the main poets of mid–nineteenth century America.

28. Galinée and Hennepin quoted in Elizabeth McKinsey, *Niagara Falls: Icon of the American Sublime* (Cambridge, UK: Cambridge University Press, 1985), 8, 11.

29. McKinsey, *Niagara Falls*, 19–21. See Patrick McGreevey, *Imagining Niagara: The Meaning and Making of Niagara Falls* (Amherst: University of Massachusetts Press, 1994), esp. ch. 2.

30. Mary Murray Journal, 14 and 15 June 1808, New-York Historical Society. Note that this method of stump removal gives a different twist to the traditional phrase describing this region, the "Burned-Over District."

31. These figures are derived from a printed "Way Bill [from] Albany to Niagara" bound into a journal attributed to a member of the Drayton family, "Journal of a Tour No. 1," 19 July 1810, item 34–36, Drayton? Mss., South Carolina Historical Society.

32. June 8 to 18, 1808; Mary Murray 1808 Travel Journal, New-York Historical Society.

33. Unknown Drayton family member, "Journal of a Tour No. 1," 1810.

34. Mary Murray Journal, 21 June 1808, New York Historical Society; Drayton? Travel Journal, 21 July 1810, South Carolina Historical Society. For a succinct summary of tourist expectations of the falls, see Patricia Jansen, "Romanticism, Modernity and the Evolution of Tourism on the Niagara Frontier, 1790–1850," *Canadian Historical Review* 72, no. 3 (September 1991): 293–96; McKinsey, *Niagara Falls*; and, for a later period, Karen Dubinsky, *The Second Greatest Disappointment: Honeymooning and Tourism at Niagara Falls* (New Brunswick, NJ: Rutgers University Press, 1999).

35. Murray Journal, 21 June 1808.

36. The embargo was a foolish attempt by President Thomas Jefferson to lessen tensions with Great Britain. In 1807, he ordered all trade with Great Britain to cease. Unfortunately, tariffs were the prime source of government revenue, and so there was suddenly very little money to pay for customs inspectors. Consequently, all border zones became vigorous areas of smuggling. Mary Murray "heard a great noise all night, which I could not account for, but which I afterward found, was occasioned by smuggling, Flour Potash &c—and proceeded from the oars & the confined sound of voices—the whole night they were crossing and recrossing," 20 June 1808, Murray Journal.

37. Jansen dates the ladder to 1795. Jansen, "Romanticism, Modernity, and the Evolution of Tourism," 297. See also William Irwin, *The New Niagara: Tourism, Technology, and the Landscape of Niagara Falls, 1776–1917* (University Park: Pennsylvania State University Press, 1996), 3; and Christian Shultz, *Travels on an Inland Voyage through the States of New York, Pennsylvania, Virginia* (1810; repr. Ridgewood, NJ: Gregg Press, 1968), 1:58–83.

38. Isaac Ball to John Ball Jr., 3 September 1806, Ball Family Papers.
39. Mary Murray Journal, 23 June 1808, New York Historical Society; Drayton? Travel Journal, 21 July 1810, South Carolina Historical Society.
40. Mentioned in Shultz, *Travels*, 1:79. See also Carroll D. Kepner, "Niagara's Water Power: The Pioneers, Part I," *Niagara Frontier* 15, no. 4 (Winter 1968): 97–105, and "Niagara's Water Power: II, The Long Frustration," *Niagara Frontier* 16, no. 2 (Summer 1969): 33–45.
41. Shultz, *Travels*, 1:79. Augustus Porter and, in particular, his brother and business partner Peter, a congressman from the Niagara district in New York, were closely involved in pressing for the war, although Peter Porter would come to regret that, as the war's planning and execution across the Niagara frontier left much to be desired. See J. C. A. Stagg, "Between a Black Rock and a Hard Place: Peter B. Porter's Plan for an American Invasion of Canada in 1812," *Journal of the Early Republic* 19, no. 3 (Autumn 1999): 385–422.
42. William Dalton, *Travels in the United States of America and Part of Upper Canada* (New York: Appleby, 1821), 184–85.
43. Mrs. John Heard Journal, 5 August 1815, Massachusetts Historical Society.
44. Ibid., 2 August, 23 and 27 July, 4 August 1815.
45. Solomon to Rachel Mordecai, 13 August 1817, folder 13, subseries 1.2, Mordecai Family Papers, Southern Historical Collection.
46. Carol Sheriff, *The Artificial River: The Erie Canal and the Paradox of Progress, 1817–1862* (New York: Hill and Wang, 1996).
47. John Pintard, *Letters from John Pintard to His Daughter* (New York: New-York Historical Society, 1940), 1:144.
48. "An Elegant Canal Barge," *Saratoga Sentinel*, 3 May 1820, 3.
49. Packet boats coordinated with coaches: "Canal Packets and Post-Coaches," *New-York Evening Post*, 15 May 1822, 3; Boat speed estimate: "Letter to a Gentleman," *Saratoga Sentinel*, 13 July 1822, 3, reprinted from the *New-York Statesman* and the *New York Evening Post*, 9 July 1822, 2. "No risk" quote: "Grand Canal," *New-York Evening Post*, 20 June 1822, 2. Miles per hour: Henry D. Gilpin to Joshua Gilpin, 3 July 1825, Henry D. Gilpin Papers, Historical Society of Delaware, Wilmington, Delaware.
50. "Letter to a Gentleman," *Saratoga Sentinel*, 13 July 1822, 3; and "Launch," *New-York Evening Post*, 19 July 1823, 2. Stephen Sirly, "Van Rensselaer, Stephen," *American National Biography Online*, Feb. 2000 (accessed October 2007).
51. Horatio Gates Spafford, *A Pocket Guide for the Tourist and Traveller, Along the Line of the Canals, and the Interior Commerce of the State of New-York* (New York: T. & J. Swords, 1824), iii–iv.
52. Ibid., 117–18.
53. Gideon Davison, *The Fashionable Tour, in 1825: An Excursion to the Springs, Niagara, Quebec and Boston* (Saratoga Springs, N.Y.: G. M. Davison, 1825), 116.
54. David P. Hillhouse Journal, 25 August 1826, 110, folder 75, Alexander-Hillhouse Papers, Southern Historical Collection.
55. Theodore Dwight, *The Northern Traveller: Containing the Routes to Niagara, Quebec, and the Springs . . .* (New York: Wilder & Campbell, 1825), vi.
56. Henry D. Gilpin to Joshua Gilpin, 1 July 1825, Henry D. Gilpin Papers.
57. Elizabeth Pierce to Rev. John Pierce, 10 August 1824, box 1, folder 5, A-132,

Poor Family Collection, Schlesinger Library, Radcliffe Institute, Harvard University.

58. John M. Duncan, *Travels through Part of the United States and Canada in 1818 and 1819* (Glasgow: Hurst, Robinson and Co., 1823), 2:12, 28.

59. Duncan, *Travels*, 2:33–34, 38.

60. Forsyth may have received a mysterious absolution through the intervention of Robert Hamilton, a powerful local figure. Robert Fraser, "Forsyth, William," *Dictionary of Canadian Biography*, vol 7 (Toronto: University of Toronto Press, 1988), 312.

61. Fraser, "Forsyth, William," 311–16.

62. William Darby praised it, but the Duke of Richmond had problems there, including an ugly dispute over his bill that tainted Forsyth's dealings with the authorities in the area for some time after. See Darby, *A Tour from the City of New York, to Detroit* (1819; repr. New York: Quadrangle Books, 1962), 163; and Fraser, "Forsythe, William," 7:313.

63. Catharine Maria Sedgwick Journal, 1821, [n.p., 43rd page], roll 7, *Microfilm Edition of the Catharine Maria Sedgwick Papers*; and Mrs. John Heard 1815 Travel Journal, entries of 3 and 4 Aug 1815.

64. Capt. Richard Langslow, who stayed at Forsyth's, mentions having to climb down "the ladder," presumably the old one, and notes that "the road onward toward the Falls was so bad, steep and wet" that he couldn't approach them. Capt. Richard Langslow Diary, typescript, 25 September 1817, New York State Historical Society, Cooperstown, New York.

65. Fraser, "Forsyth, William," 7:311–15. Darby, *Tour*, 163. Francis Hall, *Travels in Canada and the United States in 1816 and 1817* (London: Longman, 1818), 230–38.

66. "From the Niagara Patriot, Aug 3," 11 August 1819, *New-York Evening Post*, 2.

67. Frances Wright, *Views of Society and Manners in America* (1821; repr. Cambridge: Belknap Press of Harvard University, 1963), 125–26.

68. David Prall Journal, 21 July 1821, BV Sec: Prall, David Prall Papers, New-York Historical Society.

69. David Hillhouse Travel Journal, 1825, p. 118, item 11, folders 75–76, subchapter 2, subsection 6.1. Alexander-Hillhouse Papers, Southern Historical Collection.

70. Hall, *Travels*, 238.

71. Pintard, *Letters*, 1:144.

72. Jansen, "Romanticism, Modernity, and the Evolution of Tourism," 301.

6. Tourism and Literature

1. William Cullen Bryant III and Thomas Voss, eds., *The Letters of William Cullen Bryant* (New York: Fordham University Press, 1975), 1:154.

2. Wayne Franklin, *The New World of James Fenimore Cooper* (Chicago: University of Chicago Press, 1982), 176.

3. Susan Fenimore Cooper, the author's daughter, misdated this journey as 1825 in *Pages and Pictures* (1865; repr. Secaucus, NJ: Castle Books, 1980); see James Franklin Beard, introduction to *The Last of the Mohicans* (Albany: State University of New York, 1983), xx.

4. The dinner was with U.S. Navy friends, including Matthew Perry. See James F. Beard, ed., *The Letters and Journals of James Fenimore Cooper* (Cambridge, MA: Harvard University Press, 1960), 1:113.

5. Beard describes Cooper's 1823 steamboat journey north with the actor Charles Matthews in his introduction to *The Last of the Mohicans*, xix–xx.

6. Cooper, *Letters and Journals*, 1:128n2.

7. Timothy Dwight, *Travels in New England and New York* (1822; repr., with notes and edited by Barbara Miller Solomin, Cambridge, MA: Belknap Press, 1969), 3:293. We have already seen how Cooper used Dwight for *The Pioneers*; Wayne Franklin describes his use of Dwight for *Mohicans* in "The Wilderness of Words in *The Last of the Mohicans*," in *New Essays on The Last of the Mohicans*, ed. H. Daniel Peck (Cambridge, UK: Cambridge University Press, 1992), 25–45, esp. 30–32.

8. *Hudson River Port Folio*, plate 6 ("View from Cozzens' Hotel Near West Point"). Today (as noted in chapter 3), the rocks forming Glens Falls are visible and dry because the Hudson has since been dammed just above them.

9. The text for this plate, "View from Cozzens' Hotel Near West Point," describes the staircase and toll for the falls.

10. Edward Stanley, *Journal of a Tour in America in 1824–25* (London: Privately printed, 1930), 15. Another, slightly enhanced version is told in Susan Cooper, *Pages and Pictures*, 121. Both are quoted in Beard, introduction to *Last of the Mohicans*, xx. Cooper confirms this story in an 1826 letter to his British publisher. Cooper, *Letters and Journals*, 1:128.

11. For a complete history of early Lake George tourism, see Theodore Corbett, *The Making of American Resorts* (New Brunswick, NJ: Rutgers University Press, 2001), ch. 3.

12. Dwight, *Travels*, 3:247–52, 288–89.

13. Beard, introduction to *Last of the Mohicans*, xxiii.

14. Ibid., xxiv–xxvii.

15. Cooper, *Last of the Mohicans*, 119.

16. Ibid., 123.

17. W. H. Gardiner, "Cooper's Novels: *The Last of the Mohicans*," *North American Review*, n.s. 27, vol. 52 (July 1826): 156–57.

18. Cooper, *Last of the Mohicans*, 55.

19. Gardiner, "Cooper's Novels," 154. John McWilliams describes this as Hawkeye's "visual responses to the framed scene . . . the whole paragraph makes one composite picture." McWilliams, *The Last of the Mohicans: Civil Savagery and Savage Civility* (New York: Twayne Publishers, 1995), 29–30.

20. The seminal study of gift books, still the most valuable, is Ralph Thompson, *American Literary Annuals & Gift Books, 1825–1865* (1936; repr. [Hamden, CT]: Archon Books, 1967). Sales figures appear on 7, 50. For a discussion of the gift book's significance and impact as a consumer product, see Stephen Nissenbaum, *The Battle for Christmas* (New York: Alfred. A. Knopf, 1996), 140–50. For a discussion on their artistic impact, see David Lovejoy, "American Painting in Early Nineteenth-Century Gift Books," *American Quarterly* 7, no. 4 (Winter 1955): 345–61. Although it was printed in the fall of 1825, the first *Atlantic Souvenir* was postdated to 1826 to make it seem more current. See Henry

Dilworth Gilpin to Joshua Gilpin, "I send you a specimen of the Souvenir, which will be published next week," 24 November 1825, Gilpin Family Papers, Historical Society of Delaware, Wilmington, Delaware.

21. One reason that so much of that first *Atlantic Souvenir* was related to tourism was probably the influence of its editor, Henry Dilworth Gilpin. His very first literary effort, published the summer before the *Souvenir* emerged, was *The Northern Traveller*, a tourist guidebook (see chapter 7). Gilpin's editorship stretched across seven years of the annual; it is mentioned in his biographical sketches. However, although Ralph Thompson denigrates his role, noting that the publisher solicited a number of stories and all of the illustrations, it is possible that he played a larger role than has been suspected, as the preponderance of travel-related stories perhaps indicates. Thompson, *American Gift Books and Annuals*, 49.

22. P. [James Kirke Paulding], "A Tale of Mystery; Or, The Youth That Died without a Disease," *The Atlantic Souvenir; A Christmas and New Year's Offering: 1826* (Philadelphia: H. C. Carey & I. Lea, 1825), 137, 140, 142.

23. Catharine Maria Sedgwick, "The Catholic Iroquois. By the Author of Redwood," *The Atlantic Souvenir: 1826*, 72–103.

7. The First Tourist Guidebook War

1. Two other tourism-related books appeared in the interim. In 1823, A. T. Goodrich, a New York printer and one of Davison's distributors, published the anonymous *The Traveller's Guide; or A Few Weeks' Tour in the New-England States*. A small almanac-sized book, it guided tourists up the Connecticut River to the White Mountains. It is the first guidebook to New England, but it was even more obscure than Davison's guide, never having a further edition, and its author remains unknown (see note 13). In 1824, a somewhat more widely distributed guide was published, Horatio Gates Spafford's *A Pocket Guide for the Tourist and Traveller, Along the Line of The Canals, and the Interior Commerce of the State of New-York* (New York: T. & J. Swords, 1824). It followed some of the traits of Davison's book—in particular, a geographical, rather than alphabetical, listing of places—but in general it was as utilitarian and spare as an almanac.

2. A one-line notice of its publication did appear on page 284 of the July 1822 edition of the *North American Review*, but it was never reviewed.

3. Theodore Dwight signed his letters "Theodore Dwight, Junior," apparently until his father's death in 1846. Many of his papers, though, are signed and filed under Theodore Dwight, which can cause confusion between the two. His father was secretary to the Hartford Convention in 1814 and one of the "Hartford Wits." There is no biography of Dwight, but sound sketches of his life are in Timothy P. Twohill, "Dwight, Theodore," in *American National Biography*, ed. John Garraty and Mark Carnes (New York: Oxford, 1999), 7:190–91; "Dwight, Theodore," in *American Authors, 1600–1900*, ed. Stanley Kunitz and Howard Haycraft (New York: H. W. Wilson Co., 1938), 238–39; and Benjamin Dwight, *The History of the Descendants of John Dwight, of Dedham, Mass.* (New York: John Trow and Sons, 1874), 230–33. A good analysis of Dwight's philosophy and ideology is found in John Sears's introduction to the reprint of

Dwight's *Sketches of Scenery and Manners* (Delmar, NY: Scholars' Facsimiles, 1983). I am also deeply indebted to my colleague Denis Kozlov and his paper " 'The Rational Traveller': Theodore Dwight and the Authorship of Early American Travel Literature," unpublished seminar paper, University of Massachusetts Amherst, 1996.

4. Theodore Dwight Jr. to Mrs. Abigail Dwight (his mother), 13 September 1815, folder 71, Dwight Family Papers, New York Public Library.

5. Leavitt Thazter at Northampton to Theodore Dwight Jr., 15 February 1816, lamenting his absence and illness, Dwight Family Papers.

6. Theodore Dwight Jr. to John Trumbull, 24 June 1818, Theodore Dwight Jr. Papers (Misc. Mss. Dwight, T., Jr.), New-York Historical Society. See also the signed receipt Dwight collected from Luther Brandish, 7 November 1818, Luther Brandish Papers (Misc. Mss. Brandish, Luther), box 1, New-York Historical Society.

7. Theodore Dwight Jr. to Abigail Dwight, 30 and 31 December 1819, folder 32, Dwight Family Papers; Twohill, "Dwight, Theodore," 190; and "Dwight, Theodore," in Kunitz and Haycraft, *American Authors, 1600–1900*, 238. All biographies of Dwight make the point that illness required him to travel to Europe. However, his journal shows a man fit enough to undertake long journeys across the continent, and the tiny handwriting in his journal remained steady throughout. Perhaps Dwight was harkening to Lord Byron's *Childe Harold's Progress* and other romantic works, which required a wan but perceptive recorder. Dwight developed a passion for Italy that became a lifelong obsession; in the 1860s, he provided material and moral support for Italian revolutionaries such as Garibaldi.

8. C. Tuthill to Theodore Dwight Jr., 22 May 1824, Dwight Family Papers.

9. Theodore Dwight, *A Journal of a Tour In Italy, in the Year 1821* (New York: Abraham Paul, 1824). Like almost all antebellum literature, it was published anonymously, but Dwight's friends knew who had written it. One sent him a review that was glowing to the point of being tongue-in-cheek: "The author, as is evident from almost every page, is a man of the most minute observation . . . he knows how to move the more serious feelings of the heart. I have spoken thus freely . . . because as the work is anonymous, I can in no justice be supposed to know who is the author." C. Tuthill to Theodore Dwight Jr., 9 June 1824, Dwight Family Papers.

10. A review of *Journal of a Tour in Italy* appeared in the *New-York Evening Post*, 9 August 1824, 2. It is a favorable review, but it may, in fact, have been written by Dwight himself, as was customary in that day. The reviewer, who has "not yet had time to peruse the work," relies on "a friend in whose opinion we place confidence," a common device to introduce a puff piece.

11. Theodore Dwight Jr. to "Dear Brother," William R. Dwight, 13 August 1824, folder 32, Dwight Family Papers. Evidence of regular visits by the Dwight Family to Ballston can be found in Anne Royall, *The Black Book; Or, A Continuation of Travels in the United States* (Washington, D.C.: Printed for the author, 1828–29), 1:25–26. See chapter 9 for a discussion of her interaction with the Dwights.

12. Dwight may also have been inspired by *The Traveller's Guide; or A Few Weeks'*

Tour in the New-England States, an exceedingly rare 1823 guide (see note 1). The only known copy is held at the New-York Historical Society. That copy is twice inscribed with Dwight's name, once on the inner flysheet and once on the first page of the text. Although it is tempting to see him as the author of that work, there is no evidence to support that: none of the text was used in Dwight's later work. However, the guide does refer to Timothy Dwight's *Travels*, but that was the single most famous description of New England sites available in the early 1820s.

13. Theodore Dwight, *The Northern Traveller, Containing the Routes to Niagara, Quebeck, and the Springs* . . . (New York: Wilder & Campbell, 1825), 6. See note 16.
14. Dwight, *Northern Traveller* (1825), vii.
15. Ibid., 6.
16. Samples of borrowings include Dwight (1825), 12–13, and Davison (1822), 17–18 (the story of Benedict Arnold and Major John Andre); Dwight (1825), 54–55, and Davison (1822), 107–8. See also Richard Gassan, "The First American Tourist Guidebooks," *Book History* 8 (2005), 57–58 and n. 31.
17. Ibid., 100.
18. Ibid., 105–6.
19. "I understand they are filling up at Ballston, that Aldridge has not a very considerable number," Thedore Dwight to William Dwight, 13 August 1824, Dwight Family Papers. He may have met his family at Ballston Spa, as he prefaced the preceding quotation with "I shall see you on Monday or Tuesday," but is unclear whether he meant at New York or Ballston Spa.
20. [Caleb?] Sipple, 28 July 1821, Sipple Diary, New-York Historical Society. The Sipples were from Milford, Delaware (per diary), and although there is no positive identification, this may have been Caleb Sipple (1791–1829), husband of Levenia Sipple, who owned a town lot in Milford in 1820. At Saratoga, his diary showed his disdain for the fashionable life there; he found only "the gayest sort of Pride and vanity" (30 July 1821). Despite this, they remained at the resort for some time, apparently creating a zone of comfort despite all the frivolity around them. Evidence that he may have been a lawyer comes from a lengthy description of the Saratoga County courthouse (26 August 1821).
21. Dwight, *Northern Traveller* (1825), 6.
22. Ibid., 16.
23. Ibid., 100.
24. Ibid., 50.
25. Dwight, *Sketches of Scenery and Manners*, 175.
26. "The Northern Traveller," *New-York Evening Post*, 12 June 1826, 2. Dwight would also add "corrections" to the text in the 1827 edition.
27. The third edition (1828) was extensively revised, primarily to reflect the rapid changes in tourism by then.
28. *New-York Evening Post*, 10 June 1825, 3.
29. Davison, *Fashionable Tour* (1822), 13–21; Mention of the André/Arnold story was in the *Saratoga Sentinel*, 22 August 1821, 2, with a follow-up on 19 December 1821, 2. There was also extensive coverage in New York and other newspapers.

30. Davison, *Fashionable Tour* (1822), 30–31.

31. Davison, *Fashionable Tour* (1825), 41. See the descriptions of the Mountain House in Roland Van Zandt, *The Catskill Mountain House* (New Brunswick, NJ: Rutgers University Press, 1966).

32. There are no book-length biographies of Gilpin, but biographical sketches include "Gilpin, Henry Dilworth," *Dictionary of American Biography*, ed. Allen Johnson and Dumas Malone (New York: Charles Scribner's Sons, 1931); "Gilpin, Henry Dilwood [*sic*]," *National Cyclopaedia of American Biography* (New York: J. T. White, 1898); "Manuscript Collections, Index," in folder 1, box 59A, Gilpin Family Papers, Historical Society of Delaware, Wilmington, Delaware; and a profile, on which most of these biographical essays seem to be based, "Political Portraits with Pen and Pencil, No. XXIII, Henry D. Gilpin," in *U.S. Magazine and Democratic Review* 8, no. 35 (November–December 1840): 512–36. There are two significant collections of Gilpin's papers. One is at the Historical Society of Pennsylvania, composed of mostly post-1833 materials. Gilpin bequeathed his library and personal papers to the Historical Society of Pennsylvania; however, disruptions in the society's operations in the 1990s apparently made many of these materials inaccessible as of 1999; some have been transferred to other collections. Gilpin's personal papers are listed in the Historical Society of Pennsylvania's *Guide to the Manuscript Collections* (Philadelphia, 1949), item 238, "letters to his father, 1822–41," but they are apparently no longer there. They seem to have been transferred to the Gilpin Family Papers collection at the Historical Society of Delaware.

33. On Irving: Henry Dilworth Gilpin to Sarah Gilpin (sister), 1 August 1825; on Scott: Henry Dilworth Gilpin to Joshua Gilpin, 30 July 1825, Gilpin Family Papers. Gilpin read Irving's *Sketch Book* in 1819, parts of which he found "very good," as well as *Ivanhoe*, "by the best of the novel-writers." Henry Gilpin, "Extracts from a Common-Place Book," *Pennsylvania Magazine of History and Biography* 45 (1921): 230, 236.

34. Henry Dilworth Gilpin to Joshua Gilpin, 28 January 1825, box 59, folder 6, Gilpin Family Papers.

35. Henry Dilworth Gilpin to Mary Dilworth Gilpin (his mother), 25 May 1825, folder 6, box 59, Gilpin Family Papers. Henry Dilworth Gilpin, *A Northern Tour: Being a Guide to Saratoga, Lake George, Niagara, Canada, Boston, &c. &c.* (Philadelphia: Carey & Lea, 1825) was advertised in the *New-York Evening Post*, 10 June 1825, 3.

36. Gilpin, *Northern Tour*, 23.

37. Ibid., 147–48. The verses are from Canto 4 of Lord Byron's *Childe Harold's Pilgrimage*, perhaps the quintessential romantic text.

38. Gilpin, *Northern Tour*, 40–43. The verses quoted are lines 1–9 from canto 12 of Dante's *Inferno*.

39. Evidence that this was his first trip to these places is drawn from the series of letters he wrote his father, 28 June, 1, 3, 5, 9, and 22 July 1825, box 59, folder 6, Gilpin Family Papers. See, for example, 28 June, regarding the bay of New York: "I had heard a great deal of it, but I really think it exceeded all my expectations"; or 1 July: "All my expectations all that I could imagine were surpassed by the scenery" of the Hudson. He did not visit Kaaterskill Falls on this trip

and didn't travel northward again until August 1835, when he took a trip to Saratoga (Henry Dilworth Gilpin to Joshua Gilpin, 12 August 1835, Gilpin Family Papers).

40. Gilpin, *Northern Tour*, 1–2.
41. Ibid.
42. "New Publications," *United States Literary Gazette*, 1 August 1825, 361.

8. Tourism's Broader Audience

1. Nathaniel Parker Willis, "The Vacation," *The Atlantic Souvenir: A Christmas and New Year's Offering* (Philadelphia: Carey, Lea, and Carey, 1827), 41–47.
2. Thomas N. Baker, *Sentiment and Celebrity: Nathaniel Parker Willis and the Trials of Literary Fame* (New York: Oxford University Press, 1999), 19–34. Baker cites the impact of this trip, particularly his stay in New York City, as central to his development as an aesthete, that it was then that he "drifted from his evangelical moorings," 28. There was a distinct shift in his writing, from pious verse to quintessential romanticism. Willis's subsequent rise in notoriety was rapid, so much so that in 1829 he was banned from his family's church for missing services and attending the theater.
3. Willis, "The Vacation," 44–45.
4. Was he right? To a point. But Willis was unusual in presenting this picture to the general public. He would go on to have a remarkably successful career in selling himself and the idea of social climbing, rising to become one of the best-known writers of his day, as Sandra Tomc ably describes in "An Idle Industry: Nathaniel Parker Willis and the Workings of Literary Leisure," *American Quarterly* 49, no. 4 (1997): 780–805.
5. David Grimsted, *Melodrama Unveiled: American Theater and Culture, 1800–1850* (1967; repr. Berkeley: University of California Press, 1987), 56; Paul A. Gilje, *The Road to Mobocracy: Popular Disorder in New York City, 1763–1834* (Chapel Hill: University of North Carolina Press, 1987), 252. Grimsted argues that the Bowery was for the middle class by the late 1820s, while Bruce McConachie in *Melodramatic Formations: American Theater and Society, 1820–1870* (Iowa City: University of Iowa Press, 1992), 22, calls it one of six "elite" theaters in 1827, becoming downscale only by 1832. Glenn Hughes, *A History of American Theater, 1700–1950* (New York: Samuel French, 1951), 134, argues for the Park Theater's status as elite by the mid-1820s, while McConachie, "Pacifying American Theatrical Audiences, 1820–1900" in *For Fun and Profit: The Transformation of Leisure into Consumption* (Philadelphia: Temple University Press, 1990), esp. 47–54, places audience segregation by class into the 1830s.
6. Biographies of Dunlap include Robert Canary, *William Dunlap* (New York: Twayne Publishers, 1970); and Oral S. Coad, *William Dunlap: A Study of His Life and Works* (New York: Dunlap Society, 1917). A shorter profile is in Grimsted, *Melodrama Unveiled*, 1–21. *Niagara* was Dunlap's last play.
7. "A Trip to Niagara," *New-York Mirror and Ladies Literary Gazette*, 22 November 1828, 159.
8. "The Diorama at the Bowery Theater," *The Critic: A Weekly Review of Literature, Fine Arts and Drama*, 13 December 1828, 104.

9. The play was published as William T. Moncrieff, *Paris and London, or, a Trip to Both Cities: An Operatic Extravaganza in Three Acts* (New York: E. M. Murden, 1828). For a brief description of the diorama presented at the Park Theater, see George Odell, *Annals of the New York Stage* (New York: Columbia University Press, 1927), 3:320. James Callow gives a brief description of *Trip to Niagara*'s panoramas in *Kindred Spirits: Knickerbocker Writers and American Artists, 1807–1855* (Chapel Hill: University of North Carolina Press, 1967), 148–49.

10. William Dunlap, *A Trip to Niagara; or, Travellers in America. A Farce. In Three Acts* (New York: E. B. Clayton, 1830), [i].

11. As an example of this, one character is named John Bull; James K. Paulding had just published a popular book whose title was worked into this exchange:

> *Amelia:* Mr. Bull! You in America?
> *Bull:* Yes, Amelia, John Bull in America.

Dunlap, *Trip to Niagara*, 9. It was probably also not a coincidence that the play *John Bull at Home and Jonathan in England* opened just a week after *A Trip to Niagara* at the Park Theater. See *New-York Evening Post*, 2 December 1828, 3. James K. Paulding, *John Bull in America; or the New Munchausen* (New York: Charles Wiley, 1825). For more on James Hackett's *John Bull at Home . . .* see, for example, Maura L. Jortner, "Playing 'America' on Nineteenth-Century Stages; Or, Jonathan in England and Jonathan At Home" (PhD diss., University of Pittsburgh, 2005), 151–57.

12. "The Diorama," *The Critic*, 13 December 1828, 104.

13. "Bowery Theater: Friday Evening," *New-York Evening Post*, 28 November 1828, 2. The play was also advertised in the *Weekly American* that night. For a discussion of typical theater effects of the time, see Grimsted, *Melodrama Unveiled*, 78–82. The play was so popular that it was repeated the next night when the first night sold out. See "Mr Dunlap's Play of a Trip to Niagara," *New-York Mirror*, 20 December 1828, 191; and Odell, *Annals*, 3:409.

14. Dunlap, *Trip to Niagara*, 21, 26–27.

15. James Fenimore Cooper, *The Pioneers* (1821; repr. Albany: State University of New York Press, 1980), 292–93.

16. Dunlap, *Trip to Niagara*, 33–34.

17. Odell, *Annals*, 3:407, 408, 413, 472; "Trip to Niagara," *New-York Evening Post*, 2 December 1828, 3, also mentioned 1 December 1828, 2. The diorama may have burned, though, when the Bowery once again fell to fire in April 1829. Pintard, *Letters*, 3:71. (When the Bowery mounted *Niagara*, it had only very recently been rebuilt. It burned in a May 1828 fire, reopening in August 1828; *Niagara* opened in November. Fires of this regularity were quite common in the theaters of the day.)

18. For example, at Kaaterskill Falls, Amelia declares, somewhat all-inclusively, "Sublime! How bold! How picturesque!" Dunlap, *Trip to Niagara*, 37.

19. Dunlap's rendering of "house" as "housen" might point to another "antique" aspect of Leatherstocking: Dunlap is hinting at a Dutch background, which in the New York of this era, was often used to indicate conservative attitudes. Ibid., 31, 39.

20. Ibid., 53.

21. Ellouise Baker Larsen, *American Historical Views on Staffordshire China*, rev. ed. (New York: Doubleday, 1950), 2–3. General information about the American market for British china can be found in Marian Klamkin, *American Patriotic and Political China* (New York: Charles Scribner's Sons, 1973), 12–54. Most of the literature on pottery is written for collectors, and historical information can be difficult to locate, scattered among descriptions of the specific lines of individual manufacturers. The difficulty of placing particular pieces in time is also enhanced by the apparent lack of hard records kept by their manufacturers. Likewise, it is difficult to assess with any precision the quantity of production; examples of a significant number of these pieces, though, seem to have survived in collections.

22. Larsen, *American Historical Views*, lists a number of pieces based on Wall's works, especially those made by Andrew Stevenson (43–48, 50), James and Ralph Clews (58, 60–70), and Job and John Jackson (161–66). For several other Wall-illustrated pieces, see Jane Boicourt, "Some Staffordshire Views of the Upper Hudson," *Magazine Antiques* 60 (July 1951): 52–53.

23. Larsen, *American Historical Views*, 15, 144; see also Frank Stefano Jr., "American Hotels on Early Staffordshire," *Magazine Antiques* 112 (August 1977): 276. Roland Van Zandt, *The Catskill Mountain House* (New Brunswick, NJ: Rutgers University Press, 1966), reproduces both the engraving (fig. 2, p. 14) and two Staffordshire plates (fig. 10, p. 59).

24. *North American Review* 25, no. 57 (October 1827): 334, anon. review of Thomas L. M'Kenney's *Sketches of a Tour to the Lakes* (Baltimore: F. Lucas, 1827).

9. Skeptics

1. Mary Kelley, ed., *The Power of Her Sympathy: The Autobiography and Journal of Catharine Maria Sedgwick* (Boston: Massachusetts Historical Society, 1993), 3–22. There are few biographies of Sedgwick. The only other recent book-length study is Edward Halsey Foster, *Catharine Maria Sedgwick* (New York: Twayne, 1974), which is condescending at best. Somewhat more helpful is Mary Dewey, ed., *Life and Letters of Catharine Maria Sedgwick* (New York: Harper and Brothers, 1871). See also Victoria Clements, introduction to Sedgwick, *A New-England Tale* (New York: Oxford University Press, 1995), xi–xxviii.

2. Catharine Maria Sedgwick, *The Catharine Maria Sedgwick Papers, 1798–1908* (Boston: Massachusetts Historical Society, 1984), microfilm. The journal is contained in roll 7. The letters the journal was extracted from (with few omissions or additions) are found in the Catharine Maria Sedgwick Papers III, folders 2.15 and 2.16, Massachusetts Historical Society. One other letter is misdated 1819 in the collection; its content clearly places it as having been written during the 1821 journey, 5 July [1819?], folder 1.8, Catharine Maria Sedgwick Papers III.

3. Catharine Maria Sedgwick, *A New-England Tale* (New York: E. Bliss and E. White, 1822).

4. Catharine Maria Sedgwick, *Redwood: A Tale* (1824; repr. New York: Garrett Press, 1969).

5. Catharine Maria Sedgwick, *The Travellers. A Tale. Designed for Young People* (New York: E. Bliss and E. White, 1825), got favorable notices. The *United*

States Literary Gazette, 15 June 1825, 218, found that it had a "sweetness and beauty of style and sentiment"; the *New-York Review and Athenaeum Magazine*, June 1825, 34, found it an "uncommonly graceful little narrative." The book was reprinted in England, a fact noted in an anonymous review of another book in the *Atlantic Review*, n.s. 44, vol. 49 (October 1825): 458, which called it an "interesting little tale" and claimed that it "met with such success, as to be satisfactory to the publisher." This small book is her least known. Discussion of it does not appear in any of her published biographies, and it is hard to say just how widely sold it was. Like many of the novels of the 1820s, probably only five hundred or a thousand copies were printed, and it was never reprinted. Available at http://etext.lib.virginia.edu/eaf/pubindex.html (accessed 22 June 2007).

6. Sedgwick, *Travellers*, 17. Ironically, by the time the book was in print, Sedgwick herself had relocated from her country village of Stockbridge to New York City.

7. Ibid., 21.

8. Ibid., 23–24.

9. Ibid., 28–29.

10. Ibid., 77–80. Sedgwick had embraced Unitarianism (founded in New England around 1815) just a few years before.

11. Ibid., 82.

12. Ibid., 83.

13. In her 1821 travel journal, Sedgwick recorded a "a party of Greenwich Street Shopkeepers" who were entirely disappointed in their experience because "they had not seen a broiled chicken, nor a roast-pig since they left N York!!" Catharine Sedgwick Travel Journal, 3 July 1821. Catharine Maria Sedgwick Papers.

14. Sedgwick would not again directly address tourism in her later works, although she would work in a seemingly gratuitous description of the naming of Mt. Holyoke, Massachusetts, in *Hope Leslie* (1827). The mountain, a site that had only very recently been made safe for tourists, was located some distance from the main action of the novel. Sedgwick, *Hope Leslie; or Early Times in the Massachusetts*, ed. Carolyn Karcher (1827; New York: Penguin, 1998), 103–6.

15. Theodore Dwight, *The Northern Traveller: Containing the Routes to Niagara, Quebec, and the Springs* . . . (New York: Wilder & Campbell, 1825), 114, 173. Emphasis in original. Incidentally, this was perhaps the first printed exhortation to go to the White Mountains, which were then very much off the beaten path. This would change within the next five years.

16. Theodore Dwight, "Travelling to Good Purpose," in *Sketches of Scenery and Manners in the United States* (1829; repr. Delmar, NY: Scholars' Facsimiles and Reprints, 1983), 176.

17. He would remain editor of the *Souvenir* only until 1830. He then left literature temporarily to concentrate on his career as a lawyer. Soon after, he was named Andrew Jackson's attorney general, a post he held for some years, and after serving in Martin Van Buren's administration, he retired from law and government to write; his works thereafter were generally nonfiction. He died in 1860: one biography claimed that "his body was not equal to the confining life pre-

scribed by his literary tastes and after a tedious period of physical decline he died." Anon., "Henry Dilworth Gilpin," *Dictionary of American Biography* Base Set. American Council of Learned Societies, 1928–1936. Reproduced in Biography Resource Center (Thomson Gale), http://galenet.galegroup.com .silk.library.umass.edu:2048/servlet/BioRC (accessed 11 January 2008).

18. There is no surviving correspondence between the two authors discussing this transaction. Gilpin's letters for 1826 have been lost, and there is no mention of either Dwight or Gilpin's *Northern Tour* in his 1827 letters at the Historical Society of Delaware. There is a similar silence in the small number of surviving pre-1830 letters by Dwight at the New York Public Library.

19. Dwight had published a second edition, *The Northern Traveller* (New York: A. T. Goodrich, 1826), that modestly expanded the original text, adding some maps and illustrations. The third edition is Theodore Dwight, *The Northern Traveller: (Combined With The Northern Tour.) Containing the Routes to Niagara, Quebec, and the Springs. With the Tour of New-England, and the Route to the Coal Mines of Pennsylvania* (New York: G. & C. Carvill, 1828).

20. Theodore Dwight, *Sketches of Scenery and Manners in the United States* (1829; repr. Delmar, NY: Scholars' Facsimiles and Reprints, 1983).

21. Dwight, *Sketches*, 175–76.

22. Ibid., 179, 178. The source of Dwight's discomfort with leisure could be ascribed to the lingering effects of traditional attitudes inherent in some parts of New England society, particularly those derived from Puritanism. Dwight clearly had deep roots in this tradition. There seems to have also been a hardening of attitudes toward recreation in the face of the expanding consumer culture of the 1820s, which later dovetailed with the tightening moral standards of the Second Great Awakening.

23. Ibid., 182, 175–76, 180.

24. Ibid., 176.

25. James K. Paulding to Gasherie DeWitt?, 28 December 1827, in Ralph Aderman, ed., *The Letters of James Kirke Paulding* (Madison: University of Wisconsin Press, 1962), 93.

26. A few critics celebrated Paulding as one of the great authors of the nineteenth century, and as late as 1948 one placed him alongside Hawthorne and Poe: Alexander Cowie, *The Rise of the American Novel* (New York: American Book Co., 1948), dedicates fifteen pages to him. His literary star, however, has since fallen. More modern works like the *Columbia History of the American Novel*, ed. Emory Elliott (New York: Columbia University Press, 1991), either mention him only briefly or pass over him entirely. This steep decline has come as researchers have come to understand the significance of his political work, which included apologia for slavery and various other defenses of southern extremism in the period after the 1820s. One study arguing that Paulding was defending a Jeffersonian vision of Republicanism is Lorman Ratner, *James Kirke Paulding: The Last Republican* (Westport, CT: Greenwood Press, 1992). Ratner contends that Paulding was much more anti-abolitionist than pro-slavery, despite the excesses of Paulding's *Slavery in the United States* (1836), which presents a bucolic view of that institution. A fine analysis of Paulding as a social commentator and travel writer is by Beth Lueck in *American Writers and the Picturesque Tour:*

The Search for National Identity, 1790–1860 (New York: Garland Publishing, 1997), ch. 3.

27. James Kirke Paulding, *The New Mirror For Travellers; and Guide to the Springs, by An Amateur* (New York: G. & C. Carvill, 1828). Page numbers for the quotations that follow are taken from one collection of Paulding's works: *A Book of Vagaries*, ed. William I. Paulding (New York: Charles Scribner and Co., 1868), which incorporates the entirety of *The New Mirror* into its text.

28. Paulding, *New Mirror*, 289–90.

29. Ibid., 148–49.

30. Ibid., 282.

31. There are several biographies of Anne Royall. Bessie Rowland James, *Anne Royall's USA* (New Brunswick, NJ: Rutgers University Press, 1972) is clearly written and organized. Alice S. Maxwell and Marion B. Dunelvy, *Virago! The Story of Anne Newport Royall (1769–1854)* (Jefferson, NC: McFarland, 1985) is awkwardly organized but vigorously told and concentrates more on Royall's trial as a "common scold" in 1829. Finally, Sarah Harvey Porter, *The Life and Times of Anne Royall* (Cedar Rapids, IA: Torch Press Book Shop, 1908), is earnest. There are several good sketches of her life, including "Royall, Anne Newport" in *Webster's American Biographies*, ed. Charles Van Doren (Springfield, MA: Merriam-Webster, 1984). Articles include Edith B. Gelles, "Gossip: An Eighteenth-Century Case," *Journal of Social History* 22, no. 4 (1989): 667–83; Maurine Beasley, "The Curious Career of Anne Royall," *Journalism History* 3, no. 4 (1976–77): 98–102, 136; Don Dodd and Ben Williams, "A Common Scold: Anne Royall," *American History Illustrated* 10, no. 9 (1976): 32–38; Lucille Griffith, "Anne Royall in Alabama," *Alabama Review* 21, no. 1 (1968): 53–63; and Virginia Foulk, "Women Authors of West Virginia," *West Virginia History* 25, no. 3 (1964): 206–10. She is also featured in two recent dissertations, Carole A. Policy's "Status, Ideology, and Identity: Class ambiguity in the humor of the Lowell 'Factory Girls,' Anne Royall, and Fanny Fern (Massachusetts)," PhD diss., Florida State University, 2000; and Erika Maria Kreger, "Plain Speaking: American Women Writers and the Periodical Sketch Form, 1820–1870," PhD diss., University of California Davis, 2000.

32. Legal ruling from James Roane and wife Elizabeth vs. Ann Royall *et als* [*sic*], box 235, Circuit Clerk's Office, Augusta County Courthouse, Staunton, Virginia, as quoted in James, *Anne Royall's USA*, 81.

33. James, *Anne Royall's USA*, chs. 4–8.

34. "A Book of Travels," *New-York Daily Advertiser*, 20 June 1826.

35. Anne Royall, *The Black Book; Or, A Continuation of Travels in the United States* (Washington, D.C.: Printed for the author, 1828–29), 1:21.

36. Ibid., 1:21.

37. Ibid., 1:25–26.

38. Ibid., 1:22.

39. Ibid., 1:16–17. The question of Davison's numbers is an interesting one. Davison had long published estimates of the numbers of visitors at the springs, beginning in 1819. His earliest figure was derived by counting the names of visitors in the guest books of the major hotels throughout the entire season (4,219 for 1819). In the years after, though, he estimated the number of visitors

in town in any given week. These figures make comparisons difficult, but the general impression that can be derived is that the number of tourists at the hotels in Saratoga rose quickly in the early 1820s and plateaued for the remainder of the decade. The peak number of genteel tourists at the height of the season (the second week of August) as measured by Davison tended to be around 1,500. Given the general propensity for tourists of all classes to stay at Saratoga for relatively short periods, a very rough estimate of the overall number of visitors per season in an average year probably was in excess of 6,000. This, of course, takes Davison's numbers at face value; Royall's critique of them must be viewed with the same skepticism. Perhaps they balance each other out.

40. Royall, *Black Book*, 1:19. Royall's "country people" were probably a mix of residents of Saratoga County, many of them working class, and day trippers from Albany. Most of the latter would have been at least middle class. Saratoga Springs was much closer to population centers than Virginia Springs, and its much more developed transportation infrastructure made it much easier for "shoals" of non-wealthy to go there.

41. Francis J. Dallam Travel Diary, 25 July 1827. Dallam visited Bedford Springs in 1826—see Sarah Dallam to Francis Dallam, 19 and 31 July 1826. Dallam Papers, Maryland Historical Society, Baltimore, MD.

42. David Hillhouse 1826 Travel Journal, 93–96, Southern Historical Collection.

43. Mr. & Mrs. Sipple Diary, 1821, New-York Historical Society, 10. Theodore Dwight, *The Northern Traveller, Containing the Routes to Niagara, Quebeck, and the Springs* . . . (New York: Wilder & Campbell, 1825), 7.

44. *Saratoga Sentinel*, "Take Care of Your Baggage," 27 July 1824, 2; "Steam Boat Thefts," 15 May 1827, 3.

45. David P. Hillhouse Journal, folder 75, Alexander-Hillhouse Papers, Southern Historical Collection, p. 80.

46. *Ballston Spa Independent American*, 16 June 1812. In the summer tourist seasons of the 1820s the *Saratoga Sentinel* carried reports of thefts on: 12 July 1825, 3; 12 July 1825, 3; 19 July 1825, 3; 1 August 1826, 3 (two instances); 5 September 1826, 3; 15 May 1827, 3; 7 August 1827, 2; and 22 July 1828, 3.

47. John Morrison, *History of American Steam Navigation* (1903; repr. New York: Argosy-Antiquarian Ltd., 1967), 15–17, 46.

48. Donald Ringwald, *Hudson River Day Line: the Story of a Great American Company* (Berkeley: Howell-North, 1965), 4–5.

49. This discussion of the Stevens's effort with the *Albany* is heavily dependent on Kenneth John Myers, "Art and Commerce in Jacksonian America: The Steamboat *Albany* Commission," *Art Bulletin* 82, no. 3 (September 2000): 503, 510–11.

50. The twelve paintings were: Samuel F. B. Morse, *Una and the Dwarf*; John Vanderlyn, *Ariadne Asleep on the Island of Naxos*; John Sully, *Mother and Child*; Thomas Cole, *Scene from the Last of the Mohicans*; Thomas Cole, *Landscape View near the Falls of the Kauterskill*; Thomas Birch, *View of the Bay of New-York, from Castle Garden* . . . ; Thomas Doughty, *Lake Scene at Sunrise, Composition*; Doughty, *View on the Potomac at Harper's Ferry*; Thomas Birch, *View of the Coast near Sandy-Hook*; Charles B. Lawrence's copy of David's *Bonaparte Crossing the Alps*; Lawrence's copy of Sully's *Washington's Passage of the Delaware*; and Lawrence, *View from Bordentown Hill on the Delaware*. Myers, "Art and Com-

merce," 503–4. Again, I am dependent on Myers's analysis of the artistic dialogue implicit in the works and their placement. All of the paintings were painted on wooden panels.

51. In 1828 Cooper himself would commission a work from Cole. James F. Beard, ed., *The Letters and Journals of James Fenimore Cooper* (Cambridge, MA: Harvard University Press, 1960), 1:248n9, 263.

52. This painting, though, had not been in the original gallery. It had replaced John Vanderlyn's notorious *Ariadne Asleep on the Island of Naxos*, which was there only for the first season. *Ariadne* had been, no doubt, intended to please the mostly male passengers, as it depicted a voluptuous, flagrantly naked woman. Its removal was almost certainly tied in with the scandal surrounding it as one of the first non-classical nudes exhibited in America; the controversy eventually ruined Vanderlyn's career. For a discussion of *Ariadne*, see Myers, "Art and Commerce," 504–5, 524n10. The painting is now at the Pennsylvania Academy of the Fine Arts, Philadelphia.

53. Myers, "Art and Commerce," 518–19.

54. Michael Ross, *The Reluctant King: Joseph Bonaparte, King of the Two Sicilies and Spain* (London: Sidgwick and Jackson, 1976), 247; and Owen Connelly, *The Gentle Bonaparte: A Biography of Joseph, Napoleon's Elder Brother* (New York: Macmillan, 1968), 246–48. For accounts of tourists interest in Point Breeze, see, for example, Ann Jean Baker Commonplace Book, 13 November 1826, ms. 407, box 3, Graves Family Collection, Maryland Historical Society: "Went on deck to see the villages of Bristol and Burlington and was pointed out the spire of the observatory belonging to Count Survilliers the Ex-king of Spain, which brought forcibly to my mind the changes wrought by time and the mutibility [sic] of fortune experienced by the Bonaparte family." There is a similar reference is in Henry Pickering Walcott Journal, 25 May 1822, Massachusetts Historical Society.

55. Mentions of Joseph in their travel diaries include, from 1821: "We were last night at Sans Souci. Fashionable company there, and among others, Joseph Bonaparte, (formerly King of Spain) and his suite of about 15. Servants in livery," Laura (Porter) Hill Diary, 2 August 1821, New York State Historical Society; and from 1824: "evening landed us at Skenectady after tea we took the Canal boat for Utica/ J Bonaparte & suite being of the Company," S. Shulling Diary, 24 June 1824, Historical Society of Pennsylvania. See also reports in the *Saratoga Sentinel*, 25 August 1819, 25 July 1821, 2 August 1825, 18 July 1826, 8 August 1826, 17 July 1827, 8 July 1828, 5 August 1828, 11 August 1829, and 20 July 1830.

56. The fares were as high even for day boats; the cheapest night boat competitors charged only one dollar, with occasional discounts. Myers, "Art and Commerce," 520.

57. William Leete Stone, "Ten Days in the Country," *New York Commercial Advertiser*, 28 August 1824, quoted in Myers, "Art and Commerce," 522.

58. Sipple Diary, 28 July 1821.

59. Dwight, *Northern Traveller* (1825), 7.

60. For a discussion of this perception in the context of New York City, see Edwin G. Burrows and Mike Wallace, *Gotham* (New York: Oxford University Press,

1999), 699–700. The change in New York occurred around the mid-1820s. James F. Richardson, *The New York Police: Colonial Times to the Present* (New York: Oxford University Press, 1970), 15–16.

61. This was such a new phenomenon that there was not really a name for it: the term *confidence man* would not be coined until the late 1840s. See Karen Halttunen, *Confidence Men and Painted Women* (New Haven: Yale University Press, 1982), 6–7.

62. Perhaps the wealthy were at their most vulnerable while traveling, which may explain why Herman Melville set his novel *The Confidence Man* (published 1857) aboard a steamboat.

10. The Next Big Thing

1. Here is the complete route of Davison's 1822 edition: Philadelphia, Trenton, Princeton, New-Brunswick, New-York, up the Hudson to West Point (8½ pp., Arnold/André), Newburgh, Poughkeepsie, Catskill (village), Athens, city of Hudson, Albany (2½ pp.), Troy, Lansingburgh, Waterford, Cohoes, Van Schaick's Island, Ballston Spa (2 pp.), Low's Spring, Washington Fountain (1½ pp.), Ballston Boarding Houses (1½ pp.), Ballston Lake, Saratoga Springs (9 pp.), Saratoga Boarding Houses (4 pp.), Saratoga Lake, Schuylersville, Bemus' Heights (site of the Battle of Saratoga; 22 pp.), Sandy Hill, Glens Falls, Lake George (4 pp.), Herkimer, Utica, Auburn, Canandaigua, Lewiston, Niagara Falls (12 pp.), Lake Ontario, Montreal (3 pp.), William Henry (town), Three Rivers, Quebec City (10 pp.), St Johns, Lake Champlain, Plattsburgh, Burlington (3 pp.), Whitehall, New Lebanon, Pittsfield, Northampton, Worcester, Boston (9 pp.). Cambridge, Northern routes to Boston, Route from Whitehall, Vermont, through New Hamphsire to Boston.

2. Theodore Dwight, "The White Mountains," in *Sketches of Scenery and Manners in the United States* (1829; repr. Delmar, NY: Scholars' Facsimiles, 1983), 59–80, 185–88.

3. Eric Purchase, *Out of Nowhere: Disaster and Tourism in the White Mountains* (Baltimore: Johns Hopkins University Press, 1999), 25–27.

4. For a clear and coherent explanation of the disaster and its setting, see Purchase, *Out of Nowhere*, 8–13. John Sears, *Sacred Places: American Tourist Attractions in the Nineteenth Century* (New York: Oxford University Press, 1989) provides a solid introduction to White Mountain tourism, but Dona Brown, *Inventing New England: Regional Tourism in the Nineteenth Century* (Washington, D.C.: Smithsonian Institution Press, 1995) is the best overview of the creation of tourism in the White Mountains and its link to American national tourism.

5. Cole quoted in Louis Legrand Noble, *The Life and Works of Thomas Cole*, 66. Wadsworth's suggestion to Cole is in J. Bard McNulty, ed., *Correspondence of Thomas Cole and Daniel Wadsworth*, 12. Dwight, *Sketches of Scenery and Manners*, 63.

6. Visitor list from Dona Brown, *Inventing New England* (Washington, D.C.: Smithsonian Institution Press, 1995), 45.

7. Noble, *Life and Works*, 67–68.

8. Purchase, *Out of Nowhere*, 26–30.

9. Theodore Corbett, *The Making of American Resorts: Saratoga Springs, Ballston Spa, Lake George* (New Brunswick, NJ: Rutgers University Press, 2001), 80. Early racing at Saratoga was trotting or harness racing. Horse racing was initially a sport of the New York middle and upper middle class. In the early 1850s "the nouveaux riches like Cornelius Vanderbilt and Robert Bonner" took it up, making it a "respectable and prestigious amusement for the upper crust." Steven Riess, *City Games: The Evolution of American Urban Society and the Rise of Sports* (Chicago: University of Illinois Press, 1991), 32–33. Edward Hotaling claims a date of 1830 as the first race at Saratoga, citing a newspaper story from *New-York Mirror*, 14 August 1830. However, the article only describes a bet made at an informal race between two Saratoga swells rather than a staged horserace. Hotaling, *They're Off! Horse Racing at Saratoga* (Syracuse: Syracuse University Press, 1995), 16, 26–27.

10. Ibid., 27–28; George Waller, *Saratoga: Saga of an Impious Era* (Englewood Cliffs, NJ: Prentice-Hall, 1966), 81; and Hugh Bradley, *Such Was Saratoga* (New York: Doubleday, Doran and Co., 1940), 110. Neither Corbett nor Jon Sterngass mention these early gaming institutions, instead noting only the casino, built 1867–71, instrumental in Saratoga's post-Civil War revival. See Corbett, *Making of American Resorts*, and Sterngass, *First Resorts: Pursuing Pleasure at Saratoga Springs, Newport, and Coney Island* (Baltimore: Johns Hopkins University Press, 2001).

11. "Go to Saratoga!" *American Railroad Journal and Advocate of Internal Improvements* 1 (June 1833), 1.

Index